A Holocaust
Reader

A Holocaust Reader

From Ideology to Annihilation

Edited by

Rita Steinhardt Botwinick

Florida Atlantic University

Prentice Hall
Upper Saddle River, New Jersey 07458

Library of Congress Cataloging-in-Publication Data

A holocaust reader : from ideology to annihilation / edited by Rita
    Steinhardt Botwinick.
        p.   cm.
    Includes bibliographical references.
    ISBN 0-13-842238-9 (pbk.)
    1. Holocaust, Jewish (1939–1945)   2. Germany—Politics and
government—20th century.   3. Germany—Ethnic relations.
I. Botwinick, Rita S.
D804.3.H64936   1997
940.53'18—dc21   97-39843
                                                            CIP

Editor in chief: Charlyce Jones Owen
Editorial/production supervision
    and interior design: Mary Araneo
Editorial assistant: Holly Jo Brown
Buyer: Lynn Pearlman
Cover concept: Alicia Botwinick
Cover designer: Bruce Kenselaar

This book was set in 10/12 Times by A & A Publishing Services,
Inc., and was printed and bound by Courier Companies, Inc.
The cover was printed by Phoenix Color Corp.

 © 1998 by Prentice-Hall, Inc.
Simon & Schuster/A Viacom Company
Upper Saddle River, New Jersey 07458

Printed in the United States of America

10   9   8   7   6   5   4   3   2

        ISBN 0-13-842238-9

PRENTICE-HALL INTERNATIONAL (UK) LIMITED, *London*
PRENTICE-HALL OF AUSTRALIA PTY. LIMITED, *Sydney*
PRENTICE-HALL CANADA INC., *Toronto*
PRENTICE-HALL HISPANOAMERICANA, S.A., *Mexico*
PRENTICE-HALL OF INDIA PRIVATE LIMITED, *New Delhi*
PRENTICE-HALL OF JAPAN, INC., *Tokyo*
SIMON & SCHUSTER ASIA PTE. LTD., *Singapore*
EDITORA PRENTICE-HALL DO BRASIL, LTDA., *Rio de Janeiro*

To My Grandchildren and their Parents
with Abiding Love

Contents

Preface

The classroom is still, the students are motionless, stunned by the account of the massacre at Babi Yar. For a few minutes they saw that ravine where members of an SS *Einsatzgruppe* gunned down 34,000 Jews from Kiev. I look at the stricken faces before me and search for some words of comfort. But, no, I must resist the attempt to console, to ease the impact of that dreadful scene. To do so would distort its meaning. I merely remind them of the stipulation agreed upon on the first day of class: we will confront the facts without reservations. We will not justify, not rationalize, not assign God's inscrutable will to the atrocities committed by men. We will seek the truth and not dilute its reality with platitudes.

The desire to overstate the episodes of kindness and caring and miraculous survival is quite compelling. The students loved *Schindler's List*. Indeed, righteous Christians saved Jews at great peril to themselves and their families; indeed, Jews fought back with every means possible; they hid for months, even years, they passed as Gentiles, endured slave labor and concentration camps and the savage death marches. In other words, some Jews survived. But these exceptions must not be permitted to obscure the general rule. And for six million, death was the rule.

The readings selected for this book trace, as far as a slim volume can, the origins of the Third Reich and the evolution of its racial theories to their genocidal culmination. Ideologues, victims, perpetrators, and bystanders speak to us in their own voices. Documents, mostly from German sources, which add to the understanding of events are also included. Accounts by survivors were chosen not for their uniqueness but because many others shared similar experiences.

The objective of this collection is to complement the textbooks used in Holocaust studies. Although the arrangement of chapters mirrors my text, *A History of the Holocaust: From Ideology to Annihilation* (Prentice Hall, 1996), this reader will add primary dimensions to any syllabus. Our students, only a half century removed from the Holocaust, are philosophically light-years removed from it. Their questions attest to their struggle to understand: Why didn't they…How could they…Where was our government…if only…. Reared in a free, open, and multicultural society, the policy of the German government to murder millions of people for pseudoracial reasons is incomprehensible.

This anthology cannot provide the answers to the perplexing questions the Holocaust raises. We know what happened, but how it was possible remains an enigma. Psychological research and historical studies provide a glimmer of light, but they raise as many problems as they answer. Thus, while graduate students and scholars grapple with wider implications of the Holocaust, the goal of this book has a narrower focus: let the events of the Holocaust impel students to become vigilant guardians of everyone's rights. The biblical admonition to be our brother's keeper is as valid today as it has ever been.

A Holocaust
Reader

Chapter 1

Prejudice and Anti-Semitism

INTRODUCTION

The Holocaust stands as the culmination of man's capacity for inhumanity. The presence of deep-rooted prejudice toward the Jews was the starting point for this disaster. Nazi propaganda, no matter how cleverly persuasive, would not have succeeded without a bedrock of long-established hatred. Thus, it is appropriate that we begin a study of the Holocaust with some understanding of the psychological and social origins of intolerance and bigotry in general and of anti-Semitism in particular.

The debate whether or not Germans were infected with a uniquely virulent form of anti-Semitism is not part of our inquiry. Suffice it to say that they were not exempt from the general European prejudice against Jews. Many Germans, though by no means all, from university scholars to illiterate peasants, accepted anti-Semitism as their social inheritance. They wore their antipathy like a familiar suit that had undergone several alterations over the centuries. The material was old and well-worn but the fabric remained intact.

The progression from anti-Semitism as a concept to the implementing of annihilation was possible when the totalitarian Nazi regime tapped into these ancient prejudices. Those Germans, and we cannot judge their numbers, who deplored the fact that anti-Semitism was a central theme of the Third Reich, were quickly silenced. It must be remembered the Nazi Party exercised virtually unchallenged power over all aspects of German life. This total control enabled the government to carry out the complex project of identifying, transporting, and killing millions of people without serious objections from the citizenry.

Hitler chose the timing for the Holocaust carefully. The war created stressful internal and external conditions which left the ordinary German little energy beyond anxiety over his or her own immediate problems. The war also provided the justification for acts which may have been unthinkable during peacetime.

Even under Hitler's totalitarianism it was not possible to conceal the disappearance of millions. Hitler and Himmler were not certain of the reaction of the people if the truth were known and promulgated the myth of Jewish resettlement in the east. This lie required much repetition and constant justification from the propaganda ministry. Here again, in very specific ways, historic precedent had prepared the soil for Dr. Goebbels. All his incriminations to prove the Jews were a subhuman species could be found in the past. The libels, the economic restrictions, political disqualification, social ostracism, mass expulsions, and pogroms had their roots in past practices of church and state. Hitler and his followers merely intensified and modernized these longstanding precedents and adopted their use to modern technology.

During the centuries preceding Hitler's Third Reich, Germans expressed their hatred of Jews no differently than the rest of Europe. The usual pattern was one of periods of reluctant acceptance alternating with periods of oppression. The Jews reacted by retreating into lives focused on family and faith. Forced into ghettos, the gulf between them and the Christian mainstream widened. Like people under siege, they responded to the enmity of the outside world with hostility and fear.

Throughout the Middle Ages the main thrust of this hatred was based on religion. The unwillingness of the Jews to accept Christ as the Son of God resulted in their demonization. At the dawn of the modern era, during the Age of Enlightenment, most of the economic constraints were eased for western European Jews. But the change in philosophy of many educated Europeans did not spread to the masses for whom the Jews remained objects of mistrust.

As the influence of the churches waned, a new faith emerged—nationalism. It bred its own form of anti-Semitism; Jews must forever remain aliens in the body politic. The commonality that, for example, bound Frenchmen or Germans into a nation could never be attained by Jews, according to this theory. Only after a long and difficult struggle did European Jewry attain national citizenship and legal equality by the turn of the twentieth century.

The Nazis used the foundation of religious and nationalistic anti-Semitism but they emphasized its newest, so-called scientific form. Their ideology alleged that the Jews were both inferior and dangerous due to characteristics of race. How many Germans actually swallowed the "measurable genetic inferiority evidence" is impossible to say. Race, as a determining factor of a peoples' worth, complemented the social Darwinism extolled by the Nazi state: fitness to dominate is based on strength; the weak must serve the strong who have the absolute right to determine who may live and who must die.

Hate Prejudice and Racism

Milton Kleg

REFLECTIONS ON RACE AND RACIAL CLASSIFICATION

We might briefly summarize some of the salient features of racial classification as follows:

1. Human variability constitutes a continuum. Regardless of the classification system used, whether typological or geographical, there is no agreement as to the taxonomy.
2. Racial designations are merely convenient labels for discussing and comparing physical similarities and difference among populations—race as something more tangible or concrete than an abstract construct is fiction.
3. These classifications do not imply any kind of biological or cultural hierarchy, and are frequently, if not always, arbitrary.

In confronting the issue of race, racism, and hate violence, it is useful, if not necessary, to have a basic knowledge of the facts regarding race. Without this information, one may accept invalid and often racist positions. In 1964, under the auspices of the United Nations Educational, Scientific and Cultural Organization (UNESCO), a group of scientists met to examine and issued a collective statement on the nature of race. This was not the first time that scientists had issued such a statement; it had been done in 1950 and again in 1952. The more recent statement is presented here in much of its entirety because of its significance in understanding the nature of race. Since the statement repeats and emphasizes many of the points made in the preceding sections, it serves as both a summary of these points and as a concluding statement for this section on race.

Biological Aspects of Race[1]

1. All men living today belong to a single species, *Homo sapiens,* and are derived from a common stock. There are differences of opinion regarding how and when different human groups diverged from this common stock.
2. Biological differences between human beings are due to differences in heredi-

Reprinted from *Hate Prejudice and Racism* by Milton Kleg by permission of the State University of New York Press, 1993, pp. 78–100. © State University of New York Press, Albany, NY.

tary constitution and to the influence of the environment on this genetic potential. In most cases, those differences are due to the interaction of these two sets
of factors.

3. There is great genetic diversity within all human populations. Pure races—in the
sense of genetically homogeneous populations—do not exist in the human
species.

4. There are obvious physical differences between populations living in different
geographic areas of the world, in their average appearance. Many of these differences have a genetic component.

5. …Since the pattern of geographic variation of the characteristics used in racial
classification is a complex one, and since this pattern does not present any
major discontinuity, these classifications, whatever they are, cannot claim to
classify mankind into clear-cut categories.…Many anthropologists, while stress-
ing the importance of human variation, believe that the scientific interest in
these classifications is limited, and even that they carry the risk of inviting abusive generalizations.

   Differences between individuals within a race or within a population are
often greater than the average differences between races or populations.

   Some of the variable distinctive traits which are generally chosen as criteria
to characterize a race are either independently inherited or show only varying
degrees of association between them within each population. Therefore, the
combination of these traits in most individuals does not correspond to the typological racial characterization.

6. In man as well as in animals, the genetic composition of each population is
subject to the modifying influence of diverse factors: Natural selection, tending
towards adaptation to the environment, fortuitous mutations which lead to modifications of the molecules of desoxyribonucleic acid which determine heredity,
or random modifications in the frequency of qualitative hereditary characters to
an extent dependent on the pattern of mating and size of populations. Certain
physical characters have a universal biological value for the survival of the
human species, irrespective of the environment. The differences on which racial
classifications are based do not affect these characters, and, therefore, it is not
possible from the biological point of view to speak in any way whatsoever of a
general inferiority or superiority of this or that race.

7. …On account of the mobility of human populations and of social factors, mating between members of different human groups, which tend to mitigate the dif-
ferentiations acquired, has played a much more important role in human history
than in that of animals. This history of any human population or of any human
race, is in rich instances of hybridization and those tend to become more and more
numerous. For man the obstacles to interbreeding are geographical as well as
social and cultural.

   …

9. It has never been proven that interbreeding has biological disadvantages for
mankind as a whole.…The biological consequences of a marriage depend only

on the individual genetic make-up of the couple and not on their race. Therefore, no biological justification exists for prohibiting intermarriage between persons of different races, or for advising against it on racial grounds.

...

12. ...There is no national, religious, geographic, linguistic, or cultural group which constitutes a race *ipso facto;* the concept race is purely biological. However, human beings who speak the same language and share the same culture have a tendency to intermarry, and often there is as a result a certain degree of coincidence between physical traits on the one hand, and linguistic and cultural traits on the other. But there is no known causal nexus between these and, therefore, it is not justifiable to attribute cultural characteristics to the influence of the genetic inheritance.

13. Most racial classifications of mankind do not include mental traits or attributes as a taxonomic criterion. Heredity may have an influence in the variability shown by individuals within a given population in their responses to the psychological tests currently applied. However, no difference has ever been detected convincingly in the hereditary endowments of human groups in regard to what is measured by these tests. On the other hand, ample evidence attests to the influence of physical, cultural, and social environment on differences in response to these tests.

...

Neither in the field of hereditary potentialities concerning the overall intelligence and the capacity for cultural development, nor in that of physical traits, is there any justification for the concept of "inferior" and "superior" races.

The Cornerstone of Modern Racism

Joseph Arthur Gobineau, Comte de Gobineau, has been called the father of racist ideology, as the title of Michael Denis Biddiss's book *Father of Racist Ideology: The Social and Political Thought of Count Gobineau* suggests. Gobineau's *Essay on the Inequality of Races* first appeared in 1853, with additional volumes being published in 1855. His views regarding the inferiority and superiority of races were welcomed by many Europeans as well as by Americans who maintained that blacks indeed were inferior and could never function in a civilized society.

According to Gobineau, the decline of civilizations was not due to poor government, religious fanaticism, immorality, materialism, or the decline of religion. Rather, nations fell due to the disease of degeneration. This degeneration occurred when racially superior nations permitted their people to interbreed with members of inferior racial stocks. In his analysis, Gobineau pointed out that this degeneration can only occur among civilized nations. Some societies remain in an embryonic state, unable to achieve the level of a civilized nation.[2]

Those that remained in an embryonic state included "pure blooded yellow and black races," and any attempt to civilize such groups would meet with failure. Uncivilized societies could not survive the complexities of civilization.[3] Furthermore, except in the case of interbreeding, races do not change. Not unlike others of his day, Gobineau held to the belief that racial groups were physically, mentally, and morally different. In his chapter on "Characteristics of Human Races," Gobineau, a friend and colleague of Alexis de Tocqueville, sets forth descriptions of the black, yellow, and white races. Some of these traits of the "yellow" and "black" races are presented below:

> Black: "The animal character, that appears in the shape of the pelvis, is stamped on the negro from birth, and foreshadows his destiny…mental faculties are dull or even nonexistent…has an intensity of desire…taste and smell are developed to an extent unknown to the other two races. He kills willingly, for the sake of killing…"[4]
>
> Yellow: "little physical energy and inclined to apathy…desires are feeble, will-power obstinate…tends to mediocrity in everything…he understands easily enough anything not too deep or sublime. He has a love for utility and a respect for order…. He is practical, in narrowest sense of the word….does not dream or theorize;…invents little. His whole desire is to live in the easiest and most comfortable way possible."[5]

It should not come as a surprise that Gobineau's description of the white race is of a superior type in beauty, intelligence, and strength. But Gobineau laments that over time, due to race mixing, "hybrids were created, which were beautiful without strength, strong without intelligence, or, if intelligent, both weak and ugly."[6]

Finally, Gobineau determines that all civilizations were and are created from one primary source, the white race.[7] Furthermore, only ten civilizations have ever emerged throughout the history of humankind. These included the Indian ("It arose from a branch of a white people, the Aryans"), Egyptians ("…created by an Aryan colony from India…"), Assyrians ("with whom may be classed the Jews…They owe their civilizing to the great white invasions…"), Greeks ("who came from an Aryan stock as well as modified by Semitic elements"), Chinese (from an "Aryan colony from India…"), Romans ("mixture of Celts, Iberians, Aryans, and Semites"), Germanic races ("These were Aryans"), the American Alleghanian, Mexican, and Peruvian.

He ends by noting that only when the Aryan (the original and purest of which is the Germanic people) branch is present has there been any true European civilization. As for the fact that he lists no black civilization, Gobineau remarks, "…no negro race is seen as the initiator of a civilization. Only when it is mixed with some other can it even be initiated into one."[8] As for the remainder of European civilizations, Gobineau concluded that they could only survive so long as Aryan blood was not exhausted.

Despite the fact that Gobineau provided a doctrine for racist thought that would become popular among Germany's Nazis, post World War II neo-Nazis, and other racists near the end of the twentieth century, he was no more vicious in these early writings than others including Spencer. His writings did seem to influence Stewart Houston Chamberlain, who would also be lauded by twentieth century white supremacists and anti-Semites. Indeed, Hitler referred to Chamberlain as a prophet.

Racist literature and acts of violence spread like a prairie fire both in Europe and the United States during the latter half of the nineteenth century and well into the twentieth. Chamberlain's work was heavily anti-Semitic and reflected a long history of Jew-baiting in Europe. In the United States, the Ku Klux Klan and other groups produced their own brands of racism directed against Asians, Blacks, Hispanics, Catholics, and Jews. In some cases, these outbursts of hate were directed at groups across the United States in general. In other cases, they were restricted to specific geographical locations.

RACISM AND ANTI-SEMITISM IN EUROPE

In Europe, racist thought was largely directed at Jews. For centuries, Jew-baiting was common in virtually every state on the continent. Jews have been ghettoized, plundered, expelled, and murdered at various times. It has been generally accepted that early anti-Semitism was not racially motivated, but rather was the result of religious anti-Judaism including the refusal of these people to embrace Christianity.

However, Jerome Friedman argues that anti-Semitism was transformed from the religious issue to a racial one during the sixteenth century.[9] According to Friedman, the courts of the Spanish Inquisition introduced the racial factor in attempting to determine who was a Jew and who was not. Their "pure blood laws" defined a Jew as anyone with a Jewish ancestry. Such a person might be a *converso* but could not be regarded as a true Christian. The fact that Jesus and his earlier followers were Jewish led the courts to reexamine the amount of Jewish ancestry needed to be a Jew—"1/16, 1/32, or 1/64." Friedman concludes his findings by arguing that racial anti-Semitism of the sixteenth century laid the foundation for racism against Jews in the nineteenth.[10]

Notwithstanding, Friedman's position regarding the racist aspect of early anti-Semitism, it more generally has been accepted that among the main sources of anti-Semitism were: the belief that Jews were a "deicidal and perfidious race,"[11] the Jews' refusal to accept Christianity, and the belief that Jews were the offspring of Satan—the Antichrist.

The Devil's Seed.   During the middle ages the myth of Jews as descendants of Satan began to spread throughout Christian Europe. After all, were these not the killers of Christ? Certainly, it would follow that only those akin to the Devil could commit such a nefarious and putrid crime. Tales were spread that Jews had been commissioned by their Satanic father to bring havoc and destruction to Christian nations. They were accused of poisoning wells, murdering Christian children for their blood, and using Satanic magic to confound and gain supremacy over innocent Christians.[12] The goal of the Satanic Jew was world domination. Once the Jew had gained control of the world, the Antichrist, the Devil, would then appear and Christians would be enslaved by Satan and his seed.

Notwithstanding their apparent evil, some Church leaders often opposed such views and instead sought to have Jews accept Christianity. For there were those who believed that the second coming of Christ was contingent upon his acceptance by the Jews. In addition, there were those Church leaders that, from time to time, condemned Judehass (Jew hating) and noted that Jesus and his disciples were Jews. Nevertheless, the Jew remained the major target of hate throughout the history of Christendom.

The Martyrs of York.   Just how hazardous it was to be a Jew during the medieval period can be illustrated by the events in England in the twelfth century. As in other states of Europe, Jews were expected to show homage to the ruling personage. In Rome, it was the Pope; in England, obeisance was to the monarch.

On September 3, 1189, a Jewish delegation appeared at the coronation of Richard the Lion-Hearted in London. The Archbishop of Canterbury urged Richard not to accept the delegation and they were turned away, insulted and beaten. Londoners, seeing this, immediately turned upon the Jewish community in London, vandalizing and burning their homes, offering them the choice between baptism or death. The fury spread to the city of York. There Jews fled to the citadel and, after they warded off a number of assaults, the mob began to show signs of waning. A monk appeared to reignite the hatred. The siege continued until March 17, 1190.

Faced with capture or starvation, the Jewish community of York had arrived at a decision: "...the besiegers, noting the absence of the usual signs of resistance, broke into the citadel. When they reached the tower, they stood facing five hundred corpses. The men, after slaying their wives and children, had slain each other."[13] To this day, when Jews fast and lament the destruction of the Temple on the 9th of Av (usually occurring in late July or early August), they also offer an elegy for the martyrs of York: "O Awe-inspiring One! thy servants stood for judgment, fathers to be slaughtered with their children...."[14]

The Love-Hate Relationship.   The Church-State relationship with the Jews of Europe was strange and often bizarre. On one hand, the Jews were the most despised of humans—to be humiliated and destroyed, but on the other hand, they were to be saved if only they would embrace Christianity. In *From Prejudice to Destruction,* Jacob Katz summarizes Johann Andreas Eisenmenger's goal for the latter's 2,120 page anti-Semitic work entitled *Entdecktes Judentum,* published in 1700:

> Eisenmenger's declared purpose, as explained in his book, is to help the Jews recognize their error and acknowledge the truth of Christianity. In order to divert the Jews from their religion, Eisenmenger suggests several concrete steps: restricting of their economic freedom, limiting their rights, prohibiting them from writing against Christianity, and proscribing the synagogues and law courts...Above all,...to point out to the Jews the folly and blasphemy of the beliefs and opinions expressed in their writings and the immorality of their laws....[15]

Eisenmenger's work set the foundation for August Rohling's *Talmudjude* published in 1874.

Rohling, a professor of theology at the University of Prague, borrowed heavily from Eisenmenger, and it was the former's publication that spread throughout Europe. Rohling also engaged in charging Jews with using Christian blood in their religious ceremonies. The ancient blood libel had been used earlier against Jews and before that time, by Romans against Christians. In 1879, Wilhelm Marr introduced the term anti-Semitism in his publication, *Der Sieg des Judentums über das Germanentum,* that replaced the more common Judeophobia. According to Marr, the Jews were taking control of Germany and seeking world domination.[16] Marr formed the League of Anti-Semites and was joined by a number of professors who further popularized the notion that Jewish blood was mixing with the German Aryan, creating the degeneration of the latter race.

      Against this insanity, there were educated Christians who sought to combat the anti-Semitism sweeping over central Europe. In 1891, they formed an organization to combat anti-Semitism as cases of blood libel and raw violence were erupting against various Jewish communities in Germany, Austria, Hungary, and Poland. In France, anti-Semitism resulted in the Dreyfus Affair in 1894. This period from 1879 may be regarded as the beginning of modern anti-Semitism.

NOTES

[1] From "Race and Prejudice," reprinted from *The Unesco Courier,* April 1965, 8–11.

[2] Gordon W. Allport, "Attitudes," in *A Handbook of Social Psychology,* ed. Carl Murchinson (Worcester, MA: Clark University Press, 1935), 810.

[3] Ibid. Also see Robert Ezra Park, "Experience and Race Relations," *Journal of Applied Sociology* 9 (1924): 18–24.

[4] Allport also quotes Emory S. Bogardus: "An opinion may be merely a defense reaction which through overemphasis usually falsifies consciously or unconsciously a man's real attitude."

[5] Allport, "Attitudes," 809.

[6] In "The Nature of Attitudes and Attitude Change," William J. McGuire adds "and/" to Allport's definition rather than maintaining the original statement, "...directive or dynamic..."

[7] Kleg, Borgeld, and Sullivan, "An Exploration of Ethnic Attitudes," 4.

[8] Allport, "Attitudes," 806.

[9] Albert H. Hastorf, David J. Schneider, and Judith Polefka, *Person Perception* (Reading, MA: Addison-Wesley, 1970), 4.

[10] Ibid., 15

[11] Thomas F. Pettigrew, "Extending the Stereotype Concept," in *Cognitive Processes in Stereotyping and Intergroup Behavior,* ed. David L. Hamilton (Hillsdale, NJ: Lawrence Erlbaum Associates, 1981), 319.

[12] Gordon W. Allport, *The Nature of Prejudice* (Reading, MA: Addison-Wesley, 1954) 336.

[13] Ibid.

[14] Robert P. Abelson, Elliot Aronson, William J. McGuire, Theodore Newcomb, Milton J. Rosenberg, and Percy H. Tannenbaum (eds.), *Theories of Cognitive Consistency: A Sourcebook* (Chicago: Rand McNally, 1968), 769.

[15] T. W. Adorno, Else Frenkel-Brunswik, Daniel J. Levinson, and R. Nevitt Sanford, *The Authoritarian Personality* (New York: Harper & Row, 1950), 971.

[16] Ibid., 228.

The Satanizing of the Jews
Origin and Development
of Mystical Anti-Semitism

Joel Carmichael

It was during the era launched by the First Crusade that the "double vision" referred to above achieved its characteristic balance—between the intensity of a sophisticated idea, suffused with emotion, and a down-to-earth reality that enabled ordinary people to torture and kill their victims without becoming aware of invalidating the very idea by that fact alone. The mobs that fell upon Jewish communities could actually believe Jews to be embodiments of satanic power at the very moment of witnessing their total helplessness. One must assume that these mobs were incited simultaneously by horror of their satanic enemy and by glee at the ease with which they could undo him.

Thus the efforts of the Church to impress on the masses its demonic theory of the Jews created a strange counterpoint: the propaganda of the Church was emotionally so potent, from its natural links with the numerous demons already infesting the human psyche, that mass outbreaks against Jews achieved a ferocity from which the authorities themselves were bound to recoil. In social life as a whole, what for the Church was the conceptual puzzle of Jewish survival was subordinated to more down-to-earth passions. If some of the subtlety of the sophisticated explanation of Jewish survival, based on Augustine, filtered down to ordinary Christians, its only effect on them was to reinforce just this uncanny element in the bizarre metaphysical image of "The Jew," damned, a limb of Satan, yet preserved—by God himself.

When mass emotion overflowed, when the masses drew, so to speak, in ordinary life the natural conclusions of Church logic, they saw no reason why "Damned Jews" should not be treated as the awesome enemies of Christendom and of mankind that the Church itself had declared them to be. The second half of what for the Church was a syllogism—that just for that reason the Jews must be preserved—was emotionally sterile. The very concept of "sparing" the Jews because of their sacrosanct role in the Divine Plan put them still further beyond the human pale: it was like sparing Cain the Murderer because of metaphysics.

For centuries the doctrine about the Jews elaborated in the second and third centuries by the Church Fathers was confined to the small, relatively sophisticated milieu of the clergy and its educated intimates: for a long time there were no outbreaks of vio-

Joel Carmichael, *The Satanizing of the Jews: Origin and Development of Mystical Anti-Semitism,* New York: Fromm International, 1992, pps. 53–58, 82–85, 136–140. Reprinted by permission of Fromm International Publishing Corp., New York, 1992.

lence. There was no systematic persecution of Jews in Europe (except in the seventh century in Spain, under the West Goths); attacks on Jews had been sporadic (on individuals or specific communities). And while a certain background of violence is implied by occasional reactions—for example, a decree of the Mayence Town Council at the beginning of the ninth century, to the effect that the killing of a Jew was not a misdemeanor but a real murder—such incidents were rare.

By the end of the eleventh century, however, with the preparations for the First Crusade, the general situation of Jewry in Europe began to deteriorate. The Crusades, with a renewal of fervor for the Kingdom of God, were no doubt the watershed between the theoretical underpinnings, so to speak, of mystical anti-Semitism and its expression in daily life.

It would seem that Christendom was permeated by theological concepts whose symbolization had struck root in mass emotions. Christian awareness of Jews as an uncanny, powerful entity had been integrated with society as a permanent condition. From the end of the eleventh century on, Jews were there to be rejected and hated, and in addition plundered and murdered.

During the eleventh century the Church leaders, reacting against centuries of laxness, corruption, administrative indolence, and dependence on the kings and nobles who controlled Church appointments, undertook the reform of the Church, restoring its autonomy and, concomitantly, their own prestige as the spiritual elite. The purchase of ecclesiastical offices (simony) was reduced, clerical celibacy was insisted on. The laity were occasionally drawn into propaganda against recalcitrant clerics; the Church itself would denounce some of its refractory personnel as servants of Satan.

But toward the end of the century the religious energies unleashed by the Church initiative for reform overflowed into the population at large, itself now inflamed by intense plebeian fervor, a hysteria generated by the conviction of the imminent advent of the Millennium, a contemporary version of the Kingdom of God agitation of the first century that now attacked the established Church.

The fundamental Church claim, for instance, that ordination as such established the potency of the priesthood came to be overridden by ardent plebeians insisting that the function of a priest had to be complemented by personal merit, by an "apostolic" way of life (grounded in the Church's perception of Jesus' followers), of which amateur exemplars, lay "apostles" roving about Europe, had long been common.

The concept of the Millennium goes back to the Revelation of John (Chapter 20); it is the thousand-year reign of Christ and his "priests"; Satan is cooped up in the "abyss" until the cosmic battle takes place, at the end of which he is "flung into the lake of fire and sulphur...there to be tormented day and night."

This revival, or echo, of the imminent Kingdom of God was to enthrall plebeian millenarians for centuries. Beginning at the end of the eleventh century, they began agitating for the total reconstruction of society as indispensable for the World's End. The clergy came under systematic attack as "corrupt," the upper classes as oppressors.

Though some millenarians were peaceable ascetics, expecting the Millennium to be a distillation of spiritual values, the most fanatical, the most ruthless, the most extreme millenarian sects were those that focused the commonplace resentment of socio-economic distress into an intense, all-embracing revulsion against the world. For such fanatics, who for centuries were to teem throughout Western Europe, the fantasies of World's-End redemption projected a regenerated world in which blissful innocence would be achieved through an apocalyptic massacre. The people who necessarily had to be exterminated were on hand: the "rich," the clergy—and the Jews. It was only after such a cosmic slaughter that the Kingdom of the Saints—the holy executioners—could be established.

Thus, in evaluating mystical anti-Semitism as a phenomenon, the end of the eleventh century, with the First Crusade and the flood tide of plebeian Kingdom of God insurrectionaries, can be taken as the foundation of mystical anti-Semitism in its modern form. It was then that the work accomplished in the second and third centuries by the Church Fathers to establish the image of the Damned Jew began bearing fruit on a massive scale.

The tidal wave of millennial agitation showed that despite appearances and all rational perceptions, the World's End idea, which had seemed by the second century to be fossilized, retained enough latent energy to galvanize masses of people once again and generate explosive upheavals. Large parts of Western Europe were steeped in a torrent of revolutionary millenarianism.

The mass agitation was aimed at the pillars of the social order—the Church, the aristocracy, the emerging bourgeoisie. Though sometimes intertwined with Papal activity, it was essentially, in all its activist variations, hostile to the Church hierarchy as inherently corrupt, a manifestation, precisely, of the corruption of the world, and hence necessarily a target of the Kingdom of God fever aiming at a new world.

The First Crusade, for instance, launched by the Papacy in 1095 as part of a broad strategy to restore Christian unity under the aegis of Rome (by providing Byzantium with enough manpower to repel the Seljuk Turks), was transformed by hordes of fanatical plebeians into a turbulent movement of social agitation. For them, the notion of capturing Jerusalem as a way of obstructing and damaging Islam was too cold-blooded and objective. They transformed into the most acutely personal religious fervor.

And even though these new seekers of the Kingdom of God were intensely hostile to the Church, and were in fact burned at the stake in large numbers by the Church authorities, their most intense passion was directed at the Jews, who for them remained the personification of the very principle of Evil built into the current world. Their hostility to the established Church enabled them to disregard its doctrinal restraints on the murder of Jews.

If the expressed aim of the Crusades was taken at face value—wresting the Church of the Holy Sepulcher in Jerusalem from the Muslim infidels—Jews living in the small towns and villages of Europe would seem quite irrelevant. But that was not the reality perceived by the mobs inflamed by the Crusades: not merely had the Jews occupied a focal position for centuries in the world view of Christendom, they were also visible everywhere—as merchants, property holders, and money lenders. The convergence of these two factors, the ubiquitous activity of Jews interpreted by the overpowering concept of the Jews as sons of the Devil, was from then on to place them at the flash point of any social upheaval. A wide variety of political and social movements, countless currents in the endless flux of life, could find a convenient target in the Jews.

From the very outset of the First Crusade, the ardor stoked up to fuel it was fateful for the Jews. The intensification of religious fervor heightened to fever pitch the preaching for the Crusade itself; it was normal for Crusaders and the mobs accompanying them to celebrate the beginning of the arduous journey to the east by massacring small communities of Jews in France, the Netherlands, and Germany. It was evident to them that the Jews, notorious enemies of God and agents of Satan, were just as much or even more the enemies of the ardent Christians on their way to the Holy Land to free it from the infidel, indeed, were exactly the same enemy closer to home. And it was equally natural, to be sure, for the massacre of the Jews to yield material benefits by way of plunder and pillage.

It was during the Crusade of 1096 that the first great massacre of European Jews took place. It was independent of the armies of the nobility; the inflamed plebeians alone carried out the same slaughter among the Jews in Europe that they were to carry out a little later, in an even more concentrated butchery, in Palestine among the Muslims, especially in Jerusalem. The same theme was to be repeated during the Second Crusade a half century later (1146), when, for instance, masses of ordinary Jews were massacred in Normandy and Picardy.

For these plebeians the massacres of Jews in Europe and Muslims in Palestine were only the first act of a World's End enterprise on the very verge of consummation: the destruction of Satan. The plebeian hordes busily engaged in bloodshed felt themselves spurred on by the looming horror of the Anti-Christ.

The hatred of these millenarians for corrupt clerics and rapacious nobles, selected as it were functionally from the general population, was evidently different in kind from the loathing of Jews. The massacre of Jews had nothing to do with the specific activities of individual Jews, even though one real-life category, usurers, could be said to illustrate the mystical theme of "The Jew" as limb of Satan. The very existence of the entire people was taken to be a satanic activity. These plebeian massacres were of course opposed by the aristocracy and the Church summits, both in Europe and Palestine. The aristocrats leading the Crusaders generally made energetic efforts to deflect the blood lust of the mobs, and indeed saved many Jews.

It was their combination of visionary extremism and ruthless violence that distinguished these medieval Kingdom of God activists from other plebeian revolts, strictly circumscribed by low-key local aims, that also proliferated throughout the Middle Ages.

...

By 1543 Luther's stream of anti-Jewish venom had culminated in two writings dealing expressly with the Jews,* both of them outbursts of a primordial type of mys-

---

*Martin Luther, *On the Jews and Their Lies,* 1543, transl. Martin H. Bertram, in *Luther's Works,* general editor Jaroslav Pelikan, vol. 47, Philadelphia: Fortress Press, 1971, pp. 268–74, and Martin Luther, *Vom Schem Hamphoras und vom Geschlecht Christi,* Matth. 1, 1543, *Sämtliche Werke,* Polemische deutsche Schriften, Erlangen: Carl Hayder, 1842, pp. 275–358.

tical phobia buttressed by a sort of biblical erudition, by political ideas, and by the religious ferment of the day, worded with intemperate force.

Twenty years before, during his "judeophile" missionary phase, Luther had routinely scoffed at the old wives' tales of Jewish well-poisoning, ritual murder, and sorcery; now he presented all these morbid fantasies as quite believable, and while not, perhaps, factually accurate, as nevertheless an accurate expression of the soul of The Jew. Luther had by now long since given up the notion of converting Jews—"just as possible as converting the Devil": he now wanted to expose them and their lies for what they were, "so that we Germans can…know what a Jew *is*, and defend our Christianity against the Devil himself." This comparison with the Devil was a staple of Luther's rhetoric.

Luther was consumed by hatred for the God of the Torah, that is, the Jewish God Yahweh; he thought the Torah had created an unbridgeable chasm between the Jews and Christianity, and was itself the demonstration of their satanic nature. He assumed, indeed, that he was doing no more than carrying on St. Paul's struggle of fifteen hundred years before, which was possible, of course, only if he disregarded Paul's view that the "blindness" of the Jews was merely temporary.

Thus Luther's loathing of the Jews and his struggle against them were in his mind an externalization of his inner struggle against the Jewish God, Yahweh, now himself converted into a sort of Devil, like his people the Jews, and hence a menace to God's true people, the Christians, the present heirs of the chosenness of the Jews and of their mission.

In this we see again one of the conclusions endlessly to be drawn from the Incarnation: obviously there could be no place for compassion in such a struggle against the Devil: it was a struggle—as it had been since the very genesis of theology—between truth and lies, that is, between God and the Devil. Thus the cardinal motivation of Luther, as of all for whom theology could encapsulate and express pathological phobias and hatreds, was bound to exclude, more or less by definition, all "humane" factors on principle: the Jews, as the very embodiment of Evil, were inevitably counterposed to the Incarnation of God in Jesus as the quintessence of the Good. In this way Luther was merely repeating, with his characteristically ferocious boundlessness, the focal theme of Christian theology.

If Nietzsche was right in saying that Luther was a medieval phenomenon merely protesting against the Renaissance and the blossoming of the sciences, then he can be considered a typical expression of a social malaise, crystallized with special potency in an extravagant psyche.

Luther's actual views were by no means original, nor was his hatred of the Jews. His attitude merely focused a general tendency. The breakup of the Catholic monopoly, despite its apparent change in premises, was no more beneficial to the Jews, by and large, than the previous era had been. Even friends of the Jews could defend them only by refuting certain specific misstatements, falsehoods, and so on, such as, for instance, in the question of burning or conserving the Hebrew Scriptures—friends of the Jews would want the Scriptures conserved for, say, scholarly reasons—or in assessing the value of some technical Jewish view with respect to some particular area of interest to theologians. It was vital for defenders of the Jews to avoid at all costs the slightest suspicion of heresy, a matter of life and death both then and for centuries to come.

Thus Luther's view of the Jews was no different, for instance, from that of Erasmus or Johannes Reuchlin (the celebrated Hebraist of the preceding generation): for Luther, too, the dispersion of the Jews was just one more proof of their damnation, their fifteen-hundred-year exclusion from their own country—a stunning demonstration of God's verdict.

Luther's denial of protection for the Jews, which had always been incumbent on the Church, made things worse for them in many respects, since his execration of them, retained from the medieval Church, no longer had any theological mitigation. Thus his addiction to violently abusive language—his habitual references to Jews as "venomous and virulent," "thieves and brigands," "disgusting vermin"—coupled with his growing and soon enormous influence, was fatal to them.

To be sure, Luther turned the same explosive violence on all his adversaries—especially, of course, the Pope—but the position of the Jews was obviously different in kind from that of those who were more or less immune to his assaults. His lush rhetoric, rooted in a fantasy in which erotic and scatological images ran riot, made it natural for him to make much of, for instance, a preposterous sculpture of a sow suckling a Jew, a typical form of pornographic satire that was common, especially in Germany, from the thirteenth century on. He also proposed practical measures, from outright expulsion to forced labor, the burning of synagogues and houses, and so on.

Luther's fury against the Jews, after his disappointment at their reception of his ideas, was characteristically violent: "What then do we Germans want to do with this rejected, damned people of the Jews?"

Advising "sharp mercy," he recommended the following:

First, to set fire to their synagogues or schools and to bury and cover with dirt whatever will not burn, so that no man will ever again see a stone or cinder of them. This is to be done in honor of our Lord and of Christendom, so that God might see that we are Christians, and do not condone or knowingly tolerate [such] public lying, cursing, blaspheming of his Son and of his Christians....

Second, I advise that their houses be razed and destroyed. For they pursue in them the same aims as in their synagogues. Instead they might be lodged under a roof or in a barn like the gypsies....

Third, I advise that all their prayer-books and Talmudic writings, in which [such] idolatry, lies, cursing and blasphemy are taught, be taken from them.

Fourth, I advise that their rabbis be forbidden to teach henceforth on pain of loss of life and limb....

Fifth, I advise that safe-conduct on the highways be abolished completely for the Jews.

Sixth, I advise that usury be prohibited to them, and that all cash and treasure of silver and gold be taken from them....

Seventh, I recommend putting a flail, an ax, a hoe, a spade, a distaff, or a spindle into the hands of young, strong Jews and Jewesses and letting them earn their bread in the sweat of their brow, as was imposed on the children of Adam (Gen 3)....

In brief, dear princes and lords, those of you who have Jews under your rule—if my counsel does not please you, find better advice, so that you and we all can be rid of the unbearable, devilish burden of the Jews.*

...

The "racial" form of mystical anti-Semitism evidently did not replace the theological form: they ran parallel or convergently, or intertwined. The age-old stigma of the Jews was easily shifted from beliefs to genes, a shift that permitted passions to be expressed without the brake of theology.

The withering of theology had, in fact, left behind a pulsating sack of bile in people predisposed to the formation of bile. In times of tension that sack could burst. As life in the modern era grew more complex, the masses could vent on the Jews all their fury at the countless afflictions of the early and intermediate stages of industrialization. The role of scapegoat assigned the Jews, congealed in the status of outsiders, was inevitable: all the subliminal and actual content of all aspects of Christendom, alongside the religion proper, had fixed the figure of the Jew as the natural repository of the odd, the alien, the loathsome, the evil. And without the superstructure of a theological concept that made Jewry meaningful as well as degraded, there was nothing, in times of crisis and tension, to withstand destructive hostility.

Thus the abandonment of the Christian religion left a void in which all forms of outright pathology might find a foothold: Hitler may well be the outstanding example of a nontheological, mystical hatred of Jews, with all the intensity that, as we shall see, characterized his career.

An epigram may be in order: with the "racist" theory, mystical anti-Semitism became a disease of Christians, as well as an affliction of the Jews.

There were also, of course, mundane factors that intensified the emotion required to transfer the stigma on the Jews from theology to the earthier realm of biology.

The success of the Jews in permeating Western society made them extremely conspicuous. After having been abstracted, so to speak, from European society for so many centuries, and then spreading with such rapidity throughout the bourgeois world that was expanding in the wake of the Industrial Revolution, Jews were becoming more and more noticeable in Germany, Austro-Hungary, France, Great Britain, and America.

Classical Church theory, which insisted that Jews must survive, but in "abject circumstances," was now absurdly irrelevant. Though the great bulk of Jewry was far from affluent, the many Jews who had scaled the heights of society obviously made the Church's theory quite obsolete, aside from the absence of any mechanism to enforce such "abject circumstances."

And the success of many Jews was achieved against a background of social upheaval: peasants were becoming workers, traditional activities obsolescent; countless individuals were shaken up, family life was transformed. All these complex processes necessarily distressed large numbers of people. The recourse to "race" was thus a satisfying outlet for many frustrations.

On the Jews and Their Lies, op. cit.

The way Jews were depicted in the growing campaign against them in the nineteenth century came to diverge more and more from the current situation of real-life Jews, and to acquire a sort of ideology, rooted in the notion of the inherent worthlessness, as well as perniciousness of Jews, and taken to justify what was proclaimed to be an "instinctive" revulsion.

By the end of the century the anti-Jewish movements in Europe had linked up all the arguments stemming from the debates of the preceding century with respect to the emancipation of the Jews and given them an infinite scope based on "science." The growth of this pseudo-scientific view of the Jews was rapid: Wagner's attack on the Jews in music was initially published anonymously in 1850: less than twenty years later he printed it under his own name.

From the last third of the nineteenth century on, anti-Semitism spread widely among the intelligentsia and the upper classes; that growth was paralleled by its practical consequences. Anti-Semitism became part of an actual movement, first in Germany, then spreading to many other countries—to the Austro-Hungarian Empire, torn by intractable ethnic conflicts, then to France, England, and the United States. Russia too began to be preoccupied by the "problem"; by the end of the nineteenth century it was being studied in the topmost strata of the Empire. Germany, to be sure, remained the focus of the agitation concerning the Jews, sharpened, perhaps, by the stream of Jewish immigrants from the East since the 1880s.

This curious combination of political extremism and ideological mysticism produced, toward the end of the nineteenth century, an extraordinary forgery that is still current today: the Protocols of the Elders of Zion. These purport to describe a secret meeting held by "rabbis" to organize the rule of the world under international Jewry, by the use of guile, the world banking system, and the world press, and, for good measure, the infiltration of the Freemasons. The Protocols crystallize the main theories of the late Middle Ages about the Jews: the notion of a conspiracy to wipe out or enslave all Christians as an explanation of the countless tales of well-poisoning, the spreading of plagues, and similar legends.

To a receptive audience they present a seductive picture of scheming Jews, their power, their incredibly close-knit organization, and their deep hostility to all mankind, especially to Christians. The very notion of a secret conference of "rabbis"—a theme also outlined in the late Middle Ages—was to have a catalytic effect.

The legends underlying the Protocols had taken on a political flavor from the Renaissance on; after Napoleon's convocation of a Great Sanhedrin in 1807, they acquired a certain vogue in France and Germany, though without becoming very popular; in France writers also linked Jews to Freemasons as part of the same alleged plot against Christians.

Strangely enough, however, the actual text of the Protocols was composed in Paris at the end of the nineteenth century not by reworking these ancient legends in a new form, but simply by taking an entirely different composition—an attack by a French writer (Maurice Joly) on Napoleon III for his dreams of world conquest—and changing the substance of it to make it point to "international Jewry" instead of Napoleon III.

The adapter of Joly's brochure is unknown: he seems to have been working for the Tsarist Secret Police (Okhrana), perhaps in order to influence the last Tsar, Nicholas II. In any case, the forger simply took Joly's brochure, *Dialogue aux Enfers entre Machiavel et Montesquieu* (1864), which has nothing whatever to do with Jews, and turned it into something entirely different: the alleged proceedings (Protocols) of leaders of world Jewry, claimed to be already in control of many European states, and so already close to achieving world rule.

Nicholas II, not abnormally quick-witted, saw through the brochure the moment he saw it; the first Russian public printing (1905) was scarcely noticed outside a few small groups. Yet after the terrible shock of the First World War it was to have a great future. In 1920 the Protocols soared aloft. The enemies of the Bolsheviks blamed the Jews for the whole catastrophe: the Russian text was published in Europe in numerous translations. The Russian edition itself no doubt played a role in the pogroms carried out in southern Russia during the Civil War (1918–20).

The Protocols gave a seductive explanation of the upheavals and carnage of the First World War and also, of course, of the Bolshevik putsch itself, which had decapitated a great state, exiled the upper class, and no doubt destabilized Europe. The Protocols seemed to explain the reality behind the mysterious otherness of the Jews, and to create a focus for understanding the apparent variety of actual Jewish behavior.

In the modern period Jews had begun fanning out through society as individuals, rapidly achieving distinction in countless activities. It would have been evident to any observer unbiased by ideology that so many individuals could not act in unison, especially since in any given activity they might ordinarily be competing with each other. It would normally have been assumed that similar origins would be expressed in family ties, friendly coteries, a general link of a common "background," and so on—that is, that there was no *national* interest. It was just this fragmentation and chaos of Jewish life that could not be harmonized with the ideas of both mystical anti-Semites and vulgar judeophobes. The Protocols, with their description of a hidden center *behind* the chaos, satisfied the need for an explanation of the seeming diversity.

Though their authenticity was exploded almost immediately—a correspondent of the *London Times* (Philip Graves) simply demonstrated their obvious dependence on Joly's innocuous dialogue between Machiavelli and Montesquieu—so that no further attention might have been expected to be paid to them, they had an enormous impact: the text was translated into the chief languages of the world. In the United States it was sponsored and heavily subsidized by Henry Ford until 1927.

The Protocols were widely accepted, in fact, by educated opinion all over Europe as well as North America. In Germany too, the Protocols were thought by many to convey a penetrating truth about history. They were, after all, a summary of what mystical anti-Semites had been saying for generations. Since they duplicated what anti-Semites already *knew,* they carried conviction as it were automatically. But their most enduring success, ironically enough, was to be achieved after the Second World War—and in Soviet Russia.

Selection from *Mein Kampf*

Adolf Hitler

Trans. Ralph Manheim

...

The mightiest counterpart to the Aryan is represented by the Jew. In hardly any peo-ple in the world is the instinct of self-preservation developed more strongly than in the so-called 'chosen.' Of this, the mere fact of the survival of this race may be considered the best proof. Where is the people which in the last two thousand years has been exposed to so slight changes of inner disposition, character, etc., as the Jewish people? What people, finally, has gone through greater upheavals than this one—and never-theless issued from the mightiest catastrophes of mankind unchanged? What an infi-nitely tough will to live and preserve the species speaks from these facts!

The mental qualities of the Jew have been schooled in the course of many cen-turies. Today he passes as 'smart,' and this in a certain sense he has been at all times. But his intelligence is not the result of his own development, but of visual instruction through foreigners. For the human mind cannot climb to the top with steps; for every step upward he needs the foundation of the past, and this in the comprehensive sense on which it can be revealed only in general culture. All thinking is based only in small part on man's own knowledge, and mostly on the experience of the time that has preceded. The general cultural level provides the individual man, without his noticing it as a rule, with such a profusion of preliminary knowledge that, thus armed, he can more easily take further steps of his own. The boy of today, for example, grows up among a truly vast number of technical acquisitions of the last centuries, so that he takes for granted and no longer pays attention to much that a hundred years ago was a rid-dle to even the greatest minds, although for following and understanding our progress in the field in question it is of decisive importance to him. If a very genius from the twenties of the past century should suddenly leave his grave today, it would be harder for him even intellectually to find his way in the present era than for an average boy of fifteen today. For he would lack all the infinite preliminary education which our pre-sent contemporary unconsciously, so to speak, assimilates while growing up amidst the manifestations of our present general civilization.

Since the Jew—for reasons which will at once become apparent—was never in possession of a culture of his own, the foundations of his intellectual work were always provided by others. His intellect at all times developed through the cultural world surrounding him.

The reverse process never took place.

For if the Jewish people's instinct of self-preservation is not smaller but larger than that of other peoples, if his intellectual faculties can easily arouse the impression that they are equal to the intellectual gifts of other races, he lacks completely the most essential requirement for a cultured people, the idealistic attitude.

In the Jewish people the will to self-sacrifice does not go beyond the individual's naked instinct of self-preservation. Their apparently great sense of solidarity is based on the very primitive herd instinct that is seen in many other living creatures in this world. It is a noteworthy fact that the herd instinct leads to mutual support only as long as a common danger makes this seem useful or inevitable. The same pack of wolves which has just fallen on its prey together disintegrates when hunger abates into its individual beasts. The same is true of horses which try to defend themselves against an assailant in a body, but scatter again as soon as the danger is past.

It is similar with the Jew. His sense of sacrifice is only apparent. It exists only as long as the existence of the individual makes it absolutely necessary. However, as soon as the common enemy is conquered, the danger threatening all averted and the booty hidden, the apparent harmony of the Jews among themselves ceases, again making way for their old casual* tendencies. The Jew is only united when a common danger forces him to be or a common booty entices him; if these two grounds are lacking, the qualities of the crassest egoism come into their own, and in the twinkling of an eye the united people turns into a horde of rats, fighting bloodily among themselves.

If the Jews were alone in this world, they would stifle in filth and offal; they would try to get ahead of one another in hate-filled struggle and exterminate one another, in so far as the absolute absence of all sense of self-sacrifice, expressing itself in their cowardice, did not turn battle into comedy here too.

So it is absolutely wrong to infer any ideal sense of sacrifice in the Jews from the fact that they stand together in struggle, or, better expressed, in the plundering of their fellow men.

Here again the Jew is led by nothing but the naked egoism of the individual.

That is why the Jewish state—which should be the living organism for preserving and increasing a race—is completely unlimited as to territory. For a state formation to have a definite spatial setting always presupposes an idealistic attitude on the part of the state-race, and especially a correct interpretation of the concept of work. In the exact measure in which this attitude is lacking, any attempt at forming, even of preserving, a spatially delimited state fails. And thus the basis on which alone culture can arise is lacking.

Hence the Jewish people, despite all apparent intellectual qualities, is without any true culture, and especially without any culture of its own. For what sham culture the Jew today possess is the property of other peoples, and for the most part it is ruined in his hands.

---

*'*ursächlich vorhandene Anlagen.*' '*Ursächlich*' is no doubt intended as a refinement of '*urspünglich*' (originally). The phrase would then read: 'their originally existing tendencies.'

In judging the Jewish people's attitude on the question of human culture, the most essential characteristic we must always bear in mind is that there has never been a Jewish art and accordingly there is none today either; that above all the two queens of all arts, architecture and music, owe nothing original to the Jews. What they do accomplish in the field of art is either patchwork or intellectual theft. Thus, the Jew lacks those qualities which distinguish the races that are creative and hence culturally blessed.

To what an extent the Jew takes over foreign culture, imitating or rather ruining it, can be seen from the fact that he is mostly found in the art which seems to require least original invention, the art of acting. But even here, in reality, he is only a 'juggler,' or rather an ape; for even here he lacks the last touch that is required for real greatness; even here he is not the creative genius, but a superficial imitator, and all the twists and tricks that he uses are powerless to conceal the inner lifelessness of his creative gift. Here the Jewish press most lovingly helps him along by raising such a roar of hosannahs about even the most mediocre bungler, just so long as he is a Jew, that the rest of the world actually ends up by thinking that they have an artist before them, while in truth it is only a pitiful comedian.

. . .

No, the Jew possesses no culture-creating force of any sort, since the idealism, without which there is no true higher development of man, is not present in him and never was present. Hence his intellect will never have a constructive effect, but will be destructive, and in very rare cases perhaps will at most be stimulating, but then as the prototype of the "force which always wants evil and nevertheless creates good."* Not through him does any progress of mankind occur, but in spite of him.

. . .

Probably the Aryan was also first a nomad, settling in the course of time, but for that very reason he was never a Jew! No, the Jew is no nomad; for the nomad had also a definite attitude toward the concept of work which could serve as a basis for his later development in so far as the necessary intellectual premises were present. In him the basic idealistic view is present, even if in infinite dilution, hence in his whole being he may seem strange to the Aryan peoples, but not unattractive. In the Jew, however, this attitude is not at all present; for that reason he was never a nomad, but only and always a *parasite* in the body of other peoples. That he sometimes left his previous living space has nothing to do with his own purpose, but results from the fact that from time to time he was thrown out by the host nations he had misused. His spreading is a typical phenomenon for all parasites; he always seeks a new feeding ground for his race.

This, however, has nothing to do with nomadism, for the reason that a Jew never thinks of leaving a territory that he has occupied, but remains where he is, and he sits so fast that even by force it is very hard to drive him out. His extension to ever-new countries occurs only in the moment in which certain conditions for his existence are there present, without which—unlike the nomad—he would not change his residence. He is and remains the typical parasite, a sponger who like a noxious bacillus keeps spreading as soon as a favorable medium invites him. And the effect of his

*Goethe's Faust, lines 1336–1337: Mephistopheles to Faust.

existence is also like that of spongers: wherever he appears, the host people dies out after a shorter or longer period.

Thus, the Jew of all times has lived in the states of other peoples, and there formed his own state, which, to be sure, habitually sailed under the disguise of "religious community" as long as outward circumstances made a complete revelation of his nature seem inadvisable. But as soon as he felt strong enough to do without the protective cloak, he always dropped the veil and suddenly became what so many of the others previously did not want to believe and see: the Jew.

The Jew's life as a parasite in the body of other nations and states explains a characteristic which once caused Schopenhauer, as has already been mentioned, to call him the great master in lying. Existence impels the Jew to lie, and to lie perpetually, just as it compels the inhabitants of the northern countries to wear warm clothing.

His life within other peoples can only endure for any length of time if he succeeds in arousing the opinion that he is not a people but a religious community, though of a special sort.

And this is the first great lie.

In order to carry on his existence as a parasite on other peoples, he is forced to deny his inner nature. The more intelligent the individual Jew is, the more he will succeed in this deception. Indeed, things can go so far that large parts of the host people will end by seriously believing that the Jew is really a Frenchman or an Englishman, a German or an Italian, though of a special religious faith. Especially state authorities, which always seem animated by the historical fraction of wisdom, most easily fall a victim to this infinite deception. Independent thinking sometimes seems to these circles a true sin against holy advancement, so that we may not be surprised if even today a Bavarian state ministry, for example, still has not the faintest idea that the Jews are members of a *people* and not of a *'religion'* though a glance at the Jew's own newspapers should indicate this even to the most modest mind. The *Jewish Echo* is not yet an official organ, of course, and consequently is unauthoritative as far as the intelligence of one of these government potentates is concerned.

The Jew has always been a people with definite racial characteristics and never a religion; only in order to get ahead he early sought for a means which could distract unpleasant attention from his person. And what would have been more expedient and at the same time more innocent than the 'embezzled' concept of a religious community? For here, too, everything is borrowed or rather stolen. Due to his own original special nature, the Jew cannot possess a religious institution, if for no other reason because he lacks idealism in any form, and hence belief in a hereafter is absolutely foreign to him. And a religion in the Aryan sense cannot be imagined which lacks the conviction of survival after death in some form. Indeed, the Talmud is not a book to prepare a man for the hereafter, but only for a practical and profitable life in this world.

The Jewish religious doctrine consists primarily in prescriptions for keeping the blood of Jewry pure and for regulating the relation of Jews among themselves, but even more with the rest of the world; in other words, with non-Jews. But even here it is by no means ethical problems that are involved, but extremely modest economic ones. Concerning the moral value of Jewish religious instruction, there are today and have been at all times rather exhaustive studies (not by Jews; the drivel of the Jews themselves on the subject is, of course, adapted to its purpose) which make this kind of religion seem positively monstrous according to Aryan conceptions. The best characterization is provided by the product of this religious education, the Jew himself. His life is only of this world, and his spirit is inwardly as alien to true Christianity as his nature two thousand years previous was to the great founder of the new doctrine. Of course, the latter made no secret of his attitude toward the Jewish people, and when necessary he even took to the whip to drive from the temple of the Lord this adversary of all humanity, who then as always saw in religion nothing but an instrument for his business existence. In return, Christ was nailed to the cross, while our present-day party Christians debase themselves to begging for Jewish votes at elections and later try to arrange political swindles with atheistic Jewish parties—and this against their own nation.

On this first and greatest lie, that the Jews are not a race but a religion, more and more lies are based in necessary consequence. Among them is the lie with regard to the language of the Jew. For him it is not a means for expressing his thoughts, but a means for concealing them. When he speaks French, he thinks Jewish, and while he turns out German verses, in his life he only expresses the nature of his nationality. As long as the Jew has not become the master of the other peoples, he must speak their languages whether he likes it or not, but as soon as they became his slaves, they would all have to learn a universal language (Esperanto, for instance!), so that by this additional means the Jews could more easily dominate them!

To what an extent the whole existence of this people is based on a continuous lie is shown incomparably by the *Protocols of the Wise Men of Zion,* so infinitely hated by the Jews. They are based on a forgery, the *Frankfurter Zeitung* moans and screams once every week: the best proof that they are authentic. What many Jews may do unconsciously is here consciously exposed. And that is what matters. It is completely indifferent from what Jewish brain these disclosures originate; the important thing is that with positively terrifying certainty they reveal the nature and activity of the Jewish people and expose their inner contexts as well as their ultimate final aims. The best criticism applied to them, however, is reality. Anyone who examines the historical development of the last hundred years from the standpoint of this book will at once understand the screaming of the Jewish press. For once this book has become the common property of a people, the Jewish menace may be considered as broken.

Chapter 2

The World that Was Annihilated

INTRODUCTION

Approximately half of the Jews who were annihilated between 1940 and 1945 were Polish. In a land where more than 3 million Jews had lived before World War II, perhaps 5,000 remain today, a pathetic remnant of a diverse and vital culture. While the Nazis destroyed the Jewish presence in other countries, nowhere did Jews suffer greater numerical destruction and such total cultural extinction as in Poland. While tens of thousands of Jews today live in Germany, in the Balkan nations, and in western Europe, a revival on Polish soil seems beyond the realm of possibility.

Jewish life in pre-Holocaust Poland deserves a more valid assessment than the oft repeated generalization that Polish infants absorb anti-Semitism with their mother's milk. Actually, much of Polish-Jewish history was marked by long periods of tolerance, of flourishing religious creativity, and substantial population growth. Jews had originally come to the medieval kingdom of Poland by royal invitation. The rulers of the German lands had been unwilling or unable to stop the frenzy of killing and expulsion which accompanied the Crusades. Polish kings, eager to support the growth of towns and a middle class, welcomed the fleeing victims and granted them rights and privileges. Even after that initial tolerance was disturbed by intermittent anti-Jewish outbreaks and legal restrictions, the numbers reveal a successful presence; in the 150 years after 1500, the Jewish population grew from 50,000 to approximately 500,000. During the 1930s Jews constituted about 1 percent of the people in western nations, while in Poland it reached 10 percent.

For three centuries Polish Jews lived in their own, nearly autonomous communities called *stetls*. Here the people spoke Yiddish to each other and Hebrew to God. They comprised much of the petty middle class. Unlike their brethren to the west they were not restricted in their choice of livelihood. They served in the royal bureaucracy, engaged in trade, and were skilled in all handicrafts. Such favorable circumstances, however, exacted a heavy price. Whenever misery drove serfs and/or cossacks to rebel against their oppressors, the Jews were identified with the ruling class and suffered dreadful consequences. Further deterioration of the Jewish asylum was caused by the influx of German merchants who resented Jewish competition. The Catholic priesthood, by and large, inflamed anti-Jewish attitudes, particularly in their Easter deicide exhortations. Furthermore, the political disintegration of Poland required a sacrificial scapegoat, and the Jews effectively served that end. Thus, the peaceful coexistence of the Middle Ages gave way to antagonism between Jew and Christian in modern Poland.

Jewish reaction to the external threat, coupled with their physical and social isolation, resulted in ghetto life centered around faith, family, and community. This segregation was not broken until the 19th century when, at last, some Jews and some Poles found common ground. The winds of the Enlightenment were late in reaching Poland, but eventually they permitted a partial assimilation and urbanization of Polish Jewry.

The life that disappeared was not homogeneous, not in piety, not in economic conditions, not in level of education nor in political choices. When the Germans defeated Poland in 1939, Jews lived in Warsaw and in tiny villages. A few were rich, most were poor. Some were ardent Polish nationalists, others were Zionists who planned to follow the 400,000 who had already left for Palestine and America. Jewish Socialists had organized the *Bund* and worked to improve the lot of the working class. The Hasids avoided the taint of modernization but other devout Jews found it possible to bridge the conflict between tradition and modernization. Young assimilationists clashed with their orthodox parents, and girls asked to be educated in public schools. Only in the idealized recollections were family relationships perfectly harmonious.

Despite its many tensions, the interwar years were intellectually dynamic. Hundreds of Jewish newspapers and magazines found avid readers; theatrical productions and orchestras performed to full houses; scientific forums and debating societies nourished an insatiable appetite to live and learn. Zionists and Polish patriots, students of the Torah and students of the universities, youngsters who loved sports and those who thought such diversions to be sinful, all were representative of the civilization that was destroyed during the Holocaust.

Study Is the Best of Wares

Milton Meltzer

While living with his grandfather in Neshwies, young Morris Cohen went to cheder for six days in every week. The school day began at eight in the morning and ended after six, except for Friday, when the boys were dismissed a little earlier. There were few vacation days in the year, only the holiday weeks of Passover and Succoth. Looking back at his childhood in the old country, Professor Cohen recalled what he learned in cheder:

> I was taught to translate the Bible into the vernacular—Yiddish. This was a great joy, especially when we came to the narrative portions of the Book of Genesis and later to those of Judges, Samuel, and Kings. These were my first story books as well as my introduction to history, and to this day the Biblical stories have an inexhaustible liveliness for me, as if I had actually lived through them.
>
> My first rebbe in Neshwies was exceedingly poor, had four children and was very much harassed. In his irritation, he omitted the usual ritual of deliberate punishment, the letting down of the trousers and the application of the strap. Instead he lashed out his blows at the least provocation, and sometimes...even without provocation....The cheder was located on a quiet street, and the long rectangular back yard was covered with grass. I remember especially one late afternoon as the long shadows were fading with the setting sun, I ran around in the yard with a feeling of great elation....
>
> In the winter, we had to stay in the cheder until after dark and so had to light our way home by carrying lanterns. For a long time the possessing, the cleaning, and the carrying of the lantern, appealed to me as a thrilling adventure. For the rest there were few organized games among us inside or outside of the classroom....
>
> After two years in my first cheder I was sent to another rebbe, Reb Nehemiah, who was a *maskil,* that is, one who believed in bringing some of the beauty of Western learning into Hebrew studies. Indeed, he gave private lessons in grammar to advanced pupils who came to his house late in the afternoon or evening....But we, the regular pupils, were taught nothing but the traditional curriculum, the Pentateuch with the Commentary of Rashi and a few other books of the Bible. Only in an occasional comment would our rebbe's learning open up for me glimpses of the great outside world of geography and history. I remember particularly his explanation of the origin and evolution of boats and of the Franco-Prussian War of 1870....
>
> My mother, who never forgot her disappointment at not having succeeded in her ambition to learn the art of writing, was determined that I should not be similarly hand-

---

Milton Meltzer, "Study Is the Best of Wares," *A History of Jewish Life from Eastern Europe to America,* Northvale, NJ: Jason Aronson, 1996, pp. 72–79. By permission of the author.

icapped. So she had a letter written to her father that he should see to it that I receive instruction in the art of writing Yiddish. To this my grandfather replied, "My dear daughter, I am giving your son Torah—the substance of life. The trimmings come later."

In Swislocz, said Abraham Ain, boys of five were sent to cheder, which was usually in the teacher's home. They were taught the alphabet and reading for the first year and a half, then promoted to a higher grade, where they studied the Pentateuch and the rest of the Bible. The next step was the Talmud. Some teachers also gave the boys writing and arithmetic. By the age of ten, a Jewish boy knew a little of the Bible, could write Yiddish and do some arithmetic, and was studying the Talmud. Some boys were only part-time cheder students and gave several other hours a day to learning Russian, arithmetic, and writing.

Boys whose parents couldn't afford the fee went to a Talmud Torah, where the tuition was low or free. Bible and Talmud classes were mixed with reading, arithmetic, Yiddish, and Russian. Girls did not start their education until seven or eight. They were taught to read and write Hebrew and Yiddish, and to do arithmetic. At the age of thirteen or fourteen they were usually apprenticed to seamstresses. The poorer girls became domestics.

It was not until about 1900 that a general public school, running through the fourth grade, and a modern Hebrew school were opened in Swislocz, for all Jewish children.

This tradition of elementary education—centered on the Bible and Talmud—was almost universal for shtetl Jews. As early as three, and up to thirteen, boys went to school, no matter what their social or economic position. The conviction that Jewish education was for everybody went back to Rashi, the commentator on the Torah and Talmud who lived in the eleventh century. It was Rashi, said Abraham Joshua Heschel, who "democratized Jewish education; he brought the Bible, the Gemara, and the Midrash to the people, and made the Talmud a popular book, every man's book....Scholarship ceased to be the monopoly of the few and became widely disseminated. In many communities, the untutored became the rare exception."

Uncle Reuben, the itinerant tailor of Slutzk, is an example of this.

Every day Uncle Reuben awoke before dawn, washed his hands, and recited the daily portion from the Psalms. Later he went to the synagogue where he said the morning prayers and stayed on to study a chapter from the *Mishnah*. On his returning home he would open the thick leatherbound prayer book whose pages had yellowed with age and handling, and recite an additional prayer, comprising excerpts from holy writings, assigned for each day of the week. Then he would eat breakfast, and sit down to work. He sewed, as he prayed, with great dedication; he was meticulously precise, anxious to do credit to his friends, the peasants.

At one in the afternoon, Uncle Reuben would stretch out on the sofa, and nap briefly. Then he would wash his hands again, open the Midrash *Rabbah* and study the portion of the week. He had a hard time walking the muddy roads of Polesia on his rounds of the villages; but the intricate paths of the Midrash were even harder. En route he would stumble over strange words, lose his way, wander in circles, and finally stop and look desperately around. Where in the world was he! Suddenly, Uncle Reuben's face would light up. "Aha!" He had found his way out of the morass of the Midrash.

Back to the synagogue he went for the afternoon prayers, studied *The Well of Jacob,* said the evening prayers, and listened to the news from the shopkeepers and the young men who read the modern Hebrew papers. After the evening meal he read a chapter from a popular inspirational book using both the original Hebrew and the Yiddish translation in the margins. The women of the household would stop talking at their chores and listen to his loud singsong.

It is like the shtetl depicted by Mendele Mocher Sforim in one of his stories, "Shloime Red Khayims." He calls it...

a place of learning of old standing, where practically all the inhabitants are scholars, where the House of Study is full of men and youths busily pursuing their studies...where, at dusk, between the *Minha* and the *Maariv* services, artisans and other simple folk gather around the table to listen to a discourse on the Midrash, the Bible...and similar ethical and philosophical works....

Heschel asks:

What other nation has a lullaby to the effect that "study is the best of wares"? At the birth of a child, the school children come and chant the *Shema* in unison around the cradle. The child is taken to school for the first time wrapped in a *tallis.* School children are referred to as "sacred sheep," and a mother's pet name for her little boy is "*mayn tsadikl*" (my little saint). Hence, one is ready to sell all household belongings to pay tuition. Women work all their lives to enable their husbands to devote themselves to study. One shares his last morsel of food with a yeshiva *bokher.* And when the melancholy sweet tone of Talmudic study penetrates the poor alleys, exhausted Jews on their pallets are delighted, for they feel they have a share in that study....Study was a song of longing, a pouring out of the heart before the Merciful Father, a sort of prayer, a communion and an ardent desire for a purified world.

The teaching in the cheder used none of the educational methods we call progressive today. The process of learning was endless repetition. The little child had to memorize the strange Hebrew words and their meanings. He learned only the elements of reading and the prayers. Then he advanced to the second cheder, where he studied the *khumesh* (Pentateuch), learning to translate whole sentences and to understand the text. Here he worked with Rashi's commentary, going into interpretation and hidden meanings. In the next stage, the highest cheder, he undertook independent study under the guidance of a teacher more highly qualified than the elementary *melamed.* Here the study of the Talmud covered all kinds of problems, ancient and modern, religious and secular. The boring mechanical mode the youngster had begun with was now replaced by the true excitement of learning, when the mind and imagination are stretched to their full capacity. The boy was ten or eleven at this point and everyone watched closely to see if he had the intellectual power to become a Talmudic scholar.

If he did, he was sent on to the highest institution of learning, the rabbinical academy called the yeshiva.

The old one-room cheder was a "unique juvenile madhouse," says Maurice Samuel. It was supposed to be the child's second home, and the *melamed* a person to be cherished like one's father. But almost no Jew who has left a memoir of those early days mentions a rebbe with affection. Eliakum Zunser describes the bedlam in the cheder, the scolding, the spanking, the slapping, the beating with the indispensable *kantchik* (cat-o'-three-tails). In Sholem Aleichem's stories the boys speak of their teachers as "the Murderer" or "the Death-Angel."

In his novel, *The Brothers Ashkenazi,* I. J. Singer etches in acid a *melamed* in Lodz who taught older children.

> Reb Boruch Wolf is famous for his cruelty not less than for his piety and learning. Besides, he overworks the boys. He holds them in the schoolroom from early morning till late at night. On Thursday, which is repetition day, he works with them beyond midnight and sometimes until the morning hours. He crams into the children not only the Talmud with all its accepted commentaries but all kinds of super-commentaries on the commentaries themselves....He wants the boys to learn early how to carry on the heavy burden of Torah and Jewishness.
>
> He never teaches the boys the interesting parts of the Talmud, the legends and stories and adventures of the great teachers in Israel. These he considers fit only for women, or for anti-Hasidic Jews, or for others with weak heads....He avoids those tractates of the Talmud which deal with bright and cheerful things, like holy days, festivals and jolly customs....His learning is as dry and bony and harsh as his own old body. He hates the simple and straightforward, the obvious meaning of a text or interpretation. If it isn't complicated, it isn't learning to him.

The Yiddish writer I. L. Peretz, who grew up in the 1850s in Zamoscz, a town in Russian Poland, gives a more affectionate picture of his cheder teacher:

> He, too, was small in stature and frail. Though he was an angry little man, quick to fly into a temper, he didn't whip his pupils. His hands would tremble, and he would call to his wife: "Henneh, grab hold of the oven-rake and split the head of the ignoramus!"
>
> Henneh, however, remained placidly in her seat near the oven, going on with her plucking of chickens or knitting of socks.
>
> But if his angry command had to do with me, she would reply: "Listen, don't you dare touch Leibish! I'll tell Rivele on you!"
>
> To eke out a living, Henneh peddled onions and green vegetables from house to house. Rivele, my mother, was one of her customers and the two women were fast friends.
>
> "What a wonderful woman Rivele is!" said Henneh. "A female saint. She denies herself and her family necessities in order to give to the poor. And in such amounts! And this murderer wants to hit her Leibishl!"
>
> "Nu! Nu!" grumbled the rebbe. "But don't forget to tell her what a rascal he is!"

Zunser warned young men thinking of becoming *melameds:*

May God give you a better profession than teaching; but if, alas, you are doomed to teach, conduct yourselves differently. Little creatures need character training above all. So don't let a child hear oaths and curses, because these will burrow into its head like worms into a young apple. Children are wards entrusted to you, and you are paid by fathers and mothers to guard these wards against harm and to implant into them good habits. If a child sees you behaving badly, if it hears falsehood and deception within your walls, the seeds of corruption enter its soul and the beautiful flower will become a prickly thorn.

But there was another side to it, Maurice Samuel points out:

Though children were willing to play tricks on the Rebbi now and then, we never meet with genuine rancour. A Rebbi was looked upon as a natural calamity; it was in the nature of things that he should be impatient, unsympathetic, handy with the kantchik. Children learned to accept his cruelties with something like good humour, and in this they were training themselves for life as Jews. They would have much to put up with from a surrounding world more impatient, more unsympathetic and handier with the whip than even their Rebbi.

Samuel asks why the cheder, with its traditional method of teaching that remained the same generation after generation, did not cripple the children's minds. "How is it that they did not become idiots, but on the contrary maintained an astonishingly high level of intelligence and, what is more, actually learned what they were taught?"

He thinks it is because today we tend to exaggerate the sensitivity of children and to underestimate how resilient the human being is at all ages. People endure when they accept the situation, he believes. "The readiness to endure is half the trick of enduring, and those who have not known the better do not lose half their strength whimpering over the worse." Because the children in the Eastern European cheders "took for granted what they had to face in the way of training, they were immune from most of the negative effects."

There was, too, he adds, the important fact that children and parents agreed on the worth of what the cheder was teaching. "Boys were learning in cheder that which their fathers knew and cherished. They were treated as children but they were challenged as adults."

The yeshivas of the nineteenth century drew hundreds of boys from all over Eastern Europe. They were located not in the old centers of learning—Lublin, Cracow, Lemberg—but in the shtetls, the centers of Jewish spiritual life. The yeshiva at Volozhin, the outstanding center of Torah scholarship, was founded in 1802. Others developed in such small towns as Eyshisok, Mir, Slobodka, Telz, Slonim.

Education in the yeshiva rested on independent study, with the teacher used as a guide. The student relied upon himself in his deep analysis of the Talmud. The approach was to examine commentary and interpretation, always moving from the various texts back to the Biblical passages that were their ultimate sources.

The study of the Talmud was called *pilpul,* which is defined in *Life Is with People* as…

Pepper, and it is as sharp, as spicy, as stimulating as its name implies. It involves comparison of different interpretations, analysis of all possible and impossible aspects of the given problem, and—through an ingenious intellectual combination—the final solution of an apparently insoluble problem.

Penetration, scholarship, imagination, memory, logic, wit, subtlety—all are called into play for solving a Talmudic question. The ideal solution is the *khiddush,* an original synthesis that has never before been offered. This mental activity is a delight both to the performer and to his audience. Both enjoy the vigor of the exercise and the adroitness of the accomplishment. And at the same time, both relish demonstrating their ability to perform on so lofty and esoteric a level. When two accomplished scholars engage in pilpul, they will be surrounded by an admiring group that follows each sally in eager silence, and later will discuss the fine points with each other—possibly working up a new argument about which scholar carried the day.

The yeshiva teacher was respected as much as the rabbi. He was paid not by the parents of the students, as in the cheder, but by the institution. Most of the yeshiva *bokhers* (yeshiva boys) were the sons of poor parents. The Jewish community undertook to support not only the yeshiva itself, with the salary of its head and the high cost of books, but each student attending it. It was a widespread custom for students to eat in a different house every day of the week. Funds were raised throughout Eastern Europe for these purposes. Every Jew felt obliged to support the study of the law, and the small towns took great pride in their yeshivas.

No degree was given to mark the end of a phase of study. How could you complete study when "the Torah has no bottom?" A diploma was given after a few years in the yeshiva to show that the student had a right to function as a rabbi. He got no scholarly degree or title. A learned man, whether a self-taught cobbler or a yeshiva-trained intellectual, was respectfully called Reb, meaning "my teacher." The study of the law never ended. It could be interrupted for a time by circumstances, but the good Jew explored the limitless law as long as he lived, part of his day while working for a living, and all of the day after retirement.

Every shtetl had its men who did nothing but study the Talmud, night and day. The highest honors of the community went to them. They had *yichus,* they were the "beautiful Jews." If a youth showed promise of being such a scholar, everyone would help provide the opportunity for study. The father would support his son, sisters their brother, a father-in-law his son-in-law. Charnofsky offers a snapshot of such a man in Warshilovka:

Zalman Yankew David was a man in his early forties, but he had the appearance of a man in his seventies. Zalman never worked in his life. He was a Talmud student. He always prayed, he always learned, he was almost always at home or in the synagogue. He sat over a *mishnaes,* a *gemura,* a *tillum,* or other such books, reading and studying. He only took time out for eating two meals a day and sleeping and teaching his own three sons the great learning of God, the Talmud, the Torah, and everything that he knew a Jew should learn.

Zalman was well educated. He knew most of the tillim by heart. He could converse with rabbis about the deep Jewish learning, and would show them many interpretations that contradicted the holy books. He could have been a rabbi but had no such desires.

When Zalman married, his wife knew and her father knew that he would never support a family. But his father-in-law wanted him in the family. He said that Zalman was gold and diamonds to a family, so he provided full support for him and his wife.

When the father-in-law died, Zalman's wife, Ruth, took over. They already had three children that were growing up, and the needs were big. So she decided to sell *crellin* (beads) to the peasant women at the local yarids, and to travel to the nearby yarids....Ruth worked hard....But Ruth was happy. She knew that her husband had to sit at his learning and prayers and that he was shaping and building an afterlife for her and himself and the children. She thought of the *Gan Aden* and of how wonderful it would be there, with no worries, no conflicts, no disagreements, where only people with *treiag mitzvas* (613 good deeds) would be admitted. Her husband would have all of those and would be accepted without a doubt. It was worth all her efforts, all her hard work....

The study of the Talmud has long been considered to be of the highest religious and social value. It is a tradition that goes back to the days of the Second Temple. "Thou shalt study in it day and night" was like a commandment. And Jewish society has always had unlimited admiration for one who followed scholarship as the pathway to God. The sage and the scholar became the aristocrats of the Jewish world. In modern times, that prestige, authority, and position have been accorded by Jews not only to those learned in religious studies but to people of intellectual attainment in secular cultures.

Fun and Feasts

Milton Meltzer

The most fun the Jewish children of Warshilovka had came during the winter when the Bug River froze solid. Not that it didn't provide fun in the summertime too. Then they swam in the river. But they couldn't boat on it; that was strictly forbidden by their over-cautious parents. The Jewish children watched enviously as the peasants rowed or paddled up and down the stream that flowed through their town.

In the winter, the Bug froze so deep, horse and sleigh crossed the ice without fear of breaking through and people walked across freely. The youngsters turned out for skating. Charnofsky remembered the joy it gave.

Milton Meltzer, "Fun and Feasts," *A History of Jewish Life from Eastern Europe to America*, Northvale, NJ: Jason Aronson, 1996, pp. 80–86. By permission of the author.

Most of the time we all made our own skates. We took a piece of wood as long as the shoe, put a couple of holes across the width with two strings in to tie to the shoe, and a wire across the length. This made a very good skate, and all we had to do was break it in. When the wire got shiny, the skates were perfect for skating. Our sleds were also homemade. That was easy—even mothers could make sleds for their children. No one ever knew that there were so many children in town until the sleigh-riding came along. Of course the rich children also came out with a servant and a brand-new sled, bought ready-made, or with ready-made skates. We admitted that they had the nicest sleds and skates, but no one was jealous, for we were all out for a good time. The younger children would roam around the market place with their sleds but not for long, because they would get too cold.

The bigger children with their skates would go to the Bug. The skating was real exercise, and everyone was warmed up. Everybody was trying his best to outdo the other one. They skated in rings, and they skated holding hands. Then there was a great straight race that went for miles up and back....It was at this time that the Gentile and Jewish children would mix, and there were no objections from anyone. In fact, one couldn't tell the difference. They all had red cheeks, sparkling eyes, smiling faces, and sportsmanlike feelings—all alike, only some better skaters than others....When the full moon was out and reflected on the white snow and ice, and the frost was mild, our fathers would go out with us, and they too had a good time.

Play was regarded by the shtetl as a concession, says Maurice Samuel, not a right. He describes what was permitted.

On Passover you had games of chance with Brazil nuts; on *Chanukah* you could play cards, or a game resembling "put and take," with little, four-sided spinning tops, on which were inscribed letters recalling the miracle of the unspent oil in the Temple in the days of the Maccabees; on the Thirty-third Day of the Omer (*Lag b'Omer*, between Passover and Pentecost) there was actually an outing into the fields! On *Purim*...there was a play—to be exact, one of two plays, and perhaps even both: the drama of Esther and *The Sale of Joseph.*

That joyous day in the fields that took place on Lag b'Omer is described in *Life Is with People.*

This is the one day of the year when the boys, with their melamed, go out into the fields and woods to enjoy the outdoor world that otherwise is nonexistent to the cheder. Each brings his lunch in a package, and all the mothers vie to give the best "*naseray*" and the most savory tidbits, so that they will not "be ashamed" when all the food is opened and pooled in a common meal. The boys play outdoor games, long caftans flapping about their legs, earlocks bobbing as they run and jump, or shoot at a target with bows and arrows. The melamed, who all the year round bars the cheder door against any spirit of play, accepts the antics of this day as part of the approved regime. How happily he accepts it is "something else again" for occasionally it furnishes an opportunity to work off accumulated resentments against the presiding authority of the schoolroom. Excess in this direction is usually checked, however, by the realization that tomorrow the melamed will again reign in his own realm....

Even in cheder the children enjoyed some happy hours. One of them came at twilight, when the *melamed* went to shul (synagogue) for prayers. In winter, the children sat in the darkness (candles were too costly to burn) and, while waiting for their teacher's return, passed the time telling stories.

> Crowding together against the winter cold and the fear of the wonders they are describing, they tell each other tales in which themes carried over from pagan myths jostle with folklore rooted in the Talmud. In the melamed's absence the strict program of Hebrew erudition is broken into by a medley that mingles biblical miracles with the spirits and demons shared by all the folk, Jews and peasants alike. The boys tell each other in turn about the spirits who throng the shul after midnight, and the tricks they play on anyone who has to sleep there—so that a beggar would rather sleep on the floor of the humblest house than enjoy the honor of a bench in the shul. They tell about the devils who haunt the woods at night, the *sheydim,* and how some of them even get into the shtetl streets when it is very dark. They tell about the *dybbuk* who enters the soul of a person so that he becomes possessed and speaks with a voice not his own, uttering blasphemies that would be far from his true mind. They tell of Lilith, Adam's first wife, who steals children; and of children kidnapped from their parents by gypsies, or by wicked men who deliver them into Army service. Children of Hasidim will repeat tales their fathers bring from the rebbe's court, about the miracles wrought by "wonder man."

Sometimes shtetls had special celebrations. In Shklov, a village of White Russia on the Dnieper, the Burial Society—its members were all Hasidim—gave an annual bean feast. It was the only reward its members got for a whole year's hard work—washing the dead and preparing them for interment, putting on their shrouds, carrying them to the graveyard, and burying them. In hot weather or cold, in rain, snow, or ice. The money the society collected paid for shrouds for the poor, for upkeep of the cemetery, and for the lone sexton's salary. What was left went into the bean feast. It took two days to prepare it. Zalman Schneour gives this mouth-watering description of the feast held in the synagogue:

> First, the breaking of bread. For that, each member of the burial society got a large white roll, and half a loaf of fresh cornbread. Then to drink each other's health everyone was given a bottle of brandy. And to keep it company, a plate of chopped goose-liver, with a few spoonfuls of freshly melted goose-dripping over it, as an appetizer.
>
> The first course was a slice of carp weighing about a pound, stuffed, and full of onions and pepper, trimmed with soft and hard roe, and swimming in horse-radish, colored and sweetened with beetroot. Next, at least a quarter of a fat goose, roasted in its skin, with all the fat on it. And the gizzard and wings, or a stuffed neck and the feet. And to go with it, a big sour cucumber, and a baked apple.
>
> And to raise a thirst, each member of the burial society got a big stack of thin dry toast, with a thick layer of powdered spices on it and pepper and salt, or ginger. This was eaten between courses, munched so loudly that it set the palate on fire, till it had to be quenched with whatever was going in the way of drink, cold beer or dry cider.
>
> After that came a quarter of a pudding, each the size of a big drum, made of noodles, and bound with eggs and goose fat, goose brains, onions and more fat. Each pudding was

crisp and brown on the outside, like a walnut, and inside soft and yellow like calves' brains. These puddings were famed all over Shklov. The wealthiest inhabitants never enjoyed anything so rich and tasty. With the pudding went a mountain of pancakes, made with cinnamon and spices. Or dumplings. With fruit in them. Ordinary people would have called them fruit pies. But for the members of the burial society they were just dumplings.

Then the servers brought sacks of winter apples, slung over their shoulders, and handed them round to the guests. Could any of our generation have eaten all that?

Of all festivals the Sabbath was the first. The people of the shtetl worked all week to reach the Sabbath and celebrate it. To them life and religion were inseparable, and the Sabbath was the most beautiful sign of God's grace, of His gift to them. One of Sholem Aleichem's draymen tells what it meant to him:

When the Sabbath comes I'm a different man, do you hear? I get home betimes on Friday afternoon, and the first thing of course is the baths, if you know what I mean. There I sit on the top row of the steam room and get myself scalded from head to foot. That puts a new skin on me. Fresh as a newborn babe I dance home, and there on the table are the two old brass candlesticks, shining like stars, if you know what I mean, and the two big Sabbath loaves; and there, right beside them, are the winking Sabbath fish, sending out a smell that takes you by the throat. And the house is warm and bright and fresh and clean in every corner. So I sit down like a king, and open the Good Book, and go twice over the week's portion. Then I close the Book, and it's off to the synagogue.

What a homecoming after that! When I open the door and sing out "Good Sabbath" you can hear me at the other end of town. Then comes the benediction by candlelight, and the drop of good old whiskey, that sings right through me, if you know what I mean, and then the Sabbath supper—the shining fish, and the golden soup, and the good old yellow carrots in honey. That night I sleep like a lord, if you know what I mean.

And where am I going in the morning? Why, to the synagogue, of course, as I'm a man and a Jew. And back from the synagogue it's the real Sabbath meal again, the grand old chopped radish, and the good old onion, and the jellied calf's foot, if you know what I mean, with a proper smack of garlic. And when you wake up after your Sabbath afternoon nap, and your mouth's dry, and there's a sourness in your belly, if you know what I mean, what's better, I ask you, than a quart or two of cider? Then, when you're good and ready, and fresh and strong, you sit down to the Good Book again, like a giant, and off you go! Chapter after chapter, eh? Psalm after psalm, at the gallop, like the mileposts on the road, if you know what I mean....

Just how the Sabbath was prepared for and enjoyed by such a struggling shtetl family as Simche's and Molke's is depicted in detail in *Jewish Life in the Ukraine*.

For this holy day Molke would buy 30 pounds of flour to bake challah. She would have dough to take off to make noodles for soup and a kugel, to make *poplickes* (pancakes) for the children and enough twisted challahs to last through the Sabbath. Then she would get some fish and horseradish, for without fish the Sabbath would lose one custom. Then of course there was meat or, if there was enough money, chicken. She would also have a *tzimmes* of carrots, and when Simche came home, usually Friday about noon, if he had had a good week and could afford it, he would go out and buy a bottle of wine....

Molke at sunset would light four candles stuck in candelabra, put on a clean, ironed dress and a silk kerchief on her head, turned in back of her ears. With satisfaction, a sense of accomplishment and devotion, she would put her hands over the lighted candles, close her eyes and *bentsh licht* (say her prayers to open the Sabbath). The children would stay near her, and it seemed as if a divine spirit filled the room. When she ended she said, "Good Shabbos" and the children answer, "*Humain*" (so it should be).

When Simche returned from the synagogue he would repeat "Good Shabbos" and everybody would say "Humain." The table was set; the candles threw a dim light over the room. The white tablecloth glimmered and the lights showed two challahs covered with a hand-embroidered cloth, the bottle of wine and glasses around it—knives, forks, spoons, all were on the table. Simche washed his hands, opened the bottle, filled the bigger glass, put it in the palm of his hand, and said khiddush, the blessing of God for the Sabbath. He then took a drink and handed the glass to Molke. She took a sip and gave each child a sip, beginning with the oldest. Then Simche uncovered the challah and cut a piece, made a *moitza*, and sat down.

Everybody started with the fish, then soup, meat, or chicken, with kugel made of the noodles, and last the tzimmes, made of carrots sweetened with sugar. Between the courses Simche and the children would sing zmiros, a sort of thanksgiving prayer in song. Every one of the boys tried to be louder than the others and Molke would sit, her face shining brightly, and help in the harmonizing. From time to time she would say humain, and the children would follow suit. As the candles got low and began to go out only the kerosene lamp was left burning, until Vassil's son, the peasant friend of the family, would come to turn it out. Molke would hand him a big piece of challah. No Jew was allowed to turn out fire on the Sabbath.

In total darkness Simche and Molke would sit after the children were in bed, and talk about the next world and how a Jew has to prepare for it, how much good he had to do to his neighbors, to his friends, and even to his enemies to gain enough mitzvas to go right to heaven....

They sat talking until they tired and went to sleep. And when the Sabbath was gone and the grim week started, it was again the start of a struggle to make enough to live on....

The word for week was *vokh,* but it meant more, it meant everyday life, it meant hard work, it meant the return from the heavenly joy of the Sabbath to the world where one was "misunderstood, despised, and often hated." The people of the shtetl, it was said, lived from Sabbath to Sabbath, the one day each week that made all Jews equal and every man a king.

Polish Antisemitism between the Wars
An Overview

Yisrael Gutman

...

The last years of the Polish Republic, from the mid-1930s on, were marked by grave escalation in the antisemitic public mood and of anti-Jewish policies. Even a cursory examination of the Polish press from those years produces an impression that the Jewish Question stood among the central problems preoccupying the Polish society and the government. The goal of decreasing the Jewish population in Poland by immediate mass emigration became something of a national consensus. Only the Left expressed reservations, and even there some regress could be observed in its position on this question. I should mention in this context that some members of the Polish intelligentsia and the Polish Left encouraged emigration of the Jews, particularly emigration to Palestine, out of a positive approach and avowed sympathy for the Zionist venture in that land. Those liberal sympathizers always took care to make it clear that they did not want pressure put on the Jews to leave Poland and that the decision should be taken by individual Jews themselves.

Early in 1937 the Obóz Zjednoczenia Narodowego (OZON, Camp of National Unity), which was founded as a movement of regime supporters, advocated the division of the Polish population into two categories: Christians and non-Christians. OZON demanded mass emigration of Jews to Palestine and other countries, but at the same time it voiced reservations regarding violent means to speed up the process, not only out of humanitarian concerns but also out of fear that violence might destabilize the political order and result in anarchy. The option of emigration did not, of course, depend entirely on the will of the Poles and the Jews in Poland, as many of the countries thought of as possible destinations for the would-be émigrés had closed their doors to newcomers. The radical wing of the Endecja and other extremist political forces of the radical variety were not satisfied with declarations about the necessity for boycotting the Jews and removing them from the country. They argued that pressure must be applied to the Jews by initiating a campaign of violence, including pogroms. Jacob Lestschinsky mentions hundreds of victims in scores of

Yisrael Gutman, "Polish Antisemitism between the Wars: An Overview," *The Jews of Poland between Two World Wars,* Gutman, Mendelsohn, Reinharz, Shmeruk (eds.). Waltham, MA: Univ. Press of New England, 1989, pp. 105–108. © 1989 by Brandeis University Press, The Tauber Institute Series, by permission of University Press of New England.

cities and towns swept by a wave of anti-Jewish outbursts in the years 1935–37.[1] Trials conducted in the aftermath of those disturbances—the arguments put forward by the defense as well as the sentences given the offenders—also reflect the spirit of the times.

A separate question that merits further systematic research concerns the extent of the influence of National Socialism and the Third Reich on the antisemitic public climate in Poland and the anti-Jewish policies pursued during the interwar years. Szymon Rudnicki's recent study of the Obóz Narodowo Radykalny (ONR, National Radical Camp), makes a significant contribution in that direction.[2] Polish antisemitism is often portrayed, as explained above, as lacking a racist component. One of the reasons that race was not a factor was the relatively small number of Jewish converts to Christianity in Poland, as opposed to the much higher numbers in Germany and Austria. Another, and perhaps more important reason was that the Roman Catholic church regarded racism as a deviation from Christian doctrine, although this view should not obscure the part played by the church in fanning antisemitic sentiments or at the least in not restraining such sentiments. In actual fact, many priests supported the Endeks. One church leader, Cardinal August Hlond, condemned physical violence against the Jews in his 1936 pastoral letter, but at the same time he went to great lengths to underscore the sins committed by the Jews as a collectivity. In this view the Jews were seen as speculators, dealers in unfair trade practices, spreaders of permissivism and atheism, and, worse of all, supporters of the Left in general and communism in particular. The most extreme among the anti-Jewish priests, such as Stanislaw Trzeciak in Warsaw, did not refrain from seeking justification for racism in Christian doctrines.

More pronounced, however, was the influence of Nazi Germany in the political sphere. It can be seen in attempts to emulate Nazi legislation and to adapt German methods of harassing Jews to Polish conditions. Thus, for example, in September 1938, one year before the German invasion of Poland, Adolf Hitler told Józef Lipski, the Polish ambassador to Germany, of his intention to deport European Jews to colonies, indicating that Poland was to be a part of this plan. Lipski did not regard this matter as a strictly Polish internal affair, and he went so far as to declare that should the Nazi leader succeed, the Poles would erect a magnificent statue in his honor in Warsaw.[3]

The Endeks, as a traditionally anti-German party, regarded Germany as a constant threat to Poland. Consequently they preferred to follow the example of Italian fascism, though not in its lack—until 1938—of a pronounced antisemitic component. However, the contemporary Polish writer Andrzej Micewski remarked in his biography of Dmowski that the Nazi's anti-Jewish policy confused the ardent views of the Endek leader. Dmowski was a profound political thinker, and his anti-German stand remained a constant component in his analysis of the Polish political situation. But Dmowski believed, according to Micewski, that "German imperialism was promoted by freemasonry and the Jews. Since Hitler has crushed these forces Germany is no longer a threat."[4] The OZON, which went to great lengths to draw in the young generation that had allied with the radical splinter of the Endeks, did not flinch from for a time joining forces with fascist and fanatically antisemitic groups. There is no shortage of racist articles, pamphlets, and legislative proposals, copying elements of the Nuremberg Laws submitted in those years to the Sejm.

In summary, I do not think that Polish antisemitism should be regarded as a phenomenon *sui generis,* unaffected by developments throughout Europe and by the social and political dynamics of the interwar period. Antisemitism was deeply embedded in the tissue of Polish-Jewish relations as they developed over centuries. If one disregards the radical fringes, the anti-Jewish themes that had been crystallizing in the course of many generations in Poland did not evolve into forms of aggressive political action with genocidal overtones. Popular antisemitism, however, when combined with the objective conditions prevailing in interwar Poland (such as the sheer numbers of the Jews, the economic plight, and so forth) and with outside influences, particularly the rapprochement with Nazi Germany and the inspiration it provided, turned Polish antisemitism into a combustible mixture, especially in the late 1930s.

In the last months before the outbreak of the Second World War, there was some movement toward reconciliation between Poles and Jews as they perceived the threat posed by a common enemy. This reconciliation was, however, temporary and short lived. Yet I summarily reject the thesis that portrays the Poles as playing a part in initiating and implementing the extermination of Jews in the Holocaust. There is no documentary evidence to support the contention that the extermination camps were built in Poland because of the intensity of Polish antisemitism. At the same time I do not accept the opposite argument that antisemitism ceased to exist, or at least was significantly weakened, in Nazi-occupied Poland. In my view antisemitism was an active factor and to some degree had an adverse effect on the situation of the Jews in Poland, on the possibilities of Jewish defense, and on the extent of rescue of the Jews during this period.

In support of my view I would like to quote from the diary of the historian and chronicler Emanuel Ringelblum. The following was written in the Warsaw ghetto in August 1940:

> August 22. An Endek newspaper was published [clandestinely] containing the following: Jews are being beaten up and the Poles are being killed; the Jews are given several days to move out, whereas several hours were given to Poles in Poznań. The Jews are being rounded up, but the Poles are being shot at. We congratulate you [the Jews] for your new ally.[5]

This excerpt from an Endek paper is a good illustration of antisemitism beclouding the mind in a way that, in critical periods, may lead to grave consequences.

NOTES

[1]Jacob Lestschinsky, "Ha-praot be-Polin (1935–1937)," in *Dapim le-heker hashoah ve-ha-mered*, vol. 2, ed. Nahman Blumental (Tel Aviv, 1952), pp. 37–72.

[2]Szymon Rudnicki, *Obóz Narodowo-Radykalny: Geneza i dzialalno ść* (Warsaw, 1985).

[3]See Józef Lipski, *Diplomat in Berlin (1933–1939)*, ed. Waclaw Jedrzejewicz (London, 1968), p. 411.

[4]Andrzej Micewski, *Roman Dmowski* (Warsaw, 1971), p. 367.

[5]Emanuel Ringelblum, *Ksovim fun geto,* vol. 1: *Togbukh fun varshever geto (1939–1942)* (Warsaw, 1961), p. 134.

Community and Identity in the Interwar *Shtetl*

Samuel D. Kassow

The *shtetl* confronts the historian of interwar Poland with the daunting problem of reconciling symbolism with reality, implied uniformities with unmistakable diversity, assumed national exclusivity with the growing presence of another nation for whom the term *shtetl* meant absolutely nothing. Indeed the historian is tempted to plead academic rigor and leave the *shtetl* to the literary critics.

...

As an *ideal type,* the *shtetl* was a form of settlement based on a market that served as a contact point between the Jewish majority and a Gentile hinterland whose social composition and cultural level minimized the threat not only of assimilation but even of acculturation. Even in a *shtetl* with a sizable Polish population, the Jews lived in a compact mass, usually in the streets around the marketplace. The *shtetl*'s economic function dictated a specific interplay of time and space, with the market day and the Sabbath as the two main events of the week, as well as an economic relationship with the Gentiles that was complementary rather than competitive, although in practice competition from Gentile merchants, artisans, and cooperatives became more severe during the interwar period. The market day itself tended to divide into the morning hours,

---

Samuel D. Kassow, "Community and Identity in the Interwar *Shtetl*," *The Jews of Poland Between Two World Wars*, Gutman, Mendelsohn, Reinharz, Shmeruk (eds.). Waltham, MA: Univ. Press of New England, 1989, pp. 198–204, 216–219. © 1989 by Brandeis University Press, The Tauber Institute Series, by permission of University Press of New England.

when the peasants sold their products, and the afternoon, when they went into the Jewish shops to buy goods. On nonmarket days the *shtetl* was eerily quiet.

The state of communications and transportation dictated a static market: the *shtetl* mainly served peasants who could come to town with their horse-drawn wagons and return home on the same day. Unless there was a major river system or railroad, entrepreneurial opportunities were rare and credit was a persistent problem, so much so that a major function of communal organization was often the extension of credit to buy goods to sell on the market day.

Yet while the market has come to be seen as the focal point of the *shtetl*'s economic existence, there were in fact wide variations in the economic physiognomy of various *shtetlekh,* especially during the interwar period. While a *shtetl* in Polesie or the Vilna area might have conformed to the classic pattern of the market town and suffered greatly from the crisis of its agricultural hinterland, other *shtetlekh*, such as Kaluszyn in Warsaw province, found a modicum of economic security as centers of specialized handicrafts or as transfer points between larger cities and the surrounding countryside.

The *shtetl* had enough Jews to support a basic network of community institutions—a *mikveh* (ritual bathhouse), a *bes-medresh,* a *khevre kadisha,* (burial society), and a rabbi or *moreh-horaah* (religious judge). In this way it differed from smaller types of settlement such as villages, and the differences between *yishuvnikes* (village Jews) and *shtetl* Jews figured prominently in the *shtetl*'s collective sense of humor. But the Jewish community was not so big that most inhabitants were not known, ranked, exposed to social pressures, and most often fixed in the community's mind by an apt nickname. Social differences were clear and strong. Seating arrangements in the synagogue, *aliyes* (calls to the Torah), and burial sites in the cemetery all served as a constant reminder of social gradations: *sheyne yidn* (upper-class Jews), *balebatim* (well-to-do Jews), *balmelokhes* (artisans), *proste* (lower-class Jews), and so forth. Even within such comparatively modest categories as artisans, there were definite distinctions of status based on the nature of the tailoring or the shoemaking being performed. Watchmaking ranked higher still.

But if the *shtetl* nursed a strong sense of social gradation, it also maintained important "safety valves," counters to the humiliations of the caste system. *Balmelokhes* could gain prestigious *aliyes* by the simple expedient of starting their own *minyan* (quorum for public prayer), which also doubled as a fraternal organization. If a rich man showed little social responsibility, or gave too little to charity, his heirs might well face a hefty bill from the *khevre kadisha.* Especially in Congress Poland and Galicia, Hasidism was a powerful social force that established subcommunities marked by close contact between rich and poor—although often at the expense of women and family life.

If social differences and prejudices were real, they still lacked clear legal and moral underpinnings. The *shtetl* culture was pluralistic and flexible enough to nourish new social attitudes, and this tendency was especially marked in the interwar period. After World War I youth movements introduced new ferment into the *shtetl*'s life and sharply attacked the traditional *shtetl* bias toward *mishker* (trade) and against physical labor and craftsmanship. New organizations like the *handverker fareynen* (artisans' unions) fought hard to counteract this traditional prejudice by emphasizing the dignity of physical labor—*melokhe iz melukhe* (having a trade is power). The massive influx of aid from the United States after World War I gave new leaders a chance to come forward and take a prominent role in the relief effort. In the process they contested the position of the prewar elite in the *shtetl*'s politics.

This tension between social discrimination and countervailing safety valves provides a basic key to understanding the interwar *shtetl*. Another was a growing structure of organizational links between the *shtetl* and the wider Jewish community. The *landsmanshaft*, the Joint Distribution Committee, the central headquarters of the political party or youth group, the touring Yiddish theater troupe, or the daily newspaper coming from Warsaw or Vilna all helped integrate the *shtetl* into a wider network of allegiances and loyalties. The interplay of economic deprivation and these new outside currents imparted its own logic to social organizations in the *shtetl*. Young people could not afford books and newspapers but developed libraries within the framework of youth organizations, which in turn transformed patterns of social life, especially in the area of male-female relationships. The growing need for credit gave the Joint Distribution Committee (JDC) the opportunity to begin a new kind of democratic credit organization, the *gemiles khesed kase* (free-loan society), which also came to play a very important social role. Alongside traditional social events such as the banquets of long-established societies, new rituals, such as annual firemen's parades (a good example of Jewish-Gentile cooperation), Passover fund-raising bazaars (which connected the youth movements with adult politics), and amateur theater performances (often linked to the fund-raising needs of the local Tarbut or TSYSHO school) helped to mark the evolution of the interwar *shtetl* and create a sense of community.

If one accepts such integration as an index of "modernization," where traditional communities fall under the influence of universal symbols and mobilizing influences from the outside, then the inter-war *shtetl* was clearly undergoing such a process. Yet in fact there was no straight linear evolution from "tradition" to "modernity." The influence of outside institutions on the *shtetl* was filtered through traditional social organizations. While the *shtetlekh* on the eve of World War II had both caftaned Agudaniks and militant young Bundists or *halutzim* (Zionist pioneers) in blue shirts tramping off to soccer matches on Sabbath afternoons, one should not forget that most Jews in the *shtetl* fell somewhere between these two extremes. All *shtetlekh* had a *khevre shas* (study society) or its equivalent. At the same time, in most *shtetlekh* Jews could peruse advertisements for the screening of *King Kong* (a *tsvantsik meterdike malpe!* [an ape twenty meters high!]), *Captains Courageous,* and *The Blue Angel*—not to mention such uplifting rituals as "Miss Glebokie" (or Deblin or Kazimierz), complete with all the latest vicarious glitter from Atlantic City.

Traditional patterns and organizations remained strong and reflected the intertwining of social and religious issues. One example was the conflict over electing new rabbis; poorer Jews could work through organizations such as the *handverker fareyn* to ensure the election of a rabbi they perceived to be friendly to their interests. Artisans could wield power by gaining control of the *khevre kadisha*. Traditional *minyanim* and *khevres* often assumed a particular political complexion or even ran their own candidates in *kehillah* elections. One measure of their importance was that they often were the major distributors of *moes khitim* (Passover relief) and other funds sent to the *shtetl* by *landsmanshaftn* abroad. The hold of religion, if only in the form of *haltn shtat* (doing things for appearance' sake), remained strong—until the very end.

Contrary to popular perceptions, the *shtetl* saw its share of violence and chicanery. Chaim Grade's account in *Tsemakh Atlas* of a local *balebos*'s hiring thugs to destroy a library accords with real-life accounts of violence during *kehillah* elections, disputes over new rabbis and funerals, and arguments over taxes. Grudges and grievances often interrupted Sabbath prayers and even led to fights in the synagogue.

…

Of all the new changes affecting the interwar *shtetl,* one of the most significant was the advent of the youth movements. Although the great ideological movements that swept Eastern European Jewry had begun before World War I, they did not become mass movements until the postwar period, and their vital core was the youth organizations. While the latter were certainly not rebelling against the leadership of the adult parties, the fact remains that Jewish parliamentary politics in interwar Poland could not really improve the condition of Polish Jewry. But in creating a framework for new social networks and youth organizations, the political parties were more successful.

It would not be too farfetched to say that literature and theater played almost as large a role in the Jewish youth movements as ideology. Discussions of literary as well as ideological questions and an intense interest in amateur theater gave the youth movement in the *shtetlekh* its own peculiar cast—that of a counterculture, a home away from home.

A major determinant of the youth movements was the progressive decline of economic opportunity. Traditional options for young men in the *shtetl* had included taking a dowry and starting a store; going to a master, either in the *shtetl* or in a larger city, and learning a trade; studying in the *bes-medresh* in the hopes of impressing a prospective father-in-law; entering the parent's business; or emigrating. If a young woman did not marry, there was the choice of going to a larger city and becoming a maid or finding some sort of factory work. Many of these options narrowed after World War I. Economic conditions often meant that dowries which earlier would have sufficed to start a business no longer covered these costs. Only a small proportion of Polish-Jewish youth had entered trade schools, and hard-pressed artisans were taking on fewer youths as apprentices. In Glebokie a 1931 survey showed that 61 percent of the boys and 83 percent of the girls between ages sixteen and twenty had no work. Another product of the economic situation may have been a trend toward later marriage. To some extent the economic pressure on Jewish youth had been counterbalanced by the demographic impact of World War I, but the number of Jewish children turning thirteen increased from twenty-four thousand in 1930 to forty-five thousand in 1938, heightening competition for limited economic opportunities.

The youth organizations offered hope and dignity, evenings and Saturday afternoons of intense discussion about moral values, literature, and politics, and opportunities to engage in amateur theater and to travel. There was always the chance, however slim, that years of backbreaking *hakhsharah* (pioneer training) might eventually lead to a coveted Palestine emigration certificate. Youths from poorer families often found in the Bundist (and communist) youth organizations a supportive environment that not only encouraged respect for the dignity of their labor but gave them the chance to raise their self-esteem through cultivation of their dramatic and cultural talents in the language they knew best—Yiddish.

Regardless of ideology, the structure of the youth organizations was largely the same. A rented room—the *lokal*—was the center of the organization's activities. The *lokal* would probably have a library where books—too expensive for most youths to afford on their own—would be available and serve as the basis for *kestl ovntn* (debates) and discussions. The organizations sponsored amateur plays, trips to neighboring *shtetlekh,* and long hikes. All but the religious youth organizations scheduled trips on the Sabbath, thus straining relations between young people and religious parents.

As Moshe Kligsberg points out, the values encouraged by the youth movement provided a powerful antidote to traditional *shtetl* attitudes that denigrated manual work and valued commerce. If the youth movements did not entirely eliminate social divisions, they at least provided a new structure in which young people from different classes could meet on equal terms. On the whole there was more social integration in the Zionist than in the Bundist youth organizations; the latter remained primarily working class.

The youth movements played a major role in changing relationships between young men and young women. Hikes, discussion groups, and *kestl ovntn* provided opportunities for young people to meet away from the supervision of parents. Parents often tried to stop their daughters from joining youth organizations, but few succeeded. A hapless father in a *shtetl* near Vilna, told that his daughter was going on picnics in the woods on Saturday afternoon and even carrying baskets of food, replied: "Male vos zey trogn in vald iz nor a halbe tsore. Di gantse tsore vet zayn ven zey veln onheybn trogn fun vald" (I'm more worried about what she'll be carrying out of the forest than what she carries into it).

Chapter 3

The Nazi Rise to Power

INTRODUCTION

Revolutions are usually the result of a power struggle between the old and the new. When an established government is unable to defend itself against a challenge, either bloody or bloodless, a new government gains control. That model, however, does not work in the case of the German revolution of 1918. The old guard, that is, the Hohenzollern regime, fell of its own accord. The Germans were losing the Great War; four years of unprecedented losses at the fronts, the devastating effect of the British blockade on the food supply, and the seemingly boundless reserve of men and material from the United States had brought down the monarchy. The Kaiser abdicated and fled the country.

Germany's democratic revolution was a confusing affair. Although there were bloody clashes in the streets, particularly in Berlin, the conflict was not between the monarchists and the revolutionaries. The question to be decided was which of the antigovernment forces, the Socialists or the Communists, would prevail. The proclamation of a republic by one of the Socialist leaders, Philipp Scheidemann, was unplanned; he made that impromptu announcement when he learned that the Communists were about to declare themselves the German government. The structure of the republic he had called into existence was formulated later, during the constitutional convention in 1919 in the city of Weimar. Here the assembled delegates wrote a democratic and liberal constitution which combined elements of the English and American governments.

Legislative power resided mainly in the Reichstag whose members were elected by universal suffrage. Executive power was given to the chancellor who, with his cabinet, was responsible to the Reichstag. A president, chosen by direct popular vote, headed the government. One of his executive duties was the appointment of the chancellor, presumably the leader of the majority party in the Reichstag. On paper, this constitution promised to move Germany into the ranks of modern democratic nations. In reality, however, the republic was confronted with a twelve-year struggle against impossible odds.

The rise of Hitler was due to the fusion of circumstances which were tied directly to Germany's defeat in the First World War. The development and expansion of radical political parties resulted from the psychological, political, and economic difficulties which the ordinary German could not comprehend. The period between 1919 and 1933 were years of successive waves of turmoil and deprivation which embittered the people. Four years of wartime sacrifices were concluded by a humiliating peace treaty. They felt betrayed. Had not the army assured them of certain victory, but lost the war? Now, to escape the onus of failure, the generals blamed defeatists, particularly communists and Jews who "stabbed the nation in the back." The peace treaty was expected to be based on President Wilson's Fourteen Points; another lie. Was it fair that this newly constituted democratic Germany was denied acceptance and equality with other nations? How much was enough?

But more than German self-esteem was brought low after the end of the Great War. These were years of economic turmoil. Even the gifted leaders of the Weimar Republic could not save the people from the effects of a ruinous inflation followed by a severe depression. The inner security of knowing one's place in society was shaken as businesses, savings, and jobs disappeared. At the same time, the confidence that law and order could secure the streets was undermined. Hooligans, many in the uniforms of various paramilitary organizations, turned neighborhoods into battle grounds. The freedoms conferred by the constitution seemed a poor substitute for the loss of safety.

The Weimar Republic was a noble effort, doomed by its inability to make the German people cherish it. Its failings, no matter what their cause, were never forgiven. Its leaders, even when martyred, were awarded neither gratitude nor admiration. The support which a patriotic people extends to its representatives, was not forthcoming. While its democratic institutions struggled to cope with the reality of governing a defeated, unstable, and angry people, radical parties promised the quick fixes of extremism. The escape into irrational politics, the lure of emotional rather than logical solutions was tailor-made for the Nazis and their expert orators.

The wisdom of hindsight allows us now to point to a number of moments when, if a different course had been taken, the world might never have heard of Adolf Hitler. For example, the Allies should have insisted that the generals, not the civilian leaders of the fledgling Republic, sign the Treaty of Versailles. From its inception, the burden of accepting the Versailles *Diktat* haunted the signers. Any official who tried to implement its provisions was tainted in the eyes of most Germans. The constitution, so impressive in many areas, was fatally weakened by Article 48 which permitted the abrogation of civil liberties under certain circumstances. The Weimar courts were entirely too lenient with politically motivated criminals. Judges, usually held-over monarchist appointments, rarely used their full powers in punishing rebels, rioters, or assassins. Furthermore, foreign leaders might have paid closer attention to the crises in Germany, perhaps even read *Mein Kampf.* German Jews should have realized their danger and fled for their lives. There are so many crucial moments which cause one to sigh: "If only…"—and there is blame enough to break the back of every scapegoat.

The question of which radical party, the Nazis or the Communist, would bring down the government was probably settled by Hitler himself. His powers of persuasion, his ability to appeal to the masses as well as the classes, was unmatched. He built a powerful organization and won enough seats in the Reichstag to become the legitimate chancellor of the nation. His first order of business was the destruction of the Republic.

Germany Tried Democracy
A Political History of The Reich from 1918 to 1933

S. William Halperin

The occupation of the Ruhr had a most disastrous effect upon the already sagging economy of the Reich. The isolation of this supremely vital industrial area from the rest of the country brought commercial activity to a virtual standstill and robbed the German treasury of desperately needed revenue. Suffering became general as the poison of economic dislocation spread. The decision to subsidize the passive resisters in the Ruhr was, under the circumstances, unavoidable; but, its principal effect was to quicken the process of financial disorganization. The output of paper money climbed to a new high. The inflation, entering upon its climactic phase, attained the proportions of an overwhelming catastrophe. The mark sank to such fantastic depths that the barter of goods began to replace the exchange of commodities for money. Matters reached a desperate pass when farmers refused to sell their produce for worthless currency. Trucks and trains bearing food to famished city-dwellers were frequently attacked and pillaged. Such was the spectacle presented by a land that only nine years before had been one of the world's richest.

Where all this would end no one could say, but there were Germans, millions of them, who knew that their lives would never be the same again. They were the rentiers, the people with fixed incomes. They were wiped out by the inflation. Wiped out, too, were other segments of the once prosperous German bourgeoisie. Professor Arthur Rosenberg, in his *History of the German Republic,* comments as follows on this tragic development:

> The systematic expropriation of the German middle classes, not by a a Socialist Government but in a bourgeois State whose motto was the preservation of private property, is an unprecedented occurrence. It was one of the biggest robberies known to history.

These victims of the currency debacle were depressed into the ranks of the proletariat. They retained their bourgeois, white-collar psychology, and hence proved unreceptive to communist propaganda. But they had lost their faith in liberalism, in the philosophy of moderation, of which the Weimar regime was the symbol and the

S. William Halperin, *Germany Tried Democracy: A Political History of the Reich from 1918 to 1933*, New York: W.W. Norton, 1965, pp. 252–254. Reprinted by permission of Harper Collins Publishers.

embodiment. In their anguish, they turned to the gospel of extremism preached by the reactionary foes of democracy.

The middle classes were not alone in their suffering. True, the proletariat was spared the agony of seeing its savings wiped out for the simple reason that it possessed very few assets of this kind. But the drop in real wages was nothing short of calamitous. The purchasing power of paper wages sank so low that the average worker found himself unable to procure anything like adequate supplies of food and clothing for himself and his family. The inflation dealt a staggering blow to the trade unions. It undermined their financial position and thus rendered them incapable of performing their routine functions. Benefit payments to their members had to be suspended. Collective-bargaining contracts ceased to give any protection to the workers because of the rapid changes in the purchasing power of the mark. Millions of wage-earners decided that they had nothing more to gain by retaining their membership in trade associations. They sought aid and relief elsewhere.

While the laboring and middle classes were thus made to feel the full impact of runaway inflation, debtors, real-estate operators and industrial magnates were having a field day. People who had bonds to retire, mortgages to lift or notes to pay hastened to do so with worthless currency. Real-estate values soared, and immense profits were garnered by those who knew how to play this game. Speculation attained fantastic proportions. The great industrialists likewise profited enormously. They paid off loans, hired artificially cheap labor, expanded their plants and invested in up-to-date equipment. They increased their holdings at the expense of less fortunate competitors in the intermediate reaches of the economic hierarchy. Little wonder, then, that they evinced no desire to see the inflation halted until the mark had ceased to have any value whatever.

Speech of the German Delegation
Versailles, May 7, 1919

Count Ulrich Von Brockdorff-Rantzau

Gentlemen, we are deeply impressed with the great mission that has brought us here to give to the world forthwith a lasting peace. We are under no illusions as to the extent of our defeat and the degree of our powerlessness. We know that the strength of the German arms is broken. We know the intensity of the hatred which meets us, and we have heard the victor's passionate demand that as the vanquished we shall be made to pay, and as the guilty we shall be punished.

The demand is made that we shall acknowledge that we alone are guilty of having caused the war. Such a confession in my mouth would be a lie. We are far from seeking to escape from any responsibility for this world war, and for its having been waged as it has. The attitude of the former German government at the Hague peace conferences, its actions and its omissions in the tragic twelve days of July may have contributed to the catastrophe, but we emphatically deny that the people of Germany, who were convinced that they were waging a war of defense, should be burdened with the sole guilt of that war.

Nobody would wish to contend that the catastrophe goes back merely to the fateful moment when the successor to the throne of Austria-Hungary fell a victim to murderous hands. In the past fifty years the imperialism of all European states has constantly poisoned the international situation. The policy of retaliation, the policy of expansion, and a disregard of the right of national self-determination have played their part in that illness of Europe which came to its crisis in the world war. The Russian mobilization made it impossible for statesmen to find a remedy, and threw the final decision into the hands of military power.

Public opinion in every enemy country is echoing the crimes Germany is said to have committed in the war. Here, too, we are ready to admit that unjust things have been done. We have not come here to diminish the responsibility of the men who have

---

Count Ulrich Von Brockdorff-Rantzau, "Speech of the German Delegation, Versailles, May 17, 1919," *The Weimar Republic Source Book,* Anton Kaes, Martin Jay, and Edward Dimendberg, eds. Berkeley: University of California Press, 1994, pp. 9–11. Reprinted by permission of Anton Kaes, Martin Jay, and Edward Dimendberg.

First published as "Ansprache des Reichsaussenminister's Grafen Brockdorff-Rantzau bei Überreichung des Friedensvertrags-Entwurfs durch die Alliierten und Assoziierten Mächte," in Graf Brockdorff-Rantzau, *Dokumente* (Charlottenburg: Deutsche Verlagsgesellschaft für Politik und Geschichte, 1920), 113ff.

waged the war politically and economically, and to deny that breaches of the law of nations have been committed. We repeat the declaration which was made in the German Reichstag at the beginning of the war: injustice has been done to Belgium and we shall make reparations.

But in the manner of waging war, Germany was not the only one that erred. Every European nation knows of deeds and of individuals which the best of their people remember only with regret. I do not want to respond to reproaches with reproaches, but, if we alone are asked to do penance, one should remember the Armistice. Six weeks went by before we obtained an armistice, and six months before we came to know your conditions of peace. Crimes in war may not be excusable, but they are committed in the struggle for victory, when we think only of maintaining our national existence, and are in such passion as makes the conscience of peoples blunt. The hundreds of thousands of noncombatants who have perished since November 11 because of the blockade were destroyed coolly and deliberately after our opponents had won a certain and assured victory. Remember that, when you speak of guilt and atonement.

The measure of guilt of all those who have taken part can be established only by an impartial inquiry, a neutral commission before which all the principals in the tragedy are allowed to speak, and to which all archives are open. We have asked for such an inquiry and we ask for it once more.

At this conference, where we alone and without our allies are facing our many opponents, we are not without protection. You yourself have brought us an ally: that justice which was guaranteed us in the agreement as to what should be the principles governing the treaty of peace. In the days between October 5 and November 5, 1918, the Allied and Associated governments swore that there would be no peace of violence, and inscribed on their knightly banners a peace of justice. On October 5 the German government proposed that the basis of peace should be the principles set forth by the President of the United States of America, and on November 5 their Secretary of State, Mr. [Robert] Lansing, declared that the Allied and Associated Powers had accepted this basis with two definite reservations. The principles of President Wilson thus became binding for both parties to the war, for you as well as for us, and also for our former allies.

Certain of the foregoing principles call upon us to make heavy national and economic sacrifices. But by such a treaty, the sacred and fundamental rights of all peoples would be protected. The conscience of the world would be behind it, and no nation that violated it would go unpunished.

The Constitution of the German Republic

PREAMBLE

The German people, united in all their racial elements and inspired by the will to renew and strengthen their Reich in liberty and justice, to preserve peace at home and abroad, and to foster social progress, have established the following constitution:

CHAPTER I: STRUCTURE AND FUNCTIONS OF THE REICH

Section 1. Reich and States

Article 1. The German Reich is a republic. Political authority emanates from the people.

Article 2. The territory of the Reich consists of the territories of the German member states. [...]

Article 3. The Reich colors are black, red, and gold. The merchant flag is black, white and red, with the Reich colors in the upper inside corner.

Article 4. The generally accepted rules of international law are to be considered as binding integral parts of the German Reich.

Article 5. Political authority is exercised in national affairs by the national government in accordance with the constitution of the Reich, and in state affairs by the state governments in accordance with state constitutions. [...]

Article 12. Insofar as the Reich does not exercise its jurisdiction, such jurisdiction remains with the states [...] with the exception of cases in which the Reich possesses exclusive jurisdiction. [...]

Article 17. Every state must have a republican constitution. The representatives of the people must be elected by universal, equal, direct, and secret suffrage of all German citizens, both men and women, in accordance with the principles of proportional representation.

Section 2. The *Reichstag*

Article 20. The Reichstag is composed of the delegates of the German people.

Article 21. The delegates are representatives of the whole people. They are subject only to their own conscience and are not bound by any instructions.

Article 22. The delegates are elected by universal, equal, direct, and secret suffrage by men and women over twenty years of age, according to the principle of proportional representation. Election day must be a Sunday or a public holiday.

Article 23. The Reichstag is elected for four years. New elections must take place at the latest on the sixtieth day after this term has run its course. [...]

Article 32. For decisions of the Reichstag a simple majority vote is necessary, unless the constitution prescribes another proportion of votes. [...]

Article 33. The Reichstag and its committees may require the presence the Reich chancellor and every Reich minister. [...]

Section 3: The Reich President and the Reich Cabinet

Article 41. The Reich president is elected by the whole German people. Every German who has completed his thirty-fifth year is eligible for election. [...]

Article 42. On assuming office, the Reich president shall take the following oath before the Reichstag:

> I swear to devote my energies to the well-being of the German people, to further their interests, to guard them from injury, to maintain the constitution and the laws of the Reich to fulfill my duties conscientiously, and to administer justice for all.

It is permissible to add a religious affirmation.

Article 43. The term of office of the Reich president is seven years. Re-election is permissible.

Before the expiration of his term, the Reich president, upon motion of the Reichstag, may be recalled by a popular vote. The decision of the Reichstag shall be by a two-thirds majority. Through such decision the Reich president is denied any further exercise of his office. The rejection of the recall motion by the popular referendum counts as a new election and results in the dissolution of the Reichstag. [...]

Article 48. If any state does not fulfill the duties imposed upon it by the constitution or the laws of the Reich, the Reich president may enforce such duties with the aid of the armed forces.

In the event that the public order and security are seriously disturbed or endangered, the Reich president may take the measures necessary for their restoration, intervening, if necessary, with the aid of the armed forces. For this purpose he may temporarily abrogate, wholly or in part, the fundamental principles laid down in Articles 114, 115, 117, 118, 123, 124, and 153.

The Reich president must without delay inform the Reichstag of all measures taken under Paragraph 1 or Paragraph 2 of this article. These measures may be rescinded on demand of the Reichstag. [...]

Article 50. All orders and decrees of the Reich president, including those relating to the armed forces, must, in order to be valid, be countersigned by the Reich chancellor or by the appropriate Reich minister. Responsibility is assumed through the countersignature. [...]

Article 52. The Reich cabinet consists of the Reich chancellor and the Reich ministers.

Article 53. The Reich chancellor and, on his recommendation, the Reich ministers, are appointed and dismissed by the Reich president.

Article 54. The Reich chancellor and the Reich ministers require for the exercise of their office the confidence of the Reichstag. Any one of them must resign if the Reichstag by formal resolution withdraws its confidence.

Article 55. The Reich chancellor presides over the government of the Reich and conducts its affairs according to the rules of procedure laid down by the government of the Reich an approved by the Reich president.

Article 56. The Reich chancellor determines the political program of the Reich and assumes responsibility to the Reichstag. Within this general policy each Reich minister conducts independently the office entrusted to him and is held individually responsible to the Reichstag. [...]

Section 4: The *Reichsrat*

Article 60. A Reichsrat is formed to give the German states representation in the law-making and administration of the Reich.

Article 61. Each state has at least one vote in the Reichsrat. In the case of the larger states one vote shall be assigned for every million inhabitants.[*] [...] No single state shall have more than two fifths of the total number of votes. [...]

Article 63. The states shall be represented in the Reichsrat by members of their governments. [...]

Section 5: Reich Legislation

Article 68. Bills are introduced by the Reich cabinet, with the concurrence of the Reichsrat, or by members of the Reichstag. Reich laws shall be enacted by the Reichstag. [...]

Article 73. A law of the Reichstag must be submitted to popular referendum before its proclamation, if the Reich president, within one month of its passage, so decides. [...]

Article 74. The Reichsrat may protest against laws passed by the Reichstag. In case of such protest, the law is returned to the Reichstag, which may override the objection by a two-thirds majority. The Reich president must either promulgate the law within three months or call for a referendum. [...]

---

[*]Amended by law of March 24, 1921, to "every 700,000 inhabitants."

Article 76. The constitution may be amended by law, but acts…amending the constitution can only take effect if two thirds of the legal number of members are present and at least two thirds of those present consent. […]

Section 6: The Reich Administration

[Articles 78–101 cover the jurisdiction of the Reich administration in such matters as foreign affairs, national defense, colonial policies, customs, national budgets, postal and telegraph services, railroads, and waterways.]

Section 7: Administration of Justice

[Articles 102–108 provide for a hierarchy of Reich and state courts, with judges appointed by the Reich president for life.]

CHAPTER II: FUNDAMENTAL RIGHTS AND DUTIES OF THE GERMANS

Section 1: The Individual

Article 109. All Germans are equal before the law. Men and women have the same fundamental civil rights and duties. Public legal privileges or disadvantages of birth or of rank are abolished. Titles of nobility […] may be bestowed no longer. […] Orders and decorations shall not be conferred by the state. No German shall accept titles or orders from a foreign government.

Article 110. Citizenship of the Reich and the states is acquired in accordance with the provisions of a Reich law. […]

Article 111. All Germans shall enjoy liberty of travel and residence throughout the whole Reich. […]

Article 112. Every German is permitted to emigrate to a foreign country. […]

Article 114. Personal liberty is inviolable. Curtailment or deprivation of personal liberty by a public authority is permissible only by authority of law.

Persons who have been deprived of their liberty must be informed at the latest on the following day by whose authority and for what reasons they have been held. They shall receive the opportunity without delay of submitting objections to their deprivation of liberty.

Article 115. The house of every German is his sanctuary and is inviolable. Exceptions are permitted only by authority of law. […]

Article 117. The secrecy of letters and all postal, telegraph, and telephone commnunications is inviolable. Exceptions are inadmissible except by national law.

Article 118. Every German has the right, within the limits of the general laws, to express his opinion freely by word, in writing, in print, in picture form, or in any other way. […] Censorship is forbidden. […]

Section 2. The General Welfare

Article 123. All Germans have the right to assembly peacefully and unarmed without giving notice and without special permission. [...]

Article 124. All Germans have the right to form associations and societies for purposes not contrary to the criminal law. [...]

Article 126. Every German has the right to petition. [...]

Section 3: Religion and Religious Societies

Article 135. All inhabitants of the Reich enjoy full religious freedom and freedom of conscience. The free exercise of religion is guaranteed by the Constitution and is under public protection. [...]

Article 137. There is no state church. [...]

Section 4: Education and the Schools

Article 142. Art, science, and the teaching thereof are free. [...]

Article 143. The education of the young is to be provided for by means of public institutions. [...]

Article 144. The entire school system is under the supervision of the state [...]

Article 145. Attendance at school is compulsory. [...]

Section 5: Economic Life

Article 151. The regulation of economic life must be compatible with the principles of justice, with the aim of attaining humane conditions of existence for all. Within these limits the economic liberty of the individual is assured. [...]

Article 152. Freedom of contract prevails [...] in accordance with the laws. [...]

Article 153. The right of private property is guaranteed by the Constitution. [...] Expropriation of property may take place [...] by due process of law. [...]

Article 159. Freedom of association for the preservation and promotion of labor and economic conditions is guaranteed to everyone and to all vocations. All agreements and measures attempting to restrict or restrain this freedom is unlawful. [...]

Article 161. The Reich shall organize a comprehensive system of [social] insurance. [...]

Article 165. Workers and employees are called upon to cooperate, on an equal footing, with employers in the regulation of wages and of the conditions of labor, as well as in the general development of the productive forces. [...]

Concluding Provisions

Article 181.[...] The German people have passed and adopted this constitution through their National Assembly. It comes into force with the date of its proclamation.

Schwarzburg,   *August 11, 1919.*

The Reich president
EBERT
The Reich cabinet
BAUER
ERZBERGER   HERMANN MÜLLER   DR. DAVID
NOSKE   SCHMIDT
SCHLICKE   GIESBERTS   DR. BAYER
DR. BELL

The Unemployed

Heinrich Hauser

An almost unbroken chain of homeless men extends the whole length of the great Hamburg-Berlin highway.

There are so many of them moving in both directions, impelled by the wind or making their way against it, that they could shout a message from Hamburg to Berlin by word of mouth.

It is the same scene for the entire two hundred miles, and the same scene repeats itself between Hamburg and Bremen, between Bremen and Kassel, between Kassel and Würzburg, between Würzburg and Munich. All the highways in Germany over which I traveled this year presented the same aspect.

The only people who shouted and waved at me and ran along beside my automobile hoping for a ride during their journey were the newcomers, the youngsters. They were recognizable at once. They still had shoes on their feet and carried knapsacks, like the *Wandervögel. [...]*

But most of the hikers paid no attention to me. They walked separately or in small groups with their eyes on the ground. And they had the queer, stumbling gait of barefoot people, for their shoes were slung over their shoulders. Some of them were guild members—carpenters with embroidered wallets, knee breeches, and broad felt hats; milkmen with striped red shirts, and bricklayers with tall black hats—but they were in a minority. Far more numerous were those to whom one could assign no special profession or craft—unskilled young people for the most part who had been unable to find

Heinrich Hauser, "The Unemployed," *The Weimar Republic Source Book,* Anton Kaes, Martin Jay, and Edward Dimendberg, eds. Berkeley: University of California Press, 1994, pp. 84–85. Reprinted by permission of Anton Kaes, Martin Jay, and Edward Dimendberg.

First published as "Die Arbeitslosen," *Die Tat* 25, no. I (April 1933), 76–78.

a place for themselves in any city or town in Germany, and who had never had a job and never expected to have one. There was something else that had never been seen before—whole families that had piled all their goods into baby carriages and wheelbarrows that they were pushing along as they plodded forward in dumb despair. It was a whole nation on the march.

I saw them—and this was the strongest impression that the year 1932 left with me—I saw them, gathered into groups of fifty or a hundred men, attacking fields of potatoes. I saw them digging up the potatoes and throwing them into sacks while the farmer who owned the field watched them in despair and the local policeman looked on gloomily from the distance. I saw them staggering toward the lights of the city as night fell, with their sacks on their backs. What did it remind me of? Of the war, of the worst period of starvation in 1917 and 1918, but even then people paid for the potatoes. [...]

I entered the huge Berlin municipal lodging house in a northern quarter of the city. [...] Dreary barracks extended to the edge of the sidewalk and under their dripping roofs long lines of men were leaning against the wooden walls, waiting in silence and staring at a brick structure across the street.

This wall was the side of the lodging house and it seemed to blot out the entire sky. [...] There was an entrance arched by a brick vaulting, and a watchman sat in a little wooden sentry box. His white coat made him look like a doctor. We stood waiting in the corridor. Heavy steam rose from the men's clothes. Some of them sat down on the floor, pulled off their shoes, and unwound the rags that bound their feet. More people were constantly pouring in the door, and we stood closely packed together. Then another door opened. The crowd pushed forward, and people began forcing their way almost eagerly through this door, for it was warm in there. Without knowing it I had already caught the rhythm of the municipal lodging house. It means waiting, waiting, standing around, and then suddenly jumping up.

We now stand in a long hall. [...] There under yellow lamps that hang from the ceiling on long wires sit men in white smocks. We arrange ourselves in long lines, each leading up to one of these men, and the mill begins to grind. [...]

What does the man in the white smock want to know? All these fellows in white smocks belong to a very special type of official. The way they let the line flow by while they work so smoothly together is facile, lazy, almost elegant. The way they say "Mr." to the down-and-outers from the street is full of ironic politeness. [...] The whole impersonal manner of the officials makes them as incomprehensible as a cash register. [...]

Then come the questions. When and where were you born, and where have you come from? Name of your parents? Ever been in a municipal lodging house before? Where have you spent the last three nights? Where did you work last? Have you begged? The first impression that these questions and answers make on me is that it is just like the army. [...]

My second impression is the helplessness of the men on my side of the bar and the shocking ruthlessness with which the men on the other side of the bar insult this helplessness. Eight out of every ten men on my side of the bar are young fellows and about a third of these are mere boys. [...]

The official presses a white card into my hand and tells me to go to the desk of another clerk with the sign, "adjuster," over it. While waiting in line I look at my white card. It is divided into squares and has my name at the top and all kinds of mysterious symbols underneath. [...] I do not remember what the "adjuster" said to me—there was some inconsistency in my papers, I believe. [...] [Hauser was sent on to a police examiner, but eventually was cleared.]

When I come out I am holding a check that has been given me for a night's sleep and food in the lodging house. [...] The bare walls of the room that we have entered are lined with iron bedsteads. There are no windows but a sloping roof with skylights that reminds me of a factory. We sit down on the bedsteads along the middle of the room, closely packed together. A voice near me whispers, "What was the matter with you, buddy?"

"My papers."

"Say, you had luck to get out again. They kept the fellow that went in with you. He spent his dole of eighteen marks [about $4.30] in two days. Oh, boy, think of it! Eighteen marks!..."

I look at the clock again. Our reception ceremony lasted an hour and a half, and we now sit here another half hour, which makes two hours. They do not make it easy for you to get supper and a bed in a municipal lodging house.

Four Years of Political Murder

Emil Julius Gumbel

The following lines report on the political murders that have occurred in Germany since November 9, 1918. The murders committed by the left and by the right are equally represented. A case has been taken up when it concerned a premeditated, illegal killing of a well-known German by another German for domestic political motives, whereby the incident is characterized not as mass action but as an individual deed. I have addressed only those cases in which the shooting party did not maintain that he had been attacked

Emil Julius Gumbel, "Four Years of Political Murder," *The Weimar Republic Source Book*, Anton Kaes, Martin Jay, and Edward Dimendberg, eds. Berkeley: University of California Press, 1994, pp. 100–104. Reprinted by permission of Anton Kaes, Martin Jay, and Edward Dimendberg.

First published in *Vier Jahre politischer Mord* (Berlin: Verlag der neuen Gesellschaft, 1922), 145–149.

by the crowd and where it was not a matter of a lynching by a nameless crowd or some other form of mass action, but instead by a very definite perpetrator.

In the selection of cases I have proceeded much more cautiously in the murders by the right than of those by the left. I have therefore included several cases of the left which had more of the character of riots than of political murders.

I have exercised the greatest possible conscientiousness in regard to the exactness of allegations and attempted in all cases to achieve documentary precision. I have relied on court records, judgments, decisions to quash the proceedings, witness testimony, information from attorneys and from survivors, and, finally, newspaper notices. The court reports I have studied primarily in the right-wing newspapers. In all cases in which the materials were not precise I have written to the relatives and reporters. If the reports were still incomplete, then the cases in question were omitted. Thus I can document beyond question every contention offered here. In principle, I have taken up only those cases in which the victim's name was known to me. Where anonymous cases appear in the text they serve only to illustrate the proceedings in question. I have departed from this principle only in two places.

The status of the respective proceedings was the most difficult to ascertain. It is therefore possible that in cases where no proceedings were known to me that they are in fact pending or that the proceedings were already quashed. On the other hand, I believe that the number of imposed sentences I have listed is complete.

...

The present book is a continuation and expansion of my brochure, *Two Years of Murder.* I had advanced there the contention, among others, that the German judicial system had left over three hundred political murders unpunished and I expected that that could have only one of two effects. Either the judicial system would believe that I was speaking the truth, and then the murderers would be punished or it would believe that I am lying, and then I would be punished as a slanderer. In fact, something else totally unforeseen has occurred.

Although the brochure in no way went without notice, there has not been a single effort on the part of the authorities to dispute the correctness of my contentions. On the contrary, the highest responsible authority, the Reich minister of justice, expressly confirmed my contentions on more than one occasion. Nevertheless, not a single murderer has been punished,

Berlin, October 16, 1922

POLITICAL DIFFERENTIATION OF MURDER TECHNIQUES

How is the enormous difference between 354 murders by the right and 22 by the left to be explained? It would be false, in my judgment, simply to say, "Leftists are just morally superior." This cannot be concluded primarily because only a single type of crime has been researched. Thus property crimes, for example, have not been drawn into the compass of observation. Of them one could perhaps presume that, given the social structure, they are to be found more frequently in the leftist camp than in the rightist. Nor admittedly may it be forgotten that crimes against property, in contrast to crimes against the person, also have a social component, that they are for the most part produced by the fact of the present distribution of property. And in a social order that eases the individual's struggle for existence they would surely decrease considerably in number. That, however, crimes against property committed by the right are in no way rare can be seen from the numerous plunderings and robbings of the corpses. Thus, of 184 victims of fatal "accidents" in Munich, in 68 cases the corpses were plundered.

The genuine distinction between the two camps is in my judgment not a moral but a technical one. The adherents of leftist parties have gone through decades of training in the unions, which have preached to them that mass action is the sole effective means of struggle. For the leftist movements is based on the materialist conception of history, which emphasizes economic and technical aspects as the effective factors in history.

On the right there is no such union training. On the right it is a question of preserving the anarchistic economic order characterized for them by the words *peace and order.* And individual means correspond to this goal, whose effects are identical to those of the anarchist "propaganda of the deed." For the right adheres to the heroic conception of history, according to which the hero "makes" history. Correspondingy, the right is inclined to hope that it could annihilate the left opposition, which is carried by hopes for a radically different economic order, by defeating its leaders. And the right has done it: all of the leaders of the left who openly opposed the war and whom the workers trusted—Liebknecht, Luxemburg, Eisner, [Gustav] Landauer, [Leo] Jogisches, et al.—are dead. In recent times, as the assassinations of Erzberger, Auer, Scheidemann, and Rathenau demonstrate, they are also proceeding to murder the leaders of the moderate parties.

The effectiveness of this technique is for the moment indisputable. The left no longer has any significant leaders, no more people toward whom the masses have the feeling: he has suffered so much for us, dared so much for us that we can trust him blindly. The working-class movement has thereby doubtlessly been set back by years. This success is all the greater since in no case has punishment occurred.

That this method has become so widespread in the military (all of the murders by the right have been committed by officers or soldiers) naturally lies in the psychological brutalization of the war, in which the life of the individual was no longer allowed to count. In this regard the frequently spoken and unspoken order not to take prisoners has had an especially significant influence.

POLITICAL MURDERS THEN AND NOW

The indifference with which one greets political murders and the victims of turbulent street demonstrations today in Germany is to be explained by the fact that the war has numbed us to the value of human life.

The unbelievable leniency of the court is also quite well known to the perpetrators. Thus are the political murders of today in Germany to be distinguished from those common previously in other countries by two aspects: their great number and the fact that they go unpunished. Earlier a certain resolve was part of political murder. A certain heroism was not to be denied: the perpetrator risked life and limb. Flight was only possible given extraordinary effort. Today the perpetrator risks nothing at all. Powerful organizations with an extensive network of confidantes over the whole country provide him with shelter, protection, and material sustenance. "Right-minded" bureaucrats and police chiefs supply falsified papers for potentially necessary trips abroad. This technique has improved greatly since the time of Lieutenant Vogel. The beneficiaries live magnificently and happily in the best hotels. In short, political murder has gone from being a heroic deed, to becoming a daily act, an easy source of earnings for "impulsive customers."

THE COMPLICITY OF THE COURTS

These conditions would naturally be inconceivable without the perhaps unconscious assistance of the courts. This can even be proved geographically. In the occupied territory of the Rhineland the frequency of murder is much lower than in the rest of the nation. It is known that the Rhineland Commission would not share the interests and standpoint of the German judges. (If similar things occurred in their country, they would probably make the same judgments.) A further proof of the courts' unconscious complicity in the murders lies in the fact that the verbal call for the murder of well-known pacifists is in no way regarded as a crime. A fine of a few paper marks, and the one who issued the call can resume stirring up the seeds of hate. On the day following the murder of Erzberger there appeared in the *Spandauer Tageblatt*: "To the Scaffold! The Second Victim, Hello von Gerlach!" The author, Lehmann, received a two-hundred-mark fine from the second district criminal court.

This thesis of mine, that the mildness of the German courts is a precondition of political murders is also represented by most radical-right newspapers. One frequently reads sentences there like: "It is a pity that the traitor so-and-so (a pacifist, of whom not even the least of a criminal nature can even be said) lives not in Germany but in another country. There, unfortunately, the arm of punitive justice cannot reach him, as it did Erzberger." According to this, one cannot murder a political opponent who lives abroad, but not, for example, because it would be technically impossible (that is not the case) but because one would run the risk of being punished there.

Despite these horrendous facts I would not want to affirm unconditionally the assertion that German Judges consciously bend the law. They did let over three hundred murders go with no punishment. But I would like to plead mitigating circumstances for them. They lack the consciousness of the culpability of their actions. Formerly, when today's economic system was unconditionally protected against attacks from without and when the members of the right-wing parties made up uncontestedly the upper strata, the thought that there could come from this caste a bunch of murderers and instigators of murders is unimaginable to them. That is why the murderers are set free.

In the main, public opinion, for understandable reasons given the underlying interests, takes the position: *Roma locuta, causa finita;* the courts released the ones charged with murder. They are nonpartisan. The matter is settled. Only a small fraction protested, and indeed in essence always only the fellow party members of those who were murdered. This fiction of the nonpartisan nature of the German courts, incidentally, also has an extra-political origin: regarding the [Triple] Entente all doubt that just measures are being instituted against war criminals in Germany itself is to be banished.

THE TECHNIQUE OF ACQUITTAL

Virtually all of the relatively small number of assassinations of reactionaries have been atoned for through severe penalties; of the very numerous assassinations of men of the left, on the other hand, not one has been atoned. Credulousness, wrongly understood orders, or actual or purported insanity were always the bases of the defense to the extent that trials even took place. Most of the proceedings were quashed either by the prosecutor's office or the criminal court.

When the murderer and the course of the crime are known precisely then the following judicial comedy develops. An officer gave an order that could have been understood to mean that Spartacists were to be shot. The subordinate shoots people whom he takes to be Spartacists, and is acquitted because he could have believed himself to be acting on orders. He is, therefore, released on account of "putative Spartacism." Just like Lieutenant Forster in his time was released because of putative self-defense. Nothing, however, is undertaken against the officer. For either that was not what the order meant or, if that is what it meant, then it simply was not an official order. Naturally, the "Spartacist" is dead. The guilt lies with...the scapegoat. Thus do the proceedings before the prosecutor end. This process is most interesting when the treasury, in a civil proceeding being pursued simultaneously, is made to pay compensation because of a murder committed by a soldier or officer. For then it is acknowledged by a court that the killing was illegal. Nevertheless, nothing happens to the perpetrator.

Public opinion in general approves of this procedure. For clever propaganda has taught it that every enemy of militarism is a Spartacist, therefore an enemy of humanity, therefore open game.

If a member of a leftist party is murdered by the right, even the judge is instinctively incapable of ridding himself of the notion that the murdered person was his enemy and because of his, the victim's, beliefs deserved a severe penalty. Thus the murderer really only preceded criminal justice. And for that reason should be treated with lenience. Thus it frequently occurs that in the court proceedings it is not the murderer but the murdered who stands morally before the judge. The murderer comes from the same social strata, from the same life as the judge. Countless social bonds connect the murderer-officer with the judge who will acquit him, to the prosecutor who will quash the proceeding, and to the witness who depicts in detail the "attempted flight." They are flesh of their flesh, blood of their blood. The judge understands their language, their feelings, their thinking. Underneath the heavy mask of formalism, his soul resonates tenderly with the murderer. The murderer is set free.

Woe, however, to the murderer who is on the left. The judge, who himself belongs to the former upper classes, has an age-old familiarity with the thought that this economic order must be defended. His own position, after all, rests upon it. And every opponent of this economic order is reprehensible. The accused is capable of any crime. And even if he can only be nominally convicted, the most severe punishment is his certain lot.

I am not optimistic enough to believe that my work will cause even one of the murderers to be punished or that political murders will cease. Should, however, my lines have contributed at least to the atonement of the coming political murders, then I will regard my task as having been fulfilled.

Chapter 4

Hitler's Instruments
of Murder

INTRODUCTION

It is not necessary to justify a pluralistic approach to the study of the Holocaust. The work by historians, philosophers, sociologists, cartographers, and experts in law, medicine, psychiatry, and psychology, as well as scholars of economic, intellectual, and constitutional history continue to deepen and widen the research. In their published memoirs and carefully collected oral histories, the voices of the victims reach us loud and clear. In depositories all over the world, including Yale University, the United States Holocaust Memorial Museum, Florida International University, the Wiener Library in London, and Yad Vashem in Jerusalem, thousands of men and women have recorded their stories. Volunteers from the Spielberg Foundation hope to tape the experiences of all remaining survivors on every continent.

Never before have historians faced such an abundance, sometimes an overwhelming abundance, of material. We can follow the sequence of events that led to the mass graves and the heaps of ashes; we have recorded the names, even the hometowns of most of the dead. We know the location of the railroad junctions where Jews were pushed onto the death trains. We are able to reconstruct the routes of the Einsatzgruppen and are familiar with the names of their commanders. Even the caloric value of the soup fed to concentration-camp prisoners has been ascertained. We are familiar with the terror of endless roll calls. Even the stench coming from the overflowing toilets is familiar to us.

If we had no other evidence but the records compiled by the Germans, we could reconstruct the twisted road from ideology to annihilation. Besides the endless, often precise and detailed paper trail, a great deal of physical evidence exists. On public view are several crematoria, huge piles of possessions taken from the murdered Jews, many hundreds of canisters of the Zyklon B poison gas, and, finally, the remains of bodies which neither fire nor lye could eradicate completely.

Although the facts surrounding the Holocaust have been verified, the central question remains: how was it possible for ordinary Germans to commit such ghastly crimes? A study of the biographical and autobiographical material of the men who ordered the killings and those who carried out those orders does not help us to understand them. Tens of thousands of Germans were directly and indirectly involved in the Holocaust, yet the search for some common denominator has been futile.

No doubt, there were fanatical supporters of the Aryan superiority myth who believed that genocide was a legitimate right. But it is a fact that many of the most dedicated killers of Jews harbored no particularly strong anti-Semitic views. The destruction of so many helpless and innocent civilians was a job, simply a job. And doing one's duty, however unpleasant, required no further analysis. No other exoneration was needed beyond "I obeyed."

When the members of the murder squads were further pressed to explain themselves, their justifications sounded like adolescent alibis: If I didn't do it, some one else would have; If I refused I would have been sent to the Eastern front; I was only following orders; I didn't know what my job would be until I got to the camp; I needed to prove to my family that I could amount to something; I believed Hitler and his vision; I knew all Jews were Communists; It was us or them, and so on. It must be remembered that any member of the Deathhead battalions who refused to participate in the killings was merely transferred. As far as we can determine, such transfer requests were very few.

No doubt, there were psychopaths among the killers, but the great majority were legally sane. Even Hitler, whose symptoms ranged between neurosis and psychosis, would be considered responsible for his actions in an American court of law. Most of the officers of the killing squads and camp administrators were well educated and would have achieved high scores on intelligence tests. Furthermore, they usually were conventional family men who would have been incensed if they saw someone mistreat a dog.

Perhaps theologians or psychologists will some day provide an answer to the student who asks "But how could they?" In the meantime, it might serve us well to be properly alarmed about "everyman's" capacity to act with such depravity, to throw away his humanity so easily, so casually.

Otto Ohlendorf: Non-conformist, SS Leader and Economic Functionary

Hanno Sow ade

Otto Ohlendorf, born as the youngest of the four children of a well-to-do farmer on 4 February 1907 in Hoheneggelsen near Hannover, was interested in politics from his earliest days.[1] His initial inclination, influenced by his father, towards the traditional bourgeois conservative camp (the DNVP), was soon replaced by a more radical orientation. In 1925, while he was still at grammar school, Ohlendorf joined the SA, from where he was transferred to the SS in 1927 (membership number 880). He became a member of the NSDAP with the membership number 6531 (receiving the Party's Golden Badge of Honour). Thereafter he actively dedicated himself to the dissemination of National Socialism. Even while he was still at school, at the Andreanum Grammar School in Hildesheim (1917–28), Ohlendorf helped to build up the local Party Organisation in Hoheneggelsen. He abandoned this particular activity when he started to study law and political science at the Universities of Leipzig and Göttingen (1928–31), and initially became involved in the Nazi Student Association and the Party branch in Leipzig. Since he did not find the political activity there satisfactory, he moved to Göttingen after only two semesters. Here, greater political possibilities were open to Ohlendorf. From the summer of 1929 he was given the task of winning the District of Northeim for the Party. Ohlendorf was so successful that the NSDAP was able to win an absolute majority in the election, for the first time at District level, in the Region of Hannover South. Following his qualifying exams in law in the summer of 1931, Ohlendorf received a scholarship, for which the Professor of Economics, Jens Peter Jessen, had put his name forward, to go to Italy for about a year, to the University of Pavia. This stay, which was to enable him to study political science and fascist corporatist institutions, as well as to prepare him for an academic career, left a considerable mark on the future course of Ohlendorf's life. He became a convinced opponent of Italian fascism. His main criticism was directed towards what he saw as the authoritarian, autocratic features of the fascist state institutions, and against corporatism. According to Ohlendorf's ideas, the 'community of the people', as he put it, should be at the centre and take an active part through 'representatives of the people's consciousness'. He rejected the rule of individuals, which he later also regarded as exist-

Hanno Sowade, "Otto Ohlendorf: Non-conformist, SS Leader and Economic Functionary," *The Nazi Elite,* Ronald Smelser and Rainer Zitelmann eds., translation by Mary Fischer. New York: New York University Press, 1993, pp. 155–161. Reprint by permission of the editors.

ing in the 'Führer state' of the Third Reich. Ohlendorf took National Socialism's claim to embody a particular philosophy very seriously and developed his own, highly individual philosophy, particularly in the sphere of economics. By so doing he not only came into conflict with the official Party political line on various points, but occasionally even subjected it to quite bold criticism. This willingness to criticise, however, must not be allowed to conceal the fact that Ohlendorf was a convinced National Socialist who gave wholehearted support to fundamental tenets of the Nazi philosophy, like for example its racism.[2]

Alongside his political studies, Ohlendorf had intended to use the stay in Italy as a starting point for his 'lifetime's work', as he put it. By this he obviously meant rapid progress in an academic career at a German university. The scholarship was therefore to form the basis of his doctorate. Ohlendorf was also toying with the idea of a postdoctoral qualification as well. Neither came about. In the summer of 1932 he returned to Germany without having achieved his objects and, initially, proceeded with his lawyer's training. He was saved from this unwanted career by an offer from his tutor, Jessen, who in the autumn of 1933 gave him the opportunity of becoming assistant director of the Institute for International Economics in Kiel. However teacher and pupil soon came in to conflict with the local Party office and the student body. The disagreement became so serious that Jessen was finally forced to leave Kiel in the summer of 1934. Ohlendorf followed him to Berlin at the end of 1934, where he took up the post of departmental head at the Institute for Applied Economics. But in the national capital, too, Jessen and Ohlendorf failed to realise their plans—they wanted to establish a National Socialist University College of Economics. As in Kiel the failure probably had its roots less in practical than in political opposition. Be that as it may, for Ohlendorf the failure meant the final end of his hopes for an academic career.[3]

At this time there was no indication that this moderately talented, but ambitious 'intellectual' would succeed in the Third Reich. His personal ambition might have pointed to success, but his insistence on his own philosophy made it seem less likely. Nonetheless in 1936 Ohlendorf succeeded in taking the step which was to be decisive for his later career: through the intervention of Professor Jessen—and by reactivating his membership of the SS, which he had as good as suspended until then—he joined the SD as director of Department II/23 (Economy). He was fascinated by the aims the SD pursued: the establishment of an intelligence agency, which, in a system of government not accountable to public opinion, was to act as a corrective on the state leadership. As he saw it, this offered a unique opportunity, in close contact with the people, to indicate where the development of Nazi philosophy and the conduct of government had gone wrong, and at the same time to realise his own somewhat convoluted plan to influence the process of development of National Socialist philosophy, for which he believed himself to be particularly predestined by his studies of the 'model' of Italian fascism. During the subsequent period he played an influential part in building up the office for researching public opinion and advanced to be section leader of the entire Central Division. However he only held this office for a short time. He attracted the enmity of Ley and Darré with his 'uncompromisingly critical' reports about the threat posed to the middle classes by the Four Year Plan and his opposition to the National Food Corporation.

For all practical purposes he was 'left out in the cold' in the SD. In order nonetheless to realise his ideas of a Nazi middle class policy, Ohlendorf looked for a job in the economy and applied to be released from his SD duties. Heydrich did not give permission for his request to be granted but did finally agree to reducing his work in the SD to 'honorary duties'. In June 1938 Ohlendorf joined the National Trade Group and created a new platform there for his middle-class oriented economic ideology, which he was again putting forward in latent opposition to the official Party line, to the DAF and to the National Food Corporation. Within a short time he won the admiration of the majority of his colleagues and in November 1939 he was promoted to Chief Secretary of the National Trade Group. Ohlendorf probably had the imminent war to thank for the fact that Heydrich recalled him for duties in the SD in June 1939 and remembered his organisational abilities: he conferred substantial tasks in the reorganisation of the higher SS bureaucracy on him, and in September 1939 appointed him Director of Office III (German-settled areas). Thus Ohlendorf was made responsible for all research into public opinion within Germany.

It has to be asked why Heydrich catapulted Ohlendorf of all people, troublesome in many respects, into this position. One reason will undoubtedly have been the lack of economic experts in the SS. Ohlendorf probably commanded quite a reputation as an expert because of his study of political science and his close contact with the renowned economist Jessen. His 'economic policy', too, which aimed to preserve the middle class, may have recommended him to the National Trade Group. The middle class was ultimately a very important group for the NSDAP. Large sections of the membership and supporters of the Party came from it and during the years of forced rearmament they had had to endure one disappointment after another. The lofty promises the regime had made to the middle class when it seized power had all too often been reversed. It was of importance therefore to make sure of the loyalty of a man who had gained great trust among the middle class. In this context it is remarkable that Ohlendorf retained his duties at the National Trade Group and continued to perform both of his other two offices, that in the Supreme National Security Office (RHSA) and that in economic administration.

Ohlendorf will also have recommended himself to a certain extent by his nonconformism; for if the public opinion reports were really to operate as an early warning system—and this was the intention of the security plan of the SS leadership—they had to be handled by a man who dared to articulate disagreeable matters. In this the regime had completely over-reached itself, as was soon to become clear. By the time the difficult initial phase of the war was over, at the very latest, critical voices did not seem at all suited to the mood of victory and soon his superiors focused more on Ohlendorf as a presumptuous ideologue than as the economic expert and organiser. In short: Ohlendorf was in trouble again. His relationship with Himmler, especially, became worse and worse. The National Director of the SS (RFSS), who himself had high ideological pretensions, disliked Ohlendorf's 'sense of mission', which he regarded as presumptuous. Personal antipathy will also have played a part. In Himmler's eyes Ohlendorf appeared as the 'insufferable, humourless Prussian', as a 'defeatist' and 'pessimist' and as a consequence of his unwavering ideological stand as the 'keeper of the Holy Grail of National Socialism'. The disagreements never went so far, however, that Ohlendorf was forced to leave the SS. In due course his career there made steady progress, leading him to the position of SS General and Lieutenant-General of the Police.[4]

In the minds of a wider public, Ohlendorf is known less for his work on security or economic policy than for his involvement in the ideological war against the USSR. From June 1941 until July 1942 he was Leader of Task Force D, in the area of the 11th Army, which, under his command, murdered over 90,000 people. According to his own accounts Ohlendorf resisted this mission, which he traced back to an initiative by Heydrich. The Chief of the Security Office (RHSA) probably intended to force the 'unsoldierly, soft intellectual, who lacked a soldier's hardness and political clarity', into unconditional loyalty to National Socialism by involving him in mass destruction and, under the motto 'we're all in the same boat', to deprive him of the opportunity of opposition as well as making him a docile tool of the RHSA. Possibly the 'otherworldly' theoretician was also to be confronted by 'practice', as cruel as it was dirty. By all appearances Heydrich not only had Himmler's support in this but was also strengthened by the vote of Bormann, the Director of the Party Chancellery, who also disliked Ohlendorf's unorthodox inclination to anthroposophism. Ohlendorf evidently attempted to evade the assignment to Russia on several occasions by pointing out his reserved occupation at the National Trade Group. But it is questionable whether he did this to avoid becoming entangled in the planned mass destruction in Russia, about which he had information through his work in the RHSA. It is possible he was also held back by his concern for the fate of the middle class and his work in the National Trade Group. Nevertheless in the end he was no longer able to avoid the assignment.

Contrary to what might have been supposed from his initial refusal, on his own evidence Ohlendorf endeavoured 'to fulfill all the tasks he was given in Russia...honestly, to the best of his ability and with a clear conscience'. For the National Socialist Ohlendorf this meant that he put part of the core of his ideology into practice and tried to destroy life which according to Nazi ideology had no right to existence. He actively strove to deploy his Task Force as 'effectively as possible'. To this end he made efforts, for example, to improve its relationship with the High Command of the 11th Army (AOK 11), which had been bad at the beginning of the campaign, in order to expand his unit's field of action, which was severely restricted by the AOK 11 on the basis of an agreement between the overall Supreme Command of the Army (OKW) and the RFSS, which had been laid down by army officialdom. In addition to Ohlendorf's intervention, the increasing threat from partisans finally made the AOK 11 deploy to the full all the resources at its disposal, and thereby also gave Task Force D more freedom to operate. This step was taken by AOK 11 in the full knowledge of the Task Forces's activities. They had been informed about them from the beginning of the campaign by reports from Ohlendorf and his unit commanders as well as those of their own local commanders. After the initial disputes had been settled, general harmony and cooperation prevailed between Ohlendorf and his outfit and the 11th Army, which had been under the command of Manstein since September 1941. Task Force D's increasing freedom of movement is reflected in a macabre way in the 'Report on Events in the USSR'; that is the collected reports of the Task Forces, which form the basis of our own figures. While about 400 persons were murdered in the first two months, the number doubled for the period from mid-August until mid-September 1941 and reached its high point in the last two weeks of September 1941 with approximately 22,500 victims. In total, from 22 June 1941 until March 1942, Ohlendorf and his men killed around 91,000 Jews, gypsies, communists and members of persecuted groups. Ohlendorf, who by his own account made efforts to minimise the moral burden on his subordinates, did not entertain any doubts about the 'legality' of his activity. He consciously stayed on longer as chief of a task force than any of his colleagues in office who had taken up their duties at the same time as him. In his own words, to begin with, in the summer of 1941, he had been glad no longer to be exposed to the disputes and the inimical surroundings of Berlin. The real reason for his long stay in Russia was that as a convinced National Socialist, he believed in the necessity of the policy of mass extermination. Ohlendorf's racism was 'differentiated' enough to make distinctions which allowed him to recruit units of Crimean Tartars and use them as support troops. But this does not change the fact that Ohlendorf emphatically refused an early recall from Russia, since he was convinced, by his own account, that he could achieve more for National Socialism by his 'activities on population policy' than in office work for the National Trade Group. Moreover according to Ohlendorf, the accomplishment of the 'task' gave him a feeling of being right. He had several opportunities, over the entire duration of his assignment, to return early to Berlin, under 'dishonourable' or 'honourable' circumstances.[5]

He was finally brought back from Russia in the summer of 1942 by the circles which had banished him there a year earlier. To all appearances, Himmler had need of the services of his uncomfortable but tried and tested opinion researcher, Ohlendorf, on account of the smouldering crisis of confidence after the first winter of the war against Russia and after the assassination of Heydrich. The attempt to make him more docile by involving him in mass murder in the USSR had failed. Ohlendorf remained the committed and critical ideologue and his position had been additionally strengthened by having passed the 'test'. His readiness to criticise must not however be seen in the same light as the opposition to Hitler and the NSDAP which increased towards the end of the Third Reich. It was not Ohlendorf's intention to bring down the existing order, but to stabilise the system by pointing out what were in his opinion existing abuses and working against them. Even his old teacher, Professor Jessen, who was a member of the group involved in the assassination attempt on 20 July 1944, was to discover this. Since in Ohlendorf's eyes Jessen might have betrayed National Socialism, he did not use his influence to help him; it is a matter for conjecture whether or not he could have prevented the execution.

The results of the opinion research conducted by the SD Internal Affairs, which Ohlendorf directed until the end of the war, had considerable influence on the leadership of the Third Reich. Concrete measures used to stabilise the system, ranging from the deployment of the Gestapo to Hitler's speeches, can be traced back to SD reports. Nonetheless, without the criteria and orientation of the public opinion research being put into question, the 'Reports from the Reich' increasingly attracted criticism from leading National Socialists. The reason for this is probably that, along with the growing loss of confidence in the face of the threatened defeat, the reports also became more critical and admonitory and this was perceived as defeatism by various people who heard them and who did not know the facts. Since the truth and the exposure of their own mistakes were unacceptable, an attempt was made to keep them from the public. In summer 1943 (after the intervention of Goebbels, who had objected to the manner of the report of his 'Palace of Sport' speech of 18 February 1943) it reached the point where the 'Reports' were replaced by 'SD Reports on Domestic Matters', which were only available to a substantially smaller audience. After further protests in summer 1944 Bormann and Ley prohibited Party and DAF officials from cooperating with the SD. In Ohlendorf's opinion this meant that the duty of the interior intelligence service, to make available reports on the mood of the population at short notice, could no longer be fulfilled. The reports were reduced from the summer of 1944 to reports on single items, with the exception of the reaction to 20 July 1944. Nevertheless the SD-Internal Affairs continued to function until the spring of 1945 and during this time the reporting on, for example, the mood of the workers, reveals the secret fears of the regime as clearly as Office III of the RHSA. Ohlendorf continued to be a convinced believer in the concept of opinion research, and in May 1945 he made an offer to the last functioning government of the Reich to establish a new 'intelligence service on domestic affairs, covering different aspects of life'.[6]

Even after his return from Russia Ohlendorf retained his close links with the economic sphere. In the summer of 1942, Secretary of State Landfried, as the representative of a group within the Ministry of Economics which opposed Speer's economic policy, was already attempting to win Ohlendorf for the Ministry, since he was a proven proponent of policies favourable to the middle class and—as Section Head in the RHSA, a member of the powerful SS. This attempt failed primarily because of Himmler's opposition. He did not want a member of the SS to expound on economic policy in opposition to Speer, thereby allowing any set-backs in the war economy to be put at the door of the SS. One year later, in November 1943, Ohlendorf was allowed to join the Economics Ministry as a Ministerial Director and deputy to the Secretary of State, Dr. Hayler, who was newly appointed at the same time. The reason he was now available stemmed from the fact that Himmler, who had taken over the Ministry of the Interior in August 1943, planned to expand his comprehensive plan for state security by attaining potential influence in the Ministry of Economics while at the same time pursuing his ambitions in the realm of internal security. In contrast to the summer of 1942 there were now no obstacles in his way, since after the 'Führer's Decree on the concentration of the war economy' of 2 September 1943, the Ministry of Economics was released from duties relating to the armaments sector of the economy and was responsible for 'fundamental matters of economic policy' and maintaining supplies to the population.

NOTES

[1]For the dates of Ohlendorf's life: Ohlendorf's curriculum vitae dated 26.4.1936, BA NS 20 119–27 B1.106f.; Ohlendorf to Höhn, dated 18.5.1936, ibid., B1.119ff.; affidavit of SS-Brigade Leader Ohlendorf: Personal notes dated 1.4.1947, IfZ NO-2857; draft of a curriculum vitae by Ohlendorf, dated 3.1947, Nachlass Ohlendorf (Na01).

[2]Ohlendorf to his brother Heinz, dated 3.7.1932, Na01; numerous other letters to family members in Na01.

[3]USMP, Case 9, Dokumentenbuch I der Verteidigung (Dok. Buch I), Dok. 1, 1a, 36, Na01; Ohlendorf to his fiancee K. Wolpers, dated 25.11.1933, Na01. They married on 10.6.1934 and had five children.

[4]Dok. Buch I, Dok 2–4, 14–18, 20f., 26.

[5]Ohlendorf, letters from Russia Nr. 7, 11, 14, 40, 43, 46 to his wife, Na01; USMP, Case 9, Eidesstattliche Erklärung Dr Braune, Na01; much other material in Na01, for example 'Wie kam es zu meinem Russland-einsatz' (How did I come to be sent to Russia?); 'Der Ablauf meines Einsatzes in Russland' (The course of my deployment in Russia); 'Historische Tatsachen zur Aufstellung, Aufgabe und Tatigkeit der EGr. im Russlandfeldzug' (Historical facts about the setting-up, duties and activities of the Task Forces in the Russian campaign)—all undated (within the time scale of the court case!)

[6]Dok. Buch I, Dok. £f., 11, 25; USMP, Case 9, Eidesstattliche Erklärung von Dr Böhmer, Na01; Ohlendorf to Schwerin von Krosigk in May 1945, IfZ MA 660.

Inside the Third Reich
Memoirs

Albert Speer

Trans. Richard and Clara Winston

Those who took part in these table conversations were almost to a man without cosmopolitan experience. Most had never been outside Germany; if one of them had taken a pleasure trip to Italy, the matter was discussed at Hitler's table as if it were an event and the person in question was considered a foreign affairs expert. Hitler, too, had seen nothing of the world and had acquired neither knowledge nor understanding of it. Moreover, the average party politician lacked higher education. Of the fifty Reichsleiters and Gauleiters, the elite of the leadership, only ten had completed a university

Albert Speer, *Inside the Third Reich: Memoirs,* translation from German by Richard and Clara Winston. New York: Macmillan Co., 1970, pp. 121–126, 130–131. Reprinted by permission of Simon & Schuster. © 1970 by Macmillan Co.

education, a few had attended university classes for a while, and the majority had never gone beyond secondary school. Virtually none of them had distinguished himself by any notable achievement in any field whatsoever. Almost all displayed an astonishing intellectual dullness. Their educational standard certainly did not correspond to what might be expected of the top leadership of a nation with a traditionally high intellectual level. Basically, Hitler preferred to have people of the same origins as himself in his immediate entourage; no doubt he felt most at ease among them. In general he was pleased if his associates showed some "flaw in the weave," as we called it at the time. As Hanke commented one day: "It is all to the good if associates have faults and know that the superior is aware of them. That is why the Fuehrer so seldom changes his assistants. For he finds them easiest to work with. Almost every one of them has his defect; that helps keep them in line." Immoral conduct, remote Jewish ancestors, or recent membership in the party were counted as flaws in the weave.

Hitler would often theorize to the effect that it was a mistake to export ideas such as National Socialism. To do so would only lead to a strengthening of nationalism in other countries, he said, and thus to a weakening of his own position. He was glad to see that the Nazi parties of other countries produced no leader of his own caliber. He considered the Dutch Nazi leader Mussert and Sir Oswald Mosley, chief of the British Nazi party, mere copyists who had had no original or new ideas. They only imitated us and our methods slavishly, he commented, and would never amount to anything. In every country you had to start from different premises and change your methods accordingly, he argued. He had a better opinion of Degrelle, but did not expect much of him either.

Politics, for Hitler, was purely pragmatic. He did not except his own book of confessions and professions, *Mein Kampf,* from this general rule. Large parts of it were no longer valid, he said. He should not have let himself be pinned down to definite statements so early. After hearing that remark I gave up my fruitless efforts to read the book.

When ideology receded into the background after the seizure of power, efforts were made to tame down the party and make it more respectable. Goebbels and Bormann were the chief opponents of that tendency. They were always trying to radicalize Hitler ideologically. To judge by his speeches, Ley must also have belonged to the group of tough ideologists, but lacked the stature to gain any significant influence. Himmler, on the other hand, obviously was going his own absurd way, which was compounded of beliefs about an original Germanic race, a brand of elitism, and an assortment of health-food notions. The whole thing was beginning to assume far-fetched pseudoreligious forms. Goebbels, with Hitler, took the lead in ridiculing these dreams of Himmler's, with Himmler himself adding to the comedy by his vanity and obsessiveness. When, for example, the Japanese presented him with a samurai sword, he at once discovered kinships between Japanese and Teutonic cults and called upon scientists to help him trace these similarities to a racial common denominator.

Hitler was particularly concerned with the question of how he could assure his Reich a new generation of followers committed to his ideas. The general outlines of a plan were drafted by Ley, to whom Hitler had also entrusted the organization of the educational system. Adolf Hitler Schools were established for the elementary grades and Ordensburgen (Order Castles) for higher education. These were meant to turn out a technically and ideologically trained elite. To be sure, all this elite would have been good for was positions in a bureaucratic party administration, since thanks to their isolated and specialized education the young people knew nothing about practical life, while on the other hand their arrogance and conceit about their own abilities were boundless. It was significant that the high party functionaries did not send their own children into these schools; even so fanatical a party member as Gauleiter Sauckel refrained from launching a single one of his many boys on such a course. Conversely, Bormann sent one of his sons to an Adolf Hitler School as punishment.

In Bormann's mind, the *Kirchenkampf,* the campaign against the churches, was useful for reactivating party ideology which had been lying dormant. He was the driving force behind this campaign, as was time and again made plain to our round table. Hitler was hesitant, but only because he would rather postpone this problem to a more favorable time. Here in Berlin, surrounded by male cohorts, he spoke more coarsely and bluntly than he ever did in the midst of his Obersalzberg entourage. "Once I have settled my other problems," he occasionally declared, "I'll have my reckoning with the church. I'll have it reeling on the ropes."

But Bormann did not want this reckoning postponed. Brutally direct himself, he could ill tolerate Hitler's prudent pragmatism. He therefore took every opportunity to push his own projects. Even at meals he broke the unspoken rule that no subjects were to be raised which might spoil Hitler's humor. Bormann had developed a special technique for such thrusts. He would draw one of the members of the entourage into telling him about seditious speeches a pastor or bishop had delivered, until Hitler finally became attentive and demanded details. Bormann would reply that something unpleasant had happened and did not want to bother Hitler with it during the meal. At this Hitler would probe further, while Bormann pretended that he was reluctantly letting the story be dragged from him. Neither the angry looks from his fellow guests nor Hitler's gradually flushing face deterred him from going on. At some point he would take a document from his pocket and begin reading passages from a defiant sermon or a pastoral letter. Frequently Hitler became so worked up that he began to snap his fingers—a sure sign of his anger—pushed away his food and vowed to punish the offending clergyman eventually. He could much more easily put up with foreign indignation and criticism than opposition at home. That he could not immediately retaliate raised him to a white heat, though he usually managed to control himself quite well.

Hitler had no humor. He left joking to others, although he could laugh loudly, abandonedly, sometimes literally writhing with laughter. Often he would wipe tears from his eyes during such spasms. He liked laughing, but it was always laughter at the expense of others.

Goebbels was skilled at entertaining Hitler with jokes while at the same time demolishing any rivals in the internal struggle for power. "You know," he once related, "the Hitler Youth asked us to issue a press release for the twenty-fifth birthday of its staff chief, Lauterbacher. So I sent along a draft of the text to the effect that he had celebrated this birthday 'enjoying full physical and mental vigor.' We heard no more from him." Hitler doubled up with laughter, and Goebbels had achieved his end of cutting the conceited youth leader down to size.

To the dinner guests in Berlin, Hitler repeatedly talked about his youth, emphasizing the strictness of his upbringing. "My father often dealt me hard blows. Moreover, I think that was necessary and helped me." Wilhelm Frick, the Minister of the Interior, interjected in his bleating voice: "As we can see today, it certainly did you good, *mein Führer.*" A numb, horrified silence around the table. Frick tried to save the situation: "I mean, *mein Führer*, that is why you have come so far;" Goebbels, who considered Frick a hopeless fool, commented sarcastically: "I would guess you never received a beating in your youth, Frick."

Walther Funk, who was both Minister of Economics and president of the Reichsbank, told stories about the outlandish pranks that his vice president, Brinkmann, had gone on performing for months, until it was finally realized that he was mentally ill. In telling such stories Funk not only wanted to amuse Hitler but to inform him in this casual way of events which would sooner or later reach his ears. Brinkmann, it seemed, had invited the cleaning women and messenger boys of the Reichsbank to a grand dinner in the ballroom of the Hotel Bristol, one of the best hotels in Berlin, where he played the violin for them. This sort of thing rather fitted in with the regime's propaganda of all Germans forming one "folk community." But as everyone at table laughed, Funk continued: "Recently he stood in front of the Ministry of Economics on Unter den Linden, took a large package of newly printed banknotes from his briefcase—as you know, the notes bear my signature and gave them out to passers-by saying: 'Who wants some of the new Funks?'"* Shortly afterward, Funk continued, the poor man's insanity had become plain for all to see. He called together all the employees of the Reichsbank. "'Everyone older than fifty to the left side, the younger employees to the right.'" Then, to one man on the right side: "'How old are you?'—'Forty-nine sir.'—'You go to the left too. Well now, all on the left side are dismissed at once, and what is more with a double pension.'"

Hitler's eyes filled with tears of laughter. When he had recovered, he launched into a monologue on how hard it sometimes is to recognize a madman. In this roundabout way Funk was also accomplishing another end. Hitler did not yet know that the Reichsbank vice president in his irresponsible state had given Goering a check for several million marks. Goering cashed the check without a qualm. Later on, of course, Goering vehemently objected to the thesis that Brinkmann did not know what he was doing. Funk could expect him to present this point of view to Hitler. Experience had shown that the person who first managed to suggest a particular version of an affair to Hitler had virtually won his point, for Hitler never liked to alter a view he had once

*A pun in German; *Funken* = sparks.—*Translators' note.*

expressed. Even so, Funk had difficulties recovering those millions of marks from Goering.

A favorite target of Goebbels's jokes and the subject of innumerable anecdotes was Rosenberg, whom Goebbels liked to call "the Reich philosopher." On this subject Goebbels could be sure that Hitler agreed with him. He therefore took up the theme so frequently that the stories resembled carefully rehearsed theatrical performances in which the various actors were only waiting for their cues. Hitler was almost certain to interject at some point: "The *Völkischer Beobachter* is just as boring as its editor, Rosenberg. You know, we have a so-called humor sheet in the party, *Die Brennessel.* The dreariest rag imaginable. And on the other hand the *VB* is nothing but a humor sheet." Goebbels also made game of the printer Müller, who was doing his best both to keep the party and not to lose his old customers, who came from strictly Catholic circles in Upper Bavaria. His printing program was certainly versatile, ranging from pious calendars to Rosenberg's antichurch writings. But Müller was allowed considerable leeway; in the twenties he had gone on printing the *Völkischer Beobachter* no matter how large the bill grew.

Many jokes were carefully prepared, tied up as they were with actual events, so that Hitler was kept abreast of interparty developments under the guise of foolery. Again, Goebbels was far better at this than all the others, and Hitler gave him further encouragement by showing that he was very much amused.

An old party member, Eugen Hadamowski, had obtained a key position as Reichssendeleiter (Head of Broadcasting for the Reich), but now he was longing to be promoted to Leiter des Reichsrundfunks (Head of the Reich Radio System). The Propaganda Minister, who had another candidate, was afraid that Hitler might back Hadamowski because he had skillfully organized the public address systems for the election campaigns before 1933. He had Hanke, state secretary in the Propaganda Ministry, send for the man and officially informed him that Hitler had just appointed him Reichsintendant (General Director) for radio. At the table Hitler was given an account of how Hadamowski had gone wild with joy at this news. The description was, no doubt, highly colored and exaggerated, so that Hitler took the whole affair as a great joke. Next day Goebbels had a few copies of a newspaper printed reporting on the sham appointment and praising the new appointee in excessive terms. He outlined the article for Hitler, with all its ridiculous phrases, and acted out Hadamowski's rapture upon reading these things about himself. Once more Hitler and the whole table with him was convulsed. That same day Hanke asked the newly appointed Reichsintendant to make a speech into a dead microphone, and once again there was endless merriment at Hitler's table when the story was told. After this, Goebbels no longer had to worry that Hitler would intervene in favor of Hadamowski. It was a diabolic game; the ridiculed man did not have the slightest opportunity to defend himself and probably never realized that the practical joke was carefully plotted to make him unacceptable to Hitler. No one could even know whether what Goebbels was describing was true or whether he was giving his imagination free rein.

From one point of view, Hitler was the real dupe of these intrigues. As far as I could observe, Hitler was in fact no match for Goebbels in such matters; with his more direct temperament he did not understand this sort of cunning. But it certainly should have given one pause that Hitler allowed this nasty game to go on and even encouraged it. One word of displeasure would certainly have stopped this sort of thing for a long while to come.

I often asked myself whether Hitler was open to influence. He surely could be swayed by those who knew how to manage him. Hitler was mistrustful, to be sure. But he was so in a cruder sense, it often seemed to me; for he did not see through clever chess moves or subtle manipulation of his opinions. He had apparently no sense for methodical deceit. Among the masters of that art were Goering, Goebbels, Bormann, and, within limits, Himmler. Since those who spoke out in candid terms on the important questions usually could not make Hitler change his mind, the cunning men naturally gained more and more power.

...

Around 1939 Eva Braun was assigned a bedroom in the Berlin residence. It adjoined his; the windows looked out on a narrow courtyard. Here even more than in Obersalzberg she led a completely isolated life, stealing into the building through a side entrance and going up a rear staircase, never descending into the lower rooms, even when there were only old acquaintances in the apartment, and she was overjoyed whenever I kept her company during her long hours of waiting.

In Berlin, Hitler very seldom went to the theater, except to see operettas. He would never miss a new production of the by now classical operettas such as *Die Fledermaus* and *The Merry Widow.* I am certain that I saw *Die Fledermaus* with him at least five or six times in cities all over Germany. He customarily contributed considerable sums from Bormann's privy purse to have the operetta put on in lavish style.

In addition he liked revues. He went to the Wintergarten several times to attend a Berlin variety show and would certainly have gone more frequently but for the fact that he was embarrassed to be seen there. Sometimes he sent his house steward in his place and then late in the evening would look over the program and ask for an account of what had gone on. Several times he also went to the Metropol Theater which put on insipid musicals with plenty of scantily clad girls.

During the Bayreuth Festival every year he attended every single performance of the first cycle. It seemed to a musical layman like myself that in his conversations with Frau Winifred Wagner he displayed knowledge about musical matters in detail; but he was even more concerned about the directing.

Aside from Bayreuth, however, he very seldom attended performances of operas, and his initially rather keen interest in theater also dwindled. Even his enthusiasm for Bruckner never seemed very marked and imposed no obligations on others. Although a movement from a Bruckner symphony was played before each of his "cultural speeches" at the Nuremberg Party Rallies, for the rest he merely took care that Bruckner's works continued to be fostered at St. Florian. He saw to it, however, that his public image of a man passionately devoted to art was cultivated.

I never found out whether and to what extent Hitler had an interest in literature. Mostly he talked about books on military science, naval matters and architecture, which he would pore over with great interest during the night hours. On other books he made no comment.

I myself threw all my strength into my work and was baffled at first by the way Hitler squandered his working time. I could understand that he might wish his day to trail off in boredom and pastimes; but to my notion this phase of the day, averaging some six hours, proved rather long, whereas the actual working session was by comparison relatively short. When, I would often ask myself, did he really work? Little was left of the day; he rose late in the morning and conducted one or two official conferences; but from the subsequent dinner on be more or less wasted time until the early hours of the evening. His rare appointments in the late afternoon were imperiled by his passion for looking at building plans. The adjutants often asked me: "Please don't show any plans today." Then the drawings I had brought with me would be left by the telephone switchboard at the entrance, and I would reply evasively to Hitler's inquiries. Sometimes he saw through this game and would himself go to look in the anteroom or the cloakroom for my roll of plans.

In the eyes of the people Hitler was the Leader who watched over the nation day and night. This was hardly so. But Hitler's lax scheduling could be regarded as a life style characteristic of the artistic temperament. According to my observations, he often allowed a problem to mature during the weeks when he seemed entirely taken up with trivial matters. Then, after the "sudden insight" came, he would spend a few days of intensive work giving final shape to his solution. No doubt he also used his dinner and supper guests as sounding boards, trying out new ideas, approaching these ideas in a succession of different ways, tinkering with them before an uncritical audience, and thus perfecting them. Once he had come to a decision, he relapsed again into his idleness.

Reinhard Heydrich
The Chilling Story of the Man Who Masterminded the Nazi Death Camps

Edouard Calic

Trans. Lowell Bair

THE COMPOSER'S NIGHTMARE: THE JEW SUESS

Bruno Heydrich's marriage to Elisabeth Krantz in 1897 gave him the social position he wanted. His wife had been educated in a Catholic boarding school, and her parents would never have allowed her to marry outside their religion, so Bruno had converted to Catholicism, disregarding the slogan that was common in nationalistic circles at that time: "Away from Rome." He was prepared to do anything necessary to consolidate his situation in society because by now he had been forced to recognize that his singing voice and his ability as a composer were only mediocre and that he would always be a provincial in his artistic activities. It was time to head in a new direction. His father-in-law got him a post as a music teacher.

In 1899, Bruno Heydrich founded his own music school in Halle, an administrative, industrial, and university city not far from Leipzig, Dresden, and Berlin. Almost as soon as the school was opened, twenty students enrolled in it to take singing lessons. Two years later, Bruno changed its name: it became a conservatory. The number of students eventually rose to about a hundred and twenty. Elisabeth Heydrich was a member of the faculty; she taught piano.

The students came mainly from the city's rich and influential families. Heydrich kept making new contacts among those families and tried to join every organization that might be useful to him. He attached great importance to impressing his listeners with a witty remark or a wise saying whenever the opportunity arose. He liked to stud his conversation with quotations from Goethe's *Faust*. Cosima Wagner had told him that there were "inexhaustible riches of the heart and strength of soul" in Goethe. Anyone who quoted from Goethe, thought Heydrich, was sure to be known as an ardent champion of the German spirit.

When he had been drinking abundantly, he sometimes forgot the serious purpose of a meeting and told jokes. But at regular gatherings of socially prominent ladies in his house, he was on his best behavior and gratified his guests with compliments that he had prepared in advance. With important businessmen, he used flattery and servility to win their favor.

The local patricians criticized his exaggerated joviality and enviously watched his conservatory becoming more and more profitable. They were intrigued by the fact that practically nothing was known about Heydrich's background. Finally, it was learned that he regularly sent money to a Frau Ernestine Suess, and then it did not take long to discover that she was his mother. A rumor soon began circulating that Bruno Heydrich was only his professional name and that he really bore the Jewish name of Isidor Suess. When this rumor reached him, Heydrich lodged a complaint against "a person or persons unknown" in an effort to find out who had started the slanderous story.

Bruno Heydrich was not the first to be threatened with ostracism for belonging to another racial or religious group, whether the "accusation" was true or not. For centuries, German guilds of merchants and craftsmen had tried to exclude competitors from the market by depicting them as foreign elements. Newcomers who spoke Yiddish were especially hated, even when they only set up a small family business that barely made enough profits to keep them alive. They were taunted, ridiculed, and caricatured, largely on the basis of alleged customs that were actually unknown to them. Even if a Jew was totally assimilated in his language, religion, and way of living, his enemies would still claim to see "typically Jewish traits" in him.

In Halle, there was soon widespread agreement that Bruno Heydrich really did seem Jewish.

Elisabeth Heydrich regarded this story about her husband's origin as a vicious insult that could cause the whole family great harm. She tried to combat it by repeating Bruno's claim that his father, Karl Heydrich, had been a talented piano maker in Meissen. She maintained that, at the time, piano makers had been as highly respected as violin makers, and that such piano manufacturers as Bechstein and Lambert had built their fortunes on the skill of craftsmen like Bruno's father.

The Heydrichs never succeeded in putting an end to rumors about Bruno's supposed Jewish extraction. He did not understand how such an affront could have been inflicted on him when he was second to none in zealously professing German nationalism. No one in Halle had the courage to mock him to his face, but people went on calling him Isidor Suess behind his back. He was consumed with resentment, and the rest of his life was embittered by the knowledge that he was powerless to stop that slander.

BIRTH OF REINHARD TRISTAN EUGEN HEYDRICH

On March 7, 1904, the Heydrichs had a second child, the son they had been hoping for after the birth of their daughter, Maria. Bruno Heydrich had already decided to give him the name of Reinhard, the main character in his opera *Amen,* who because of his love was killed by the vindictive peasant, Thomas. It was a name intended to symbolize courage, loyalty, honor, and undying love.

A son with dark hair and eyes would have been a disaster for Bruno Heydrich, that fanatical racist who was tortured by rumors that attributed Jewish ancestry to him. When he saw that his baby was blond and blue-eyed, he must have taken it as a sign that he was worthy of the three prenames he had chosen for him: Reinhard Tristan Eugen.

Four months after Reinhard's birth, the family moved into a new home. The number of students had increased to the point where a larger building was needed for the conservatory. The new building, at 21 Poststrasse, had many classrooms and a concert hall with a stage.

In 1905, another son, Heinz Siegfried, was born.

Elisabeth Heydrich gave her three children a rigorously Catholic upbringing. Bruno taught them that they must respect soldiers and that the army was the concentrated embodiment of the people. Hoping to counter the effects of the Isidor Suess rumors, he saw to it that everyone noticed his family's militaristic Prussian spirit, which he confirmed by maintaining close relations with his friend Major Ernst von Eberstein and the latter's entourage of career officers. He often told anecdotes beginning with such phrases as "When my opera *Amen* was performed in Cologne…" or "When I was with Cosima in Bayreuth…." The implication was that his close friendship with Cosima Wagner entitled him to refer to her by her first name only.

With Major von Eberstein, his conversations were almost exclusively political. He railed against the Social Democrats, accusing them of trying to weaken the Reich with their campaigns against military spending. He never forgot to make some laudatory mention of "the Iron Chancellor" (Bismarck) and present himself as a stalwart supporter of the glory of Prussia.

But his efforts to show his devotion to Prussianism brought him only short-lived successes. When he asked the authorities to grant him the rank of Professor, since many students had graduated from his conservatory and some had become well-known musicians, his request was denied. His conservatory, he was told, was not an official institution. He felt that this was only a pretext and that the real reason for his rejection was the cloud that hung over his origin.

Meanwhile, however, he was prospering financially. In 1906, when Reinhard was two, the family moved into a building at 20 Gütchenstrasse, in a well-to-do residential neighborhood.

As Reinhard and his brother, Heinz, grew older, fighting with wooden swords became their favorite game. They were later to become enthusiastic athletes. Their father encouraged their growing inclination toward developing physical strength and skills. In Reinhard, it was an inclination that lasted all his life and made him tend to judge men by their athletic ability.

The two boys soon became interested in everything military, and when Major von Eberstein came for a visit, they looked him over admiringly, from the tips of his boots to his epaulets. They also admired their father because he was an accomplished fencer and belonged to the Fencing School of the German Reich.

Reinhard, of course, had to study music. But it soon became apparent that he would never be an opera singer: the poor boy had a falsetto voice. So Bruno Heydrich's favorite son studied piano and violin in the family conservatory.

Reinhard was only ten when World War I began. From then on, every phase of the war was discussed at length in the Heydrich household. "Uncle Ernst" von Eberstein's son Karl had just turned twenty and therefore had the good luck of being able to fight for the Kaiser and the Fatherland. The assassination of Ferdinand, Archduke of Austria, cried out for vengeance. Karl's and Reinhard's mothers began collecting gifts that the Red Cross distributed to soldiers at the front. Bruno Heydrich supported their efforts by organizing patriotic meetings at which music was provided by the Patriotic Singing Association.

Reinhard cared very little about those activities: it was weapons that aroused his passionate interest, and especially the warships he had seen with his own eyes during vacations on the Baltic shore at Warnemünde. His childish view of the war was centered on those formidable ships that could take their gigantic cannons all over the world.

"HEIL, EMPEROR OF GERMANY, HEIL!"

When it was time for Reinhard to enroll in a *Gymnasium* ("high school"), his parents chose a "reformed" *Gymnasium* in which the curriculum stressed technical subjects and modern languages, rather than the humanities. Emperor Wilhelm II, who was regarded almost as a god by German nationalists, had urged educators to give priority to technology, for understandable reasons. He was not satisfied with having the largest army on the European continent: he needed a transatlantic fleet strong enough to compete with those of other countries and bring from the colonies the raw materials necessary for the further development of German industry.

When Reinhard looked in his atlas and was surprised by the great number of British colonies throughout the world, he asked his father how the English had acquired them.

"It's simple," he was told. "The English have more than enough warships."

"Could we build even more warships than the English?" asked the boy.

"Of course. Uncle Ernst says it's only a question of money."

Reinhard's interest in seafaring, and particularly the navy, did not diminish. He dreamed of someday being a shipbuilder, or a ship's captain, or even an Admiral. He decorated the walls of his room with colored pictures of warships.

His teachers at the reformed *Gymnasium* were pleased by the interest he showed in mathematics and chemistry, as well as German and history. He was a boy who would amount to something when he grew up, especially since his parents had taught him to respect the authorities in general and the Emperor in particular. The people of Halle still remembered that for the twenty-fifth anniversary of Wilhelm II's accession to power Bruno Heydrich had organized a celebration at which his conservatory students performed an "authentically German program" of works by German composers from George Frederick Handel to Richard Wagner. He had also composed a march for the occasion, and written the words himself. Reinhard, nine years old at the time, had learned those words by heart:

Lord God, give thy blessing…
Lead us on all paths
And protect the Emperor as always.
May unity and peace
Always uplift us in this world.
Look upon us in thy grace.
Without thee, nothing is done.
Heil, land of Germany!
Heil, Emperor of Germany, heil!

Reinhard keenly felt the tragedy of the loss inflicted on the Austrians by the assassination of Archduke Francis Ferdinand at Sarajevo, in Bosnia, which was part of the vast Austro-Hungarian empire. "There's nothing surprising about it," his father told him. "Those Serbs even killed their own King Alexander Obrenovich and replaced him with a puppet who made it possible for them to have good relations with France. Then there was that anarchist Luchieni, who killed Empress Elisabeth, Franz Josef's wife, at Geneva in 1898." And Bruno Heydrich explained to his two sons that such outrages could only come from the pernicious ideas that had become widespread, especially in France.

Bruno Heydrich, the "absolute Wagnerian," naturally knew every sentence that Wagner had written against the Jews. Wagner was of the opinion that the Jews really belonged in Palestine, and since he hated "Judeo-French democracy," he had recommended destroying Paris during the Franco-Prussian War of 1870–71. The Heydrichs were sure that this time Wilhelm II would accomplish what his grandfather had not been able to do in 1870.

As the World War continued, Reinhard's developing mind became better able to understand what was happening. His father explained events to him, as he saw them. He also imbued Reinhard with contempt for the Jews, considering it his duty to bring up his children to be zealous anti-Semites, and hoping that this would help to protect them against the effects of the Isidor Suess rumors. Things had reached the point where the two Heydrich boys were sometimes taunted in the street with shouts of "Isi! Isi!" (Isi was the diminutive of Isidor.) Their father urged them to silence their tormentors with their fists, and Heinz once went so far as to threaten one of them with a knife.

Because of his family's special situation and the intense interest with which the course of the war was followed in his home, Reinhard acquired a certain political awareness at an earlier age than his classmates. As he grew older, he often displayed an arrogant attitude, and he was generally criticized for his aggressiveness. This tendency toward physical violence was fully manifested whenever one of the other boys dared to call him a goat, a teasing he received because of the bleating quality of his high-pitched voice. His brutality was nourished by discussion with his parents concerning the war and the best way of annihilating the hated enemy.

In 1916, the Heydrich family's hopes for a German victory in the near future began to fade: the French were defending Verdun with unexpected tenacity, and it became clear that the German Navy had no chance of wiping out the British fleet. But Bruno could still look forward to a personal victory: a new edition of Hugo Riemann's *Musiklexikon* ("Dictionary of Music") was about to be published, and he hoped that it would recognize his worth as an artist.

He was outraged when the dictionary appeared and he saw that the entry concerning him began as follows: HEYDRICH, BRUNO (REAL NAME SUESS)...."

Elisabeth Heydrich had great difficulty calming her husband. By threats of legal action he was finally able to obtain the assurance that the words REAL NAME SUESS would be omitted from the next edition of the dictionary. But the experience left its mark on him; from then on he was more and more determined to be recognized by everyone as a pure Aryan.

While the German people became increasingly tired of the war, Bruno Heydrich maintained his unshakable belief in victory; he wrote articles describing how the enemy could be overcome. But suddenly the workers began demanding an end to the war, and there was a sailors' mutiny in the seaport of Kiel. The German Army was headed for collapse, but the bourgeois citizens of Halle continued to believe that it would finally triumph. After all, German soldiers were still in enemy territory. All they had to do was hold their positions and eventually they would be victorious. Reinhard acquired this conviction from his parents, and it influenced his military thinking the rest of his life.

EXTERMINATION

In 1940, after the fall of France, Heydrich knew that the following year Hitler would take his next step toward world mastery: conquest of the Soviet Union, that "satanic creation of international Jewry." Besides gaining the "living space" it needed, the Third Reich would have access to the grain of the Ukraine, the petroleum of the Caucasus, and a labor force composed of a hundred million slaves. Then all the resources of the European continent could be used for subduing Britain and the United States. Heydrich had carefully studied each phase of this project because he would have to develop the structure of an enormous system of domination and supervise its functioning.

To him, the struggle against Britain was primarily a matter of psychological warfare. He believed that the British would hold out as long as they had any hope of help from the armed forces of other European countries. France had already been disarmed, and the Soviet Union would soon meet the same fate.

The German plan for an invasion of Britain (code name Sea Lion) was now well known in the world of international espionage. Military attachés in Germany and other countries regularly received supposedly secret information intended to fill them with respect for the enormous war machine that Hitler was going to use in the invasion. According to Nazi propaganda, German submarines in the Atlantic would increase their activity to a devastating level, then the Luftwaffe would launch massive bombing attacks that would wipe British cities off the face of the earth.

These dire prospects were supposed to make the British negotiate a peace settlement. As early as November 1940, Heydrich had said that peace with Britain was certain. After the defeat of the Soviet Union, at the very latest, the British would accept the inevitable, especially since some political circles and part of the aristocracy already disapproved of Churchill's war policy.

While final preparations for the invasion of the Soviet Union were being made, Hitler ordered Himmler, and therefore Heydrich, to begin preparing for the total elimination of the Jews.

All those in the zone controlled by the Reich would be deported. The operation would begin suddenly but would last for three or four years, until the death of the last Jew. At the same time, the vanquished Soviet Union would be completely pacified. For the Generalissimo of that racial war, the extermination of eleven million human beings posed only a technical problem.

To carry it out, Heydrich enlisted the services of doctors, chemists, transportation experts, truck drivers, commanders of concentration camps, administrators, accountants, crematory designers, engineers, carpenters, guards, and others. Murder squads, known as Einsatzgruppen, were created to follow combat troops into occupied territories. They, in turn, were followed by trucks carrying collapsible barracks, gasoline, drinking water, and tools, such as shovels, picks, and rakes. Whenever they stopped to set up a camp, they used forced labor from the local population. The four thousand murder experts of the Einsatzgruppen, their technical personnel, and their slaves constituted an army of more than a hundred thousand men.

We have no official documents giving an exact description of those death camps where the Einsatzgruppen operated; we have only accounts by survivors. I will not repeat those that are already well known, but I think the reader will be interested by the story of a thirteen-year-old boy named Mendel, who lived in Poland:

> The police surrounded the streets and houses. My father hid my mother, my two sisters, and me, making us lie on the ground, then he went off by himself to see what was happening....We never saw him again....The first people were taken into the forest in cars....A very big grave was dug, and people were thrown into it after being shot. Children were thrown into it alive. This was on a Thursday; the grave was not filled in till Friday morning. Ten children and several women who had been only wounded were able to crawl out of the grave during the night, after lying under dead bodies.

A few Nazi murderers later confirmed these facts by their own statements, and others took photographs that have been preserved.

We know that Heydrich began developing his methods of annihilation as soon as German troops marched into Czechoslovakia, that he developed them further in Poland, and that in preparation for the invasion of the Soviet Union he organized the largest and most efficient mass-murder system of all time. He acted in accordance with specific principles that followed from his nationalistic (*voelkisch*) attitudes: "We do not want to conquer the souls of the Jews, Catholics, and Marxists; we want to conquer living space. We want to settle Germanic peasants on that land."[1]

Besides the victims who were killed directly, others died "naturally," from epidemics, starvation, and cold. Inhuman conditions in ghettos and concentration camps did part of the work; gas chambers and bullets did the rest.

After the war, apologists for the Nazis tried to disguise the real nature of their murderous system. They often spoke of individual crimes committed by subordinates who, exasperated by the situation in the occupied territories, were driven to acts that went beyond their duty. According to those apologists, the killings occurred only because of the chaos that resulted from the state of war. But the fact is that, long before the invasion of the Soviet Union, the Nazi leaders already knew how their civilian "enemies" were going to be slaughtered.

The four Einsatzgruppen—designated A, B, C, and D—their four thousand specialists and some hundred thousand assistants, had complete autonomy of action but were officially under the supervision of the Wehrmacht. On March 26, 1941, Field Marshal Walther von Brauchitsch, the Wehrmacht Commander in Chief, issued directives to his subordinates concerning the operations of the Einsatzgruppen. They were first to exterminate "inferior Asians," Gypsies, and Jews. An order from Heydrich designated some of the victims more specifically: Red Army People's Commissars; Jews holding positions in the Communist party and the state; warmongers, guerrillas, and propagandists.

Heydrich repeatedly explained to SS leaders and Einsatzgruppen commanders how the extermination operations were to proceed. The "great suppression of the Jews" was to begin within hours after a piece of territory had been occupied. The Einsatzgruppen would try to stir up the local population to the point where they would take part in killing the Jews. The whole territory had to be carefully searched to make sure that not one Jew was left alive, and an especially close watch had to be kept on young people, because they had a tendency to run away and join Resistance groups.

Here are the operational results of those elite SS units: Einsatzgruppe A (commanded by Stahlecker) reported killing 229,052 Jews by the end of August 1941; Einsitzgruppe B (Nebe): 45,467 by mid-November; Einsatzgruppe C (Rasch): 95,000, also by mid-November; Einsatzgruppe D (Ohlendorf): 92,000 by the beginning of April 1942.

On December 20, 1941, Heydrich informed the Fuehrer that 363,211 other Jews had been killed.

Most victims of that extermination campaign led by Himmler and Heydrich were killed in death camps, usually by means of gas chambers, and in mass executions by the Einsatzgruppen, but there were also many who died while they were being transported under bestially cruel conditions.

It is not true that Hitler persecuted only Jews, as his propagandists tried to make the Eastern peoples believe. Slavs and "inferior Asians" were also slaughtered. The invasion of the Soviet Union provided an opportunity to wipe out several million people and clear the way for German colonization. This plan had been adopted even before the invasion began.

Hitler stated on April 30, 1941, that the Red Army would be annihilated within four weeks. He expected half of its ten million men to be taken prisoner, yet no plans were made for feeding or sheltering that great mass of human beings.

The historian Christian Streit has calculated that of the 5,734,528 Soviet prisoners of war, about 3,300,000, more than 57 percent, were either executed or died of starvation, disease, or cold.[2] That is, the death rate was twenty times higher than among prisoners in World War I. In World War II, the Soviet Union lost more than twenty million people.

NOTES

[1]Friedrich Zipfel, communication to the author.

[2]Christian Streit, *Die Wehrmacht und die sowjetischen Kriegsgefangenen 1941–1945,* Stuttgart, 1978.

Chapter 5

Life in Nazi Germany, 1933–1940

INTRODUCTION

The leaders of the Nazi state served Hitler faithfully up to the day of the collapse of the Reich. The Fuehrer induced and seduced some able and many mediocre men to join his government and his army. They vied for positions because they loved power, or wealth, or sought ego gratification. Although the regime wanted a businesslike approach to the final solution, a number of sadists joined the ranks of the SS, but the majority were conventional, commonplace men. Judging from their actions rather than the self-serving statements they parroted after the fall of Hitler, most of the Nazi officials embraced the doctrine of the racial inferiority of the Jews. Many members of the Nazi elite were motivated by extreme nationalism and supported Hitler's foreign policy enthusiastically. A powerful incentive to support Hitler, the restoration of German pride and greatness, cut across all levels of German society.

A question that is raised in every classroom where the Holocaust is studied concerns the acquiescence of the German population at large. Their votes had brought Hitler the chancellorship in 1933. Once the Nazis achieved power, the German masses were generally supportive of the regime during the prewar years and largely passive and obedient between 1939 and 1945. How can we understand their compliance and submission in light of the vast changes instituted during the Third Reich? That the turbulence of the Republic was translated into the rise of the Nazis is intelligible, but why did Hitler continue to retain his hold on the people? Certainly, the Weimar years had witnessed a great deal of political participation from the electorate. What happened to the hundreds of thousands of activists who had rallied, marched, gone on strikes and fought battles in the streets to either support or bring down the Republic? Their activities contradict the claim that Germans were "by nature" submissive and apolitical. During the pre-Nazi decade, they had joined dozens of political parties, had challenged the status quo with their votes, and with their voices, and with their fists. Nonetheless, these same Germans never organized a viable opposition to the Nazis once they were in power. The quarrel between Hitler and the SA, resolved in the "Night of the Long Knives," had been an intra-Party feud, barely affected the general public. The 1943 assassination attempt on Hitler by the Kreisau Circle was not a popular uprising. It was an effort by a small, elite group to restore Christian morality to the government and sue for peace to end the military disasters suffered by the army. Even when the war was surely lost, 80 million Germans continued to work and fight and suffer for a catastrophic regime.

The following readings pertain to conditions in peace-time Germany. What changed and what remained the same? How did the people feel about a dictator whose qualifications had never enabled him to get a job? How much or how little of Dr. Goebbels' verbiage did they believe? Was it true, as so many Germans later claimed, that the Third Reich resembled an immense prison? Were the people helpless victims, paralyzed by fear? Or did they adapt quite readily to the new order because that was the road of least resistance?

The German population, consciously or subconsciously, applied a balance sheet to the Nazi style of governance. Hitler's achievements were weighed against his deficiencies. Simply put: what did we gain and what did we lose? We, who have the wisdom of hindsight, may wonder how the German people could possibly have exercised such poor judgment. The fact that the well educated were among the most avid Nazis further confounds the issue. Did they not miss their freedom of speech, of action, of press and assembly? Never mind the fate of the Jews, what about the regimentation of the children, the loss of fair trial? To an American such deprivation would have been intolerable and would have aroused furious opposition. But in the 1930 most Germans gauged their government on a different scale. To clarify the point, the following list may be helpful.

Among the benefits experienced and/or perceived during the first seven years of the Third Reich were the following:

1. The restoration of law and order; the turmoil of the Weimar years was stopped.
2. The virtual end to unemployment; at its height, joblessness had reached 6,000,000.
3. The revival of the military; improvements were effected in both quality and quantity of the vaunted forces.
4. The return of patriotic pride, brought about particularly by Hitler's diplomatic successes and the abrogation of the Versailles Treaty.
5. The expectation of unlimited opportunities for advancement for themselves and their children, as rank and class lost much of its traditional rigidity.
6. The simplification of politics; Germans were good, others were evil; to fight against evil—in whatever shape—was right and honorable.
7. Pageantry and spectacle on the grand scale of Nazi rallies created a sense of solidarity and power.

8. The idealization of workers and farmers and their contribution to society was a welcome sop for the underclass.
9. The glorification of the German past as rationale for future greatness satisfied a sense of history.
10. Such visible accomplishments as the Autobahn, the extensive building program, and the industrial revival made Germans proud.

These assets were not attained without a balance on the other side of the ledger. The losses included the following:

1. Freedom of speech, press, political association, economic associations were nullified.
2. The individual was subordinated to the state, culture and creativity were subjected to official censorship.
3. The breach between parents and their Hitler Youth children became wider and deeper.
4. Christian worship and doctrine were demeaned and an attempt was made to elevate Nordic myths to religious doctrine.
5. Fear of concentration camps for opposing the regime was a reality.
6. The anti-intellectual stance of the authorities and promotion of racial ideology undermined educational quality.
7. The demands of the government on the private time of families was excessive.
8. Nazi Party membership rather than merit was the key to advancement.
9. Women were valued only in relationship to their childbearing services to the fatherland.

Two components of Hitler's regime, namely the persecution of the Jews and the elimination of the Communists met with mixed responses. Many Germans believed that the revocation of citizenship of the Jews and their expulsion from the economic life of the nation "went too far"; others applauded the action. (In 1939 the physical annihilation of the Jews was not yet an issue.) The virtual disappearanc of members of the Communist Party was greeted as a victory by many and as a shame by some. These authorized abuses were openly and publicly carried out without provoking any public reaction or action. Minding one's own business was, after all, an attribute of decent people.

Winzig, Germany, 1933–1946
The History of a Town under the Third Reich

Rita S. Botwinick

Winzig's political life had its moments of melodrama during the thirties. The political waters were not as quiet as the weekly paper so endlessly proclaimed. Not even in Winzig. Resistance to the Nazi power structure came from two widely divergent sources—a man and a woman with very little in common. Neither would have conceded that their struggle against Lang and Schaube were in any way comparable. They were never friends. In fact, they moved in very different social circles. Both, however, had made assumptions that right actions will bring right results. They were wrong, of course.

The lady was tall and blond. She wore her hair in a braid twisted around her head, and she carried her large frame with a straight back and a purposeful stride. Her name was Martha Hildebrandt, but she was always called Hulda, a name that suited her *Walkuerian* bearing. Her husband owned the Black Eagle Inn on the Ring. Hulda was the dominant member of the pair, both in business and in their private lives. It was Hulda who would star in the "Hildebrandt affair" while Herr Hildebrandt was cast in a supporting role.

Hulda was one of the few Winzigers who could call herself an "old fighter," since she had joined the NSDAP before 1930. The Black Eagle, quite naturally, became a favorite gathering place for the local Nazi clique, and Hitler's victories were celebrated with countless steins of brew. Hulda, outspoken and completely at ease among the men, was a respected member of the group. But not for long.

When power had been transferred from Winzig's conservative leadership to the Lang and Schaube duo, Hulda was disappointed. She should have been jubilant; instead she became critical and sharply faultfinding. She was an idealist, uncompromising in the expectation that the new Germany would be led by warriors, men whose idealism matched her own. Behind the bar at the inn she displayed a picture of Hitler, always adorned with fresh flowers. The fuehrer's eyes seemed to admonish her to set things right in Winzig. Lang in particular, Schaube and Juerke to a lesser extent, did not meet her standards of government in the new Reich.

She heard and saw much as she served the tankards of beer at the inn. The

Rita S. Botwinick, *Winzig, Germany, 1933–1946: The History of a Town under the Third Reich*, Westport, CT: Praeger Publishers, 1992, pp. 47–59. © by Rita S. Botwinick, reproduced with permission of Greenwood Publishing Group, Inc., Westport, CT.

mayor and his cohorts were no better, in fact much worse, than the pettifoggers they had replaced. Where she expected to see supermen, she found only self-serving bunglers. Her indignation was fueled by rumors of mismanagement of funds, of the wrongful use of the official car, tales of stupidity and abuse of power. Hulda could not stand by while Winzigers sneered at the Nazi administration. This was an intolerable state of affairs that she must set right. So she became an informer. The county officials were kept abreast of every infraction she could charge against Winzig's administrators. Her accusations grew into a bombardment of letters and phone calls. She traveled to the county seat in Wohlau to file her complaints in person. But she was ignored, and no action was taken.[1] In the world of reality, Nazi officials were not eager to make enemies of comrades based on the carping of an overzealous woman. Since Hulda made no secret of her intention to cleanse Winzig of its nest of drones, a small group of like-minded neighbors gathered about her. She was no longer a lone woman who "ought to stop meddling in men's affairs and get back into the kitchen." Among her intimates were several prominent members of the party: Dr. Mueller, the physician, and also Dr. Giesel, the dentist. These men, and others, shared in the embarrassment that the town was run by a former nature healer and a grave digger. It was unseemly, unGerman, and created disrespect for the regime. The mayor and his friends were furious with Hulda, but other than declaring the Black Eagle out-of-bounds for the party faithful, there was nothing they could do. They probably hoped that Frau Hildebrandt would realize that she was unable to force the authorities to investigate her complaints. But they misjudged Hulda. Her failures merely aroused her passion to create her world in Hitler's image. The county, the Silesian district authorities, and the Prussian state bureau in charge of official misconduct continued to receive salvos of her angry protests. The townspeople, for the most part, watched with gleeful curiosity. One morning Hulda received a token of encouragement. One of the street signs had been painted over during the night to read "Huldaplatz."[2]

How many times did Hulda sigh, "If only the fuehrer knew…"

Clearly a new approach was needed. If the lower echelons of the party ignored her, well, there was only one thing left to do. She must tell the fuehrer. She must go to Berlin and place her grievance before the all-highest himself. In 1934 personal audiences were still granted by Hitler. Hulda went to work and set into motion the complicated machinery that made this possible. She persevered through the lengthy and trying screening process, and her persistence paid off—she was granted an audience.

With head and hopes held high, Hulda boarded the train to Berlin. Rektor Spieler, although not a party member, was privy to the events and recalled Frau Hildebrandt's account of this extraordinary day in her life:

> After several hours of waiting, one of Hitler's aides informed me that I would be permitted three or four minutes of the fuehrer's time. This was not enough for a presentation of my prepared indictment, but I was determined to do my utmost to set matters right in Winzig. I was ushered into Hitler's presence and his first question was unexpected:
> "Who paid for your trip to Berlin?"
> I answered that I had paid out of my own funds. Hitler seemed pleased and he then

inquired into the purpose of my trip. As rapidly as I could, I described the situation in Winzig. Before I had finished, Hitler interrupted me with the comment that he did not have such local leaders in the Reich. He then extended his hand with the assurance that matters would be put in order. I handed him a written statement I had brought and said, "I guess this will end up in the wastebasket with all the others."

Hitler reacted to this criticism with a sign of real interest. He rang for an aide, a certain von Blankenburg, and instructed him to give special attention to my problems and thanked me for coming. Already dismissed, I nonetheless fired one more shot on behalf of Winzig, "Why have we failed to receive an army garrison as did the neighboring towns?" Hitler replied that this was a subject I ought to discuss with the army ministry. And with that the audience was over.[3]

Hulda returned on a cloud of optimism. Redress was surely close at hand. Indeed, shortly after her trip, two gentlemen from Berlin arrived in town. They conducted interviews, took notes and left. Hulda and her friends congratulated one another, but their euphoria was short-lived. Days of waiting turned into weeks and then the weeks stretched into months. There simply was no further action.

The little group of dissidents was uncertain about continuing the struggle. Was it not time to get on with their lives? But Hulda would not hear of it; her determination had become an obsession. To their credit, her friends stood by her as she entered into the final phase of her battle to make Winzig representative of all she so naively assumed Nazi ideology had pledged.

After all the failures, the only remaining weapon against the scoundrels, the *Halunken,* was to bring them to court and charge them with abuse of office. Such a case would fall under the jurisdiction of the special courts of the NSDAP. The Nazis had established a separate administration of justice that dealt with party matters. Cases concerning such complaints as membership qualifications, party discipline, use of party funds, and so forth were tried here. The system consisted of a series of lower courts whose decisions could be appealed, if necessary, to a higher tribunal.[4] Hulda brought suit against Winzig's, top three Nazi officials for behavior detrimental to the party and the fatherland. Her accusations were backed by a number of specific charges. She collected affidavits and depositions attesting to the malfeasance of the accused. The fact that she also had corroborating testimony from witnesses attested to her persuasive powers. A personal appearance in such a court was nerve-racking at best, dangerous at worst.

The court was convened in Wohlau. The county leader of the party, von Ridder, sat as judge. The issues of the case were represented and countered by the defendants over several sessions lasting twenty-three hours. Hulda presented a closely argued case against Lang, Schaube and Juerke. The trio used their position in their own, not the town's, best interest. The most startling appearance was that of the school principal, Rektor Spieler. Fortunately, the *Rektor* was a prudent man. Long ago he had established the habit of carefully recording events pertaining to his career. When, to his great surprise, he received a subpoena to appear, he made notes for use in his own testimony, and he also kept a record of the proceedings. His meticulousness permits the reconstruction of the trial which took place in 1935.

Spieler's appearance at the hearing chamber created quite a stir. Tall, thin, with iron gray hair and glasses, in his dark suit and white shirt, he was out of place among all the uniforms. He was the only person not dressed in party brown. The presiding official asked him if he was a member of the party. Spieler's "No" created more confusion. It was most unusual to have a nonmember appear at party court. "Perhaps you prefer that I withdraw?" suggested the *Rektor.*

The court deliberated for a few moments and then requested that he stay. The charges were read: "Frau Hildebrandt, together with a number of respected party members, accuse these named officials of Winzig of misconduct, of lacking the higher principles of the NSDAP and of representing a danger to the Reich."[5] Spieler was asked to take the stand. Because he was well aware that his evidence might be altered to conform with the outcome of the trial, he had made some preparations. He now said: "I will speak only if certain of my conditions are met."

The court was aghast: "We are not accustomed to have witnesses dictate conditions to us!"

"But I am not a party member, therefore the usual rules do not apply to me," Spieler replied.

Again heads were bent in consultation. Then the judge inquired into the nature of Spieler's conditions.

"First, I will speak only if my words are taken down by the court typist and if I will receive a copy of my statement at the conclusion of my testimony. Second, I wish to know beforehand how much time has been allotted to me."

Another hurried conference resulted from the *Rektor's* insistence on knowing how much time the court planned to allow for his testimony. The court requested to hear the reason for this demand.

"Because I have prepared my statement according to the limitations you may set for me. If you give me ten minutes, then I will read the lines I have marked in blue, if I have twenty minutes, then the paragraphs in red. Should there be no restraints on time, then I will read my entire paper."[6]

This time the magistrate and his associates withdrew to another room. After some moments they returned and declared themselves willing to permit Spieler to speak as long as he wished.

Spieler was on the stand for an hour and a half. His testimony concerned his own struggle with Winzig's leading Nazis. He had been defamed by them, hounded and persecuted. By means of treachery and trickery the three accused men had deprived him of his position as *Rektor* of Winzig's school, and their chicanery had very nearly cost him his health.

Upon conclusion of his statement, Spieler submitted the corroborating affidavits. Inasmuch as no one had asked him to leave he was able to observe the testimony of the next witness, Dr. Mueller.

From the witness stand the doctor pointed his finger at Lang and shouted, "Here sits our town leader! I know him to be guilty of three cases of illegal abortion!"

"Such an accusation must be supported," the judge admonished the doctor.

Thereupon Dr. Mueller placed sworn affidavits that attested to the facts of the charge upon the table. Von Ridder now declared that this issue was a criminal matter, not under the jurisdiction of a party court. He added that he would submit pertinent documents to the district attorney for further action.[7]

The two most serious indictments against the trio concerned mismanagement of public funds and misuse of authority. One of the lesser charges brought against Schaube was not without its ironic note. Schaube was accused of insincerity in his hatred of the Jews. Had he not lived, for a time, in the house of the Jewess Schlesinger? Had he not been seen in said Jewess's store buying children's clothing? If the court had questioned the Jewish families in Winzig, they could have exonerated the maligned Schaube, testifying to the fact that he persecuted them with complete devotion.

The trial was over. What was the verdict? Hulda, her friends and the rest of Winzig waited and waited and waited. At long last, even the most sanguine of her circle had to face the truth. There would be no verdict! Unofficially and obliquely a decision was rendered when von Ridder was removed as county leader of the party and replaced by none other than Winzig's Schaube.[8]

Hulda paid dearly for her romantic illusion of a Germany created in the image of Goebbels's propaganda campaigns. Her party membership was revoked. Then the Hildebrandts lost the inn. Soon thereafter they moved away.

In 1954, not long before her death, she received a letter from her old enemy, Schaube. He was dying but could not face his maker without her forgiveness for the wrong he had done her. He was contrite and full of remorse. Hulda accepted his penitence. Perhaps this kindness eased the final days for both, victim and victor of justice in the style of the Third Reich.[9]

With Hulda's defeat and the capitulation of the Stahlhelm, all open opposition against the Nazis in Winzig was ended. On an individual basis, however, conservative and NSDAP personalities continued to clash. There was, for example, the matter of the *Schandsaeule,* a tree trunk placed on the west side of the Ring. Schaube was said to have originated the idea of shaming so-called enemies of the Reich by publicly exposing their misdeeds. Only one inscription was ever placed on this Nazi version of the pillory. It referred to the local Stahlhelm leader and read: "*Walter Kahl—Deutsch Fatal.*" Just why Walter was fatal to Germany was not very clear, even to Winzigers. One night some of the townsmen expressed their disapproval of the *Schandsaeule* by dousing it with tar. There was a good deal of huffing and puffing to bring the suspected Stahlheimers to trial for the destruction of public property. But the county organization of the party had heard quite enough on that subject and suggested that the contentious column simply disappear. And so it did, Cebulla and his SA carried it off after dark. The mayor placed this new crime upon the convenient heads of the Stahlhelm. Hulda, however, knew better. She told one and all to look for the cursed pillar in the basement of party member Otto Schumann's house.[10]

Whereas most Winzigers regarded this incident as yet another example of official absurdity, the ordeal faced by their *Rektor* was another matter entirely. For two years Rektor Spieler, the head of the public school, battled the party for his job, his reputation, and his future. The attempt to discredit and remove him from office emanated from three sources.

Locally, Mayor Lang was on the attack and, in fact, had initiated the proceedings. On the next level, von Ridder's party organization had joined the battle, and finally, the county Nazi Teachers' Association aligned itself against Spieler. The teachers group was headed by Superintendent of Schools (*Schulrat*) Tretz, whose name was spoken with reverence because his son was a member of Hitler's personal bodyguard.

The *Rektor's* prolonged struggle, which he called his "battle against slander for honor and right," was the result indirectly of his democratic political views. But the fire and smoke of the case were produced by one of Winzig's teachers, Georg Mai. Mai was a Nazi. He was ambitious. He had money problems and he wanted Spieler's job. The mayor was eager to Nazify the town completely, to make it a model of conformity with the ideals of the new regime. To achieve this goal, all nonparty members had to be removed from positions of authority. Spieler was one of the most visible and most respected men in Winzig. His very presence was a thorn in Lang's brown-shirted side. The mayor's desire dovetailed neatly with that of Mai, who was in the perfect position to attack the *Rektor*. If necessary, Mai could swear that Spieler's leadership of the school was out of step with the Third Reich. The alliance of Lang and Mai was clearly a matter of mutual need and shared hypocrisy.

Spieler had given Winzig twenty-five years of service. He had come as a teacher and been promoted to principal. His family life was exemplary. He had a devoted wife and two handsome children. They had built one of the town's showcase homes across the street from the school—a neat white house with colorful shutters and flowers all around. Spieler was an active citizen and had been involved in the politics of Reichsbanner Schwarz-Rot-Glid. He had acted as a consultant for the juvenile court and was an officer in the pre-Nazi teacher's union. When Lang became mayor, Spieler was vice chairman of the school board. In that capacity he collided with Lang, whose position automatically entitled him to be the chairman of the school board. Thus the board meetings became the stage for their conflict.[11]

Lang officiated at the meetings. He ignored Spieler completely, even refusing to acknowledge his existence. Consequently the *Rektor's* judgments were effectively blocked. Next, Lang moved to undermine Spieler's position. He circulated lists of complaints to all associations in which the *Rektor* held a membership. The reaction was predictable. Within a few months Spieler was removed from all the honorary and paid appointments save that as head of the school. All offices he vacated were filled by Mai!

But the mayor did not have the power to remove Spieler from his post. Such action was under the jurisdiction of the *Schulrat,* the superintendent of schools. It was clear that Lang expected Spieler would resign rather than endure continued harassment. But Spieler was not a willing victim. For months Mai had leveled accusations against his principal to the regional administrator. The educational system was dominated by Nazis, and the *Rektor* was refused the opportunity to answer the charges. In order to force a confrontation that would permit the accused to face his accusers, Spieler requested a disciplinary hearing—against himself! But the petition was denied, with the excuse that "there is no case against you."

Nevertheless, a few weeks later the *Schulrat,* Herr Daunert, called at Spieler's office. He placed before the *Rektor* a long list of charges. All were filed by Mai.

DAUNERT: I want your immediate comment on each of these charges.
SPIELER: That is impossible. But I will agree to a face-to-face confrontation with my accuser. This should be done in the presence of the faculty and the superintendent.
DAUNERT: Your request is denied.[12]

Spieler was able to delay Daunert long enough to make some notes and comments concerning the indictment:

1. The *Rektor* had displayed an un-German sympathy toward the Jewish children in Winzig. For example, he had permitted the itinerant Jewish religion teacher the use of his office for instruction. He had permitted a Jewish girl to be crowned at the *Kinderfest.* He had punished an Aryan boy for beating up a Jewish child, Siegfried Steinhardt.
   (All of the above charges were basically true.)
2. The *Rektor* had refused to fly the swastika from the school's flagpole after the election of 1932.
   (True. The school did not yet possess a Nazi flag.)
3. The minutes taken by Spieler when he was secretary of the teachers' association revealed anti-Nazi commentaries.
   (True. These were quotations from topics under discussion at the meetings.)
4. Spieler was a longtime Socialist.
   (Untrue. He was a democrat.)
5. Spieler conducted a patriotic assembly in the rear school yard instead of beneath the swastika in front of the building.
   (True. There was not enough room in front.)
6. Spieler replaced signs reading "Shut the door" with signs requesting, "Please, close the door." This revealed an un-Aryan attitude. Children must be commanded, not asked to obey.
   (No comment.)
7. Spieler had failed to attend a meeting featuring an important Nazi speaker.
   (True. His wife had collapsed that day at her mother's funeral.)
8. Spieler no longer had the confidence of the student body.
   (A lie.)

The *Rektor's* frustration over his inability to defend himself against the allegations was wearing him down. He found it particularly difficult to face Mai day after day. Physically and emotionally drained, he applied for and was granted a month's leave of absence. The county physician was aware of the stress and consented to five more months of sick leave.

The temporary withdrawal of the *Rektor,* however, settled nothing. A visit from the district leader of the Nazi Teachers' Association failed to bring about a solution.

Once more, Mai's complaints were discussed and Spieler's defense fell on deaf ears. The district leader declared that, in essence, Mai was acting in the best interest of the party. Yes, on several counts the young teacher had been excessive and would be reprimanded. But that was all. A renewed request for disciplinary action by Spieler against himself was again rejected. He was not to have the opportunity to appear in a public forum. Spieler became ill. The strain was becoming unbearable, and he soon suffered a nervous breakdown. Steadfast friends and students eased his isolation for brief moments. One day a group of students noticed the *Rektor* at his open window. They set up a chant: "one, three, five, nine, our *Rektor* is just fine, two, four, six, eight, ten, and we want him back again."[13]

There could no longer be any doubt that the county school officials were more concerned with pleasing the party than with the merits of the case. When Spieler was well enough, he appealed to the next level of authority, the Provincial School Council, which had the power to override county decisions. But in order to get a hearing in Breslau, the detestable county *Schulrat* had to endorse the request. Daunert refused to give his permission. The rope tying the *Rektor*'s, hands was beginning to tighten like a noose. But not quite yet. Spieler used Daunert's rebuff as a wedge to pry open a door of the Provincial Education Department. Would someone explain what his remaining options were? Surprisingly, he was granted an interview by the head of the Silesian School Administration, Dr. Ruchatz. It was an astonishing meeting. Ruchatz proved to be representative of the best in the tradition of the German civil service. He was not a member of the party and as late as 1939 had not been removed from his position. Ruchatz was not impressed by political connections. He judged people and events on their merit. That such a man had retained his professional post was a small miracle. Finally, after so many rejections, Spieler found an official who listened with sympathy and increasing indignation. Ruchatz assured the *Rektor* that he would lift his petition from the net of personal intrigue and place it before the highest authority: the national minister of education, Rust. The *Rektor* addressed a bitterly worded demand, not a plea, for justice to Minister Rust in support of this action.

Once more, it was a time for waiting. Several weeks after Spieler's visit to Breslau, the long awaited reply arrived. The family gathered around to hear the verdict. Spieler read it and joined his wife and children in a joyful hallelujah. Rust's investigation resulted in a complete exoneration. All charges were dismissed. The minister concluded that it was unlikely that Spieler could derive any satisfaction from further service in Winzig and asked if he would accept the position of principal in the city of Guhrau. Since Guhrau had twice the population of Winzig, this transfer was, in fact, a promotion.[14] His vindication restored the *Rektor* in mind and body. He went to Guhrau to make the obligatory call on the mayor, followed by the amenities of protocol with the school authorities. He found a house and returned to Winzig to prepare for his move. But his enemies were not yet defeated. The news of Spieler's victory reached the party, and once again unseen wheels were set into motion. In the midst of packing for his relocation to Guhrau, the *Rektor* received the devastating news that the offer had been withdrawn. It was a blow that left Spieler close to despair. Such a long struggle, so many defeats, and now, with victory apparently assured, again he faced professional and personal ruin. The world had become unrecognizable. Those sworn to uphold justice had become agents of injustice. Why continue the hopeless contest? The well-informed Daunert (no doubt, Mai had kept him abreast of all developments concerning the *Rektor*) now requested a meeting with Spieler.

The two men confronted each other in a restaurant. Daunert, eager to exploit the *Rektor*'s frame of mind, alternately offered him a carrot and showed him the stick:

> The party is instituting a suit against you. Your action against members of the NSDAP can be interpreted as treachery. Specifically, we have lodged the charge of "seditious agitation against a personage of the state." You have used up all possible sick leave. If you do not go back to work, you will be dismissed. Perhaps you should forget about school administration and return to teaching. There is just one alternative to save you, a position of principal in the town of Maltsch. Take that and stop fighting so many windmills.[15]

Spieler said little. In the end, he wearily pushed aside the cups and saucers on the table and signed his acceptance of the offer. Maltsch was not a bad place, not very different from Winzig. The students gave Spieler a farewell dinner. Friends called to wish him and his family Godspeed and expressed regrets to see them go. But the Spielers derived little pleasure from these visits. They were too tired and heartsick. Essentially, they had fought alone.

Few Winzigers appreciated the broader implication of Spieler's removal from a job well done. After all, everyone had troubles of his own. Everyone was busy. Especially Georg Mai. He moved into the *Rektor*'s office and ordered that signs on the doors throughout the school be changed to a single word: "SHUT."

NOTES

[1] Johannes Spieler, *Mein Kampf um Recht*, p. 4.

[2] Ibid.

[3] Ibid., p. 5.

[4] Dr. Otto Ganweiler and Dr. Anton Lingg, eds., *Der Partei Richter* (Munich: NSDAP Verlag, 1938), p.15.

[5] Johannes Spieler, *Als Nichtparteigenosse vor dem Parteigericht,* (unpublished), trans. Rita S. Botwinick, p. 1.

[6] Ibid., p. 2.

[7] Ibid.

[8] Ibid., p. 3.

[9] Wittmann, *Winziger Geschichte,* pp. 3–4.

[10] Ibid., p. 4.

[11] Spieler, *Mein Kampf um Recht,* p. 5.

[12] Ibid.

[13] Ibid.

[14] Ibid., p. 6.

[15] Ibid.

Helmut Schmidt

Johannes Steinhoff, Peter Pechel, and Dennis Showalter

*Born 1918; officer in the anit-aircraft artillery; after the war became a
career politician (SPD) and a member of the Bundestag; is the former Federal Minister of Defense and of Finance and Economic Affairs; was a
Chancellor of the Federal Republic from 1974 through 1982; resides in
Hamburg.*

"Since I was the captain of the club, I automatically became a Hitler Youth leader."

I grew up in a very lower-middle-class family. My father's natural father was a Jew, and
his mother was from Mecklenburg. My grandfather, who was actually my father's foster father, was an unskilled longshoreman who spoke only dialect. My father was
able to work himself up and out of this class. Not only did he become an apprentice,
which at this time was unheard of, but he became an apprentice in a law firm. Apparently he must have made an impression on somebody because he was ultimately
given a scholarship. He entered a teachers college and majored in elementary education. After the First World War ended, he continued with his studies in night school and
eventually received a degree in economics. He then became a certified business and economics teacher. During the first 40 years of his life my father had succeeded in rising
out of the lowest class of the proletariat into the bourgeoisie. He was, therefore, in a
position to send his two sons to higher schools.

My father's political influence on me, his oldest son, was minimal. He didn't
believe in political activities by youth. He even forbade me to join a youth group, which
was an extremely popular thing to do at the time. Naturally, he refused to let me join
the Hitler Youth. He couldn't, however, prevent my school's rowing club from being
incorporated into the Hitler Naval Youth in 1934. Since I was the captain, the president,
of the club, I automatically became a Hitler Youth leader.

My parents avoided any political involvement after the Nazis came to power and
the Nuremberg Laws went into effect. It was obvious that they wanted nothing to do
with the Nazis. I knew how terrified they were of somehow someone finding out that
they had been concealing their Jewish descent.

Johannes Steinhoff, Peter Pechel, Dennis Showalter, "Helmut Schmidt," *Voices from the Third
Reich: An Oral History.* Washington, DC: Regnery Gateway, 1989, pp. 24–26. Copyright © 1989
by J. Steinhoff, et al. All rights reserved. Reprinted by special permission of Regnery Publishing, Inc., Washington, DC.

My father sent me to a school that even by today's standards would be considered extremely progressive. Some of the teachers were Communists, some were Nazis, some were German Nationalists, while others were anti-Semites. But none of this mattered much to us, because they were all dedicated educators. Strong emphasis was placed on the more artistic subjects such as music, art, sketching, and literature. We spent many, many school hours in these subject areas. All of this influenced me in developing a great interest for modern and expressionist art, and for music, baroque as well as modern.

Our time at school was shortened by one year, because Adolf Hitler needed soldiers. As a result, we all received our diplomas one year early. My parents had told me that according to the Nuremberg Laws, I was a one-quarter Jew, so I decided to leave Germany. I was in contact with the German Shell Oil Company and had intentions of going to Indonesia where they were drilling for oil. But nothing came of it.

Because I had changed my mind about going to Indonesia, and I wanted to study, I decided to enlist and get the two years I had to serve in the military over with. I wanted to study either in Munich or in Vienna. I planned to study simultaneously at the Technical University and the Arts Academy, and in no way did I want my studies to be interrupted by the draft. So in 1937, I volunteered to serve the mandatory two years.

During my two years as a draftee, I spent one year as a rank-and-file gunner. I was a Private First Class during the following six months, and an NCO the last six months of my initial tour of duty. All this time I was planning to become an architect. I sought out friends and contacts accordingly.

I had no real ambition as far as the military was concerned. I didn't have the slightest interest in achieving any great accomplishments or becoming somebody. The fact that I became a reserve officer was due to my previous education. Promotion to reserve officer was largely an automatic process for those of us who had the *Abitur.* Of course, I didn't have any complaints about becoming a reserve officer, but I never had any interest in becoming a career officer. I wanted to be an architect. Then the war started. As young as I was, I only hoped that the episode wouldn't last too long.

Inge Aicher-Scholl

Johannes Steinhoff, Peter Pechel, and Dennis Showalter

Born 1917; her sister and brother were key members of the White Rose resistance group; they were condemned to death by the Volksgerichtshof *and executed on February 22, 1943; now lives in Bavaria.*

"From that day on, I was afraid of prison."

Shortly before the Nazi takeover, we moved to Ulm. There were five of us brothers and sisters. I was 16, Hans 15, and Sophie was 12 years old. Politics became an issue for the first time in our lives. There was a great deal of talk about the fatherland, of comradeship, of the love of our homeland and the unity of the German people. It impressed us because we loved our home very much; also our home in the larger sense, the fatherland, though we wouldn't have been able to say why. And Hitler, or so we heard, wanted to bring greatness, fortune, and prosperity to this fatherland. He wanted to see that everyone had work and bread, that every German became a free, happy, and independent person. We thought that was wonderful, and we wanted to do everything we could to contribute. So it was no wonder that all five of us joined the Hitler Youth.

We just could not understand why our father was against it from the beginning. He even compared Hitler to the Pied Piper. All of his attempts to hold us back failed in the face of our excitement.

Hans was the first to have doubts. They were little things, but they added up: an injustice toward one of his friends here, the ban on the books of his favorite poet, Stefan Zweig, there. This seed of doubt soon sprouted in all of us. On one of our spring walks we had a long discussion with our father, who explained to us what was really going on in Germany. He said that Hitler wanted war. This conversation made father and us friends again, and the family became a small, secure island in a world that was becoming increasingly strange and hard to understand. It wasn't as if Hans decided from one day to the next that he was against National Socialism; it was a gradual develop-

Johannes Steinhoff, Peter Perbel, Dennis Showalter, "Inger Aicher-Scholl," *Voices from the Third Reich: An Oral History.* Washington, DC: Regency Gateway, 1989, pp. 26–29. Copyright © 1989 by J. Steinhoff, et al. All rights reserved. Reprinted by special permission of Regnery Publishing, Inc., Washington, DC.

ment. Although Hans was a year younger than me, he had an aura; what he had to say interested you.

One morning in the autumn of 1937, the Gestapo knocked at our door just as Sophie was ready to leave for school. Elisabeth, our middle sister, had already left home to complete her studies as a kindergarten teacher. Werner, Sophie, and I were there when the two Gestapo men arrived—they usually operated in twos. They searched the apartment, confiscated our diaries, and took us away. I was 19 years old.

The Gestapo took only us children, not our parents. We were accused of continuing the activities of disbanded youth groups. They kept us in the local Gestapo prison at Ulm that day, and when it got dark they put us into an open truck and drove us to Stuttgart on the newly finished Autobahn. Of course, we weren't dressed warmly enough, and the next morning, we arrived helter-skelter at the Gestapo headquarters. They put each of us into a separate cell. We were completely flabbergasted. We could not take it very seriously. We knew that we had not done anything bad, so we thought we would just be interrogated and set free again.

They left me sitting in that cell for eight days before coming to question me. I heard footsteps above me and footsteps in the courtyard. Once I heard a woman's voice which I thought could be my mother's. Perhaps they had picked her up too. And sitting there in prison, I wondered if they had already shot my father. Heaven only knew. I was very afraid of what would happen to my brother Werner; he was only 15. I was only 19 at the time, and it was such a shock that from then on I was always afraid. I was afraid of anything that might lead to my being taken to prison again, and that was exactly what they wanted.

On the last day, I was called for questioning—two Gestapo men once again— and they asked about all kinds of things. At one point, I said that I had read a tiny article in the newspaper about a resistance group in Berlin. And the Gestapo men asked me what I thought resistance was. I answered that I thought resistance was against bad people. With that they roared with laughter, and thought I was so naive that I would not be able to tell them much at all.

Gradually, I learned that the more naive, the more innocent and stupid you answered, the better. When they burst out laughing, I laughed along with them. And then they let me go, after I signed a paper which said that I would not discuss this interrogation with anyone, and if I did, it would be grounds for another arrest. I signed it, and they let all of us go.

But from that day on, I was afraid of prison, and this fear made me very timid and passive, just completely inactive.

My father was arrested in early February 1942, picked up in the early morning, the second time for our family. I was just coming back from a visit in Munich and my mother met me at the door: "Your father has just been taken away by the Gestapo." As she spoke, another Gestapo man, who had just finished searching the house, appeared. He had rooted through all of our books. He asked us a few questions. He wanted to know names. He even asked us for the address of Rainer-Maria Rilke. Thank God I told him that Rilke had long been dead. And then the Gestapo man seemed to lose interest.

I wanted to bring a few things to the prison for my father. I happened to see him being escorted between two Gestapo men. His face was pale as a sheet, and he looked at me mutely. Later we learned that one of his employees had reported him. She had asked him what he thought of the war and of Hitler. He said he thought Hitler was the biggest scourge with which God had ever punished humankind, and if he didn't end the war soon the Russians would be sitting in Berlin inside a few years. She had talked about this, probably with the district Nazi officers, and they had informed the Gestapo. Naturally, this kind of testimony by an employee carried a lot of weight. In August 1942, my father was tried and sentenced to four months in prison. At that, he got off fairly easily. It could have been much worse.

Marianne Hoppe

Johannes Steinhoff, Peter Pechel, and Dennis Showalter

Born 1911; movie and stage actress; met both Hitler and Goebbels; after the war continued to act in many films and television series; lives in Bavaria.

"This man was sickening. I left and never went back."

I was young and pretty, I think you could say that. I had made two or three films when I received the phone call: "The Führer would like to invite you to dinner." Leni Riefenstahl, Sybille Schmitz, and a few other well-known actresses were there. Hitler sat across from me and didn't talk at all. Actually, we were all pretty quiet. After dinner, we stood up and he said to me, "I am glad you were able to come. May I show you my apartment?" I said, "Yes, that would be nice." After he showed me a few rooms, he opened the door to another. "This is my bedroom," he said. "Oh," I said, "how gloomy." I will never forget it; the room was really dismal. "Can't you do something to cheer this room up?" I asked. "No" was the only thing he said.

Hitler in person made just about the same impact on me as his picture on a postcard did. As a man, he had absolutely no flair, at least, not to me. People talked about his sincere interest in the arts. He had his own concept of the arts and he was most likely interested in that, but it wasn't our kind of art. I was invited back much later. And what happened on that evening is a really strange story.

The film *The Rebel* was being shown. It was about the people's revolt in the Tyrol against the French in 1809. In one scene, the French army had to march through a very narrow pass. From above, the Tyrolians had set up some boards loaded with stones, When the French came through, the Tyrolians cut the ropes, and all of the rocks fell on the French. Hitler became terribly excited and started to rub his knee. He started to moan as the rocks started to roll. I don't know if he was crazy or what, but he had a kind of orgasm.

I remember standing up in the dark room. This man was sickening. I left and never went back.

One day in 1936, the doorbell rang. There was an SS soldier at the door. "Hello," he said, "the Reich Propaganda Minister is on his way up the steps." And a few moments later, he really was there. The driver went back downstairs and Goebbels walked into my apartment and closed the door. I was 25, old enough, you'd think, but I was still relatively naive. In a situation like that you're speechless, totally baffled. What was I going to do? How was I going to get this man out of here?

Goebbels sat down and said he thought the two of us could get together, and he hoped we could make some kind of arrangement. For example, he told me he was giving a speech in Dresden, and would naturally have a plane ready to fly me there. "You fly over, I'll give my speech, and then we'll dine together." I began to feel a bit queasy and thought: "He can't really mean he's going to pick me up with an airplane and flowers. Surely others will be going along too!" Although it wasn't easy, I told him, "You know we both have our reputations to lose. I don't think it will work out." I had a reputation to lose in any case, something I had absolutely no desire to do. Then I had to think of a way to get him out of my apartment. He started to make advances. He told me how much influence he had in the film industry, and so on. I didn't like that one bit. He was trying to blackmail me! I don't think I was really aware of what I was saying, but I told him, "And you seriously think I would fall for a person like you?" Hearing that, he turned pale, took his cap, and left.

Selection from *Mein Kampf*

Adolf Hitler

...

The function of propaganda does not lie in the scientific training of the individual, but in calling the masses' attention to certain facts, processes, necessities, etc., whose significance is thus for the first time placed within their field of vision.

The whole art consists in doing this so skillfully that everyone will be convinced that the fact is real, the process necessary, the necessity correct, etc. But since propaganda is not and cannot be the necessity in itself, since its function, like the poster, consists in attracting the attention of the crowd, and not in educating those who are already educated or who are striving after education and knowledge, its effect for the most part must be aimed at the emotions and only to a very limited degree at the so-called intellect.

All propaganda must be popular and its intellectual level must be adjusted to the most limited intelligence among those it is addressed to. Consequently, the greater the mass it is intended to reach, the lower its purely intellectual level will have to be. But if, as in propaganda for sticking out a war, the aim is to influence a whole people, we must avoid excessive intellectual demands on our public, and too much caution cannot be exerted in this direction.

The more modest its intellectual ballast, the more exclusively it takes into consideration the emotions of the masses, the more effective it will be. And this is the best proof of the soundness or unsoundness of a propaganda campaign, and not success in pleasing a few scholars or young aesthetes.

The art of propaganda lies in understanding the emotional ideas of the great masses and finding, through a psychologically correct form, the way to the attention and thence to the heart of the broad masses. The fact that our bright boys do not understand this merely shows how mentally lazy and conceited they are.

Once we understand how necessary it is for propaganda to be adjusted to the broad mass, the following rule results:

It is a mistake to make propaganda many-sided, like scientific instruction, for instance.

The receptivity of the great masses is very limited, their intelligence is small, but their power of forgetting is enormous. In consequence of these facts, all effective propaganda must be limited to a very few points and must harp on these in slogans until the last member of the public understands what you want him to understand by your slogan. As soon as you sacrifice this slogan and try to be many-sided, the effect will piddle away, for the crowd can neither digest nor retain the material offered. In this way the result is weakened and in the end entirely cancelled out.

···

The folkish state must make up for what everyone else today has neglected in this field. *It must set race in the center of all life. It must take care to keep it pure. It must declare the child to be the most precious treasure of the people. It must see to it that only the healthy beget children; that there is only one disgrace: despite one's own sickness and deficiencies, to bring children into the world, and one highest honor: to renounce doing so. And conversely it must be considered reprehensible: to withhold healthy children from the nation. Here the state must act as the guardian of a millennial future in the face of which the wishes and the selfishness of the individual must appear as nothing and submit. It must put the most modern medical means in the service of this knowledge. It must declare unfit for propagation all who are in any way visibly sick or who have inherited a disease and can therefore pass it on, and put this into actual practice. Conversely, it must take care that the fertility of the healthy woman is not limited by the financial irresponsibility of a state regime which turns the blessing of children into a curse for the parents. It must put an end to that lazy, nay criminal, indifference with which the social premises for a fecund family are treated today, and must instead feel itself to be the highest guardian of this most precious blessing of a people. Its concern belongs more to the child than to the adult.*

Those who are physically and mentally unhealthy and unworthy must not perpetuate their suffering in the body of their children. In this the folkish state must perform the most gigantic educational task. And some day this will seem to be a greater deed than the most victorious wars of our present bourgeois era. By education it must teach the individual that it is no disgrace, but only a misfortune deserving of pity, to be sick and weakly, but that it is a crime and hence at the same time a disgrace to dishonor one's misfortune by one's own egotism in burdening innocent creatures with it; that by comparison it bespeaks a nobility of highest idealism and the most admirable humanity if the innocently sick, renouncing a child of his own, bestows his love and tenderness upon a poor, unknown young scion of his own nationality, who with his health promises to become some day a powerful member of a powerful community. And in this educational work the state must perform the purely intellectual complement of its practical activity. It must act in this sense without regard to understanding or lack of understanding, approval or disapproval.

A prevention of the faculty and opportunity to procreate on the part of the physically degenerate and mentally sick, over a period of only six hundred years, would not only free humanity from an immeasurable misfortune, but would lead to a recovery which today seems scarcely conceivable. If the fertility of the healthiest bearers of the nationality is thus consciously and systematically promoted, the result will be a race which at least will have eliminated the germs of our present physical and hence spiritual decay.

For once a people and a state have started on this path, attention will automatically be directed on increasing the racially most valuable nucleus of the people and its fertility, in order ultimately to let the entire nationality partake of the blessing of a highly bred racial stock.

The way to do this is above all for the state not to leave the settlement of newly acquired territories to chance, but to subject it to special norms. Specially constituted racial commissions must issue settlement certificates to individuals. For this, however, definite racial purity must be established. It will thus gradually become possible to found border colonies whose inhabitants are exclusively bearers of the highest racial purity and hence of the highest racial efficiency. This will make them a precious national treasure to the entire nation; their growth must fill every single national comrade with pride and confidence, for in them lies the germ for a final, great future development of our own people, nay—of humanity.

In the folkish state, finally, the folkish philosophy of life must succeed in bringing about that nobler age in which men no longer are concerned with breeding dogs, horses, and cats, but in elevating man himself, an age in which the one knowingly and silently renounces, the other joyfully sacrifices and gives.

Chapter 6

German Jews
or Jews in Germany?

INTRODUCTION

German Christians had lived with their Jewish neighbors for many hundreds of years. In the 19th and 20th century economic and cultural assimilation of the Jewish minority (always less than 1 percent of the population) seemed to be proceeding toward full integration. Intermarriage was a common phenomenon and the Jews had every reason to be proud of their contributions to the fatherland. Until the Nazi rise to power, they were optimistic that they would become accepted as Germans who were Jewish, like others who were Lutheran or Catholic. Because many German Jews had Gentile business associates and friends, they believed that anti-Semitism was an anachronism surely on the wane and would disappear in time. The resurgence of active hatred and tacit consent to their persecution was a great shock. Only about half their total number realized their peril in time to flee the country.

Hitler declared war against the Jews just two months after achieving power as chancellor. On April 1, 1933, Julius Streicher, editor of the anti-Semitic *Stuermer,* was delegated by Hitler to organize a boycott of all Jewish businesses and professional offices. Its purpose was twofold: first, the SA was restless and had clamored to "smash some Jewish heads" and second, this was an experiment to test the reaction of the German people. Would there be serious protests? When customers and clients noticed the brown-shirted SA troupers at the doors of Jewish-owned or operated concerns, they stared, then shrugged their shoulders and left. Of course, there were exceptions to that response but not enough to disturb the calm of the nation. It is important to remember that in 1933 the Nazis did not have an iron grip on the country. The *Gleichschaltung,* which led to the achievement of dictatorship, was only in its early stages. But the message communicated to Berlin from large cities and small hamlets was clear: the boycott is proceeding without incident. The fact that it was called off was not due to the reaction of the German citizens, but was to the negative response from the foreign press and their governments. The Fuehrer was not yet ready to risk the censure of the non-German world.

The boycott assured the government that the people would not rally in defense of the Jews. Thus an opportunity to moderate Hitler's anti-Jewish passion had slipped by. The 1938 pogrom known as *Kristallnacht* was also conducted in full view of the public. This *Aktion* resulted in extensive destruction of property by arson and dynamite. Jewish men were beaten, tens of thousands were arrested and shipped to concentration camps. These assaults on a peaceful minority living in their midst made some Germans ashamed, others were gleeful, but the majority found the spectacle frightening and turned away. The notion that by their acquiescence, their silent inactivity, they shared in the crimes of the government would have astounded them. They would have argued that the attacks were carried out by a legitimate government whose leaders alone were responsible. Again, Hitler was assured that he could proceed to make Germany *Judenrein* without arousing domestic opposition.

German Jewry's reaction to Hitler's persecution was, at first, muffled and confused. When no doubt remained that Hitler's words were not mere propaganda but the prologue to further persecution, they prepared to pull up their roots and leave. But eagerness to emigrate was not enough—they had to find countries willing to provide havens. And that was very difficult. The waiting lists were measured in years. When Jewish children were barred from attendance in public schools, many families moved from small towns and villages to the larger cities where Jewish schools were organized. Berlin, with its foreign embassies, was the most sought-after destination. Saving the children became the priority, even if the youngsters must go alone to whatever country would accept them. More often than not, the Holocaust made these separations permanent.

The Jewish community tried valiantly to meet the needs of its people. Among the national organizations, the *Central Verein* (CV, Central Union) played the most important role in coordinating a number of self-help agencies. The Nazis encouraged this development; it simplified their dealings with the Jewish people. The leadership of the CV was charged with enforcing government orders and was held responsible for compliance.

Despite the fact that the CV tried to serve two completely divergent masters, the German government and its victims, its accomplishments were considerable. Its various agencies ran schools for children and adults; doled out their dwindling financial resources to support the destitute; opened soup kitchens and medical clinics. When it was still permitted, CV lawyers defended Jews in the courts. Specialists aided hopeful emigrants through the morass of red tape. When Jews were forbidden to attend public cultural performances, the CV sponsored musical and theatrical performances, films and art shows. Despite the fact that the Nazis continuously curtailed the Committee's ability to provide assistance, it remained active until German Jewry had vanished, either to foreign lands or to the camps in the east.

Wear It with Pride, the Yellow Badge

Robert Weltsch

The first of April, 1933, will remain an important date in the history of German Jewry—indeed, in the history of the entire Jewish people. The events of that day have aspects that are not only political and economic, but moral and spiritual as well. The political and economic implications have been widely discussed in the press, though of course the need for agitation has frequently obscured objective understanding. To speak of the *moral* aspect, that is *our* task. For however much the Jewish question is now debated, nobody except ourselves can express what is to be said on these events from the Jewish point of view, what is happening in the soul of the German Jew. Today the Jews cannot speak except as Jews. Anything else is utterly senseless….Gone is the fatal misapprehension of many Jews that Jewish interests can be pressed under some other cover. On April 1 the German Jews learned a lesson which penetrates far more deeply than even their embittered and now triumphant opponents could assume….

We live in a new period, the national revolution of the German people is a signal that is visible from afar, indicating that the world of our previous concepts has collapsed. That may be painful for many, but in this world only those will be able to survive who are able to look reality in the eye. We stand in the midst of tremendous changes in intellectual, political, social and economic life. It is for us to see how the Jews will react.

April 1, 1933, can become the day of Jewish awakening and Jewish rebirth. If the Jews will it. If the Jews are mature and have greatness in them. If the Jews are not as they are represented to be by their opponents.

The Jews, under attack, must learn to acknowledge themselves.

Even in these days of most profound disturbance, when the stormiest of emotions have visited our hearts in face of the unprecedented display of the universal slander of the entire Jewish population of a great and cultural country, we must first of all maintain: composure. Even if we stand shattered by the events of these days we must not lose heart and must examine the situation without any attempt to deceive ourselves. One would like to recommend in these days that the document that stood at the cradle of

Robert Weltsch, "Wear It with Pride, the Yellow Badge," *Jüdische Rundschau*, No. 27, April 4, 1933. From *Documents on the Holocaust: Selected Sources on the Destruction of the Jews of Germany and Austria, Poland, and the Soviet Union*, Yitzhak Arad, Yisrael Gutman, Abraham Margaliot eds. Jerusalem: Yad Vashem, 1981, pp. 44–47.

Zionism, Theodor Herzl's "Jewish State," be distributed in hundreds of thousands of copies among Jews and non-Jews....

They accuse us today of treason against the German people: The National-Socialist Press calls us the "enemy of the Nation," and leaves us defenseless.

It is not true that the Jews betrayed Germany. If they betrayed anyone, it was themselves, the Jews.

Because the Jew did not display his Judaism with pride, because he tried to avoid the Jewish issue, he must bear of the blame for the degradation of the Jews.

Despite all the bitterness that we must feel in full measure when we read the National-Socialist boycott proclamations and unjust accusations, there is one point for which we may be grateful to the Boycott Committee. Para. 3 of the Directives reads: "The reference is...of course to businesses owned by members of the Jewish race. Religion plays no part here. Businessmen who were baptized Catholic or Protestant, or Jews who left their Community remain Jews for the purpose of this Order." This is a [painful] reminder for all those who betrayed their Judaism. Those who steal away from the Community in order to benefit their personal position should not collect the wages of their betrayal. In taking up this position against the renegades there is the beginning of a clarification. The Jew who denies his Judaism is no better a citizen than his fellow who avows it openly. It is shameful to be a renegade, but as long as the world around us rewarded it, it appeared an advantage. Now even that is no longer an advantage. The Jew is marked as a Jew. He gets the yellow badge.

A powerful symbol is to be found in the fact that the boycott leadership gave orders that a sign "with a yellow badge on a black background" was to be pasted on the boycotted shops. This regulation is intended as a brand, a sign of contempt. We will take it up and make of it a badge of honor.

Many Jews suffered a crushing experience on Saturday. Suddenly they were revealed as Jews, not as a matter of inner avowal, not in loyalty to their own community, not in pride in a great past and great achievements, but by the impress of a red placard with a yellow patch. The patrols moved from house to house, stuck their placards on shops and signboards, daubed the windows, and for 24 hours the German Jews were exhibited in the stocks, so to speak. In addition to other signs and inscriptions one often saw windows bearing a large Magen David, the Shield of David the King. It was intended as dishonor. Jews, take it up, the Shield of David, and wear it with pride!...

Organization of the Anti-Jewish Boycott of April 1, 1933— Instructions Given by the National-Socialist Party

AN ORDER TO THE WHOLE PARTY!

The following order is accordingly issued to all Party offices and Party organizations.

Point 1: *Action Committees for the Boycott against the Jews*

In every local branch and organizational section of the NSDAP [National-Socialist German Workers' Party] Action Committees are to be formed immediately for the practical systematic implementation of a boycott of Jewish shops, Jewish goods, Jewish doctors and Jewish lawyers. The Action Committees are responsible for making sure that the boycott will not affect innocent persons, but will hit the guilty all the harder.

Point 2: *Maximum Protection for all Foreigners*

The Action Committees are responsible for ensuring maximum protection for all foreigners, without regard to their religion, origin or race. The boycott is solely a defensive measure, directed exclusively against the German Jews.

Point 3: *Propaganda for the Boycott*

The Action Committees will immediately use propaganda and information to popularize the boycott. The principle must be that no German will any longer buy from a Jew, or allow Jews or their agents to recommend goods. The boycott must be general. It must be carried out by the whole nation and must hit the Jews in their most sensitive spot.

"Organization of the Anti-Jewish Boycott of April 1, 1933—Instructions Given by the National-Socialist Party," *Völkischer Beobachter (Süddeutsche Ausgabe)*, No. 88, March 29, 1933. From *Documents on the Holocaust: Selected Sources on the Destruction of the Jews of Germany and Austria, Poland, and the Soviet Union*, Yitzhak Arad, Yisrael Gutman, Abraham Margaliot eds. Jerusalem: Yad Vashem, 1981, pp. 32–35.

Point 4: *Central Direction: Party Comrade Streicher*

In doubtful cases the boycott of the store concerned is to be postponed until definite instructions are received from the Central Committee in Munich. The Chairman of the Central Committee is Party Member Streicher.

Point 5: *Supervision of Newspapers*

The Action Committees will scrutinize newspapers most stringently with a view to observing the extent to which they take part in the information campaign against Jewish atrocity propaganda abroad.* If any newspaper fails to do this or does so to a limited extent only, then they are to be excluded immediately from every house in which Germans live. No German person and no German business may place advertisements in such newspapers. They [the newspapers] must be subjected to public contempt, as written for members of the Jewish race, and not for the German people.

Point 6: *The Boycott as a Measure for the Protection of German Labor*

The Action Committees, together with Party cells in industry, must carry into the enterprises explanatory propaganda on the consequence of Jewish atrocity campaigns for German production, and therefore for the German worker, and explain to the workers the need for a national boycott as a defensive measure to protect German labor.

Point 7: *Action Committees Right Down into the Smallest Village!*

The Action Committees must reach out right into the smallest peasant village in order to strike particularly at Jewish traders in the countryside. On principle, it is always to be stressed that this is a matter of a defensive measure which has been forced on us.

Point 8: *The Boycott Will Start on April 1!*

The boycott is not to begin piecemeal, but all at once; all preparations to this end are to be made immediately. Orders will go out to the SA and SS to post guards outside Jewish stores from the moment that the boycott comes into force, in order to warn the public against entering the premises. The start of the boycott will be made known with the aid of posters, through the press and by means of leaflets, etc. The boycott will start all at once at exactly 10:00 a.m. on Saturday, April 1. It will continue until the Party leadership orders its cancellation.

---

*This was the phrase used by the Nazis for press accounts of atrocities against Jews in the Third Reich.

Point 9: *Mass [meetings) to Demand the Numerus Clausus!*

The Action Committees will immediately organize tens of thousands of mass meetings, reaching down to the smallest village, at which the demand will be raised for the introduction of a limited quota for the employment of Jews in all professions, according to their proportion in the German population. In order to increase the impact of this step the demand should be limited to three areas for the time being:
   a) attendance at German high schools and universities;
   b) the medical profession;
   c) the legal profession.

Point 10:: *The Need for Explanations Abroad*

The Action Committees also have the task of ensuring that every German who has any kind of connections abroad will make use of these in letters, telegrams and telephone calls. He must spread the truth that calm and order reign in Germany, that the German people has no more ardent wish than to go about its work in peace and to live in peace with the rest of the world, and that its fight against Jewish atrocity propaganda is solely a defensive struggle.

Point 11: *Quiet, Discipline and No Violence!*

The Action Committees are responsible for ensuring that this entire struggle is carried out in complete calm and with absolute discipline. In future, too, do not harm a hair on a Jew's head! We will deal with this atrocity campaign simply through the incisive weight of the measures listed. More than ever before it is now necessary for the whole Party to stand in blind obedience, as one man, behind the leadership....

From Goebbels' Diary on the Boycott

J. Goebbels

APRIL 1, 1933

The boycott against the international atrocity propaganda has burst forth in full force in Berlin and the whole Reich. I drive along the Tauentzien Street in order to observe the situation. All Jews' businesses are closed. SA men are posted outside their entrances. The public has everywhere proclaimed its solidarity. The discipline is exemplary. An imposing performance! It all takes place in complete quiet; in the Reich too....

In the afternoon 150,000 Berlin workers marched to the Lustgarten, to join us in the protest against the incitement abroad. There is indescribable excitement in the air.

The press is already operating in total unanimity. The boycott is a great moral victory for Germany. We have shown the world abroad that we can call up the entire nation without thereby causing the least turbulence or excesses. The Führer has once more struck the right note.

At midnight the boycott will be broken off by our own decision. We are now waiting for the resultant echo in the foreign press and propaganda.

APRIL 2, 1933

The effects of the boycott are already clearly noticeable.
The world is gradually coming to its senses. It will learn to understand that it is not wise to let itself be informed on Germany by the Jewish émigrés. We will have to carry out a campaign of mental conquest in the world as effective as that which we have carried out in Germany itself.

In the end the world will learn to understand us.

J. Goebbels, *Vom Kaiserhof zur Reichskanzlei* ("From the Emperor's Court to the Reich Chancelry"), Munich, 1937, pp. 291–92. From *Documents on the Holocaust: Selected Sources on the Destruction of the Jews of Germany and Austria, Poland, and the Soviet Union,* Yitzhak Arad, Yisrael Gutman, Abraham Margaliot eds. Jerusalem: Yad Vashem, 1981, pp.35–36.

The German Authorities and the Cultural Association of German Jews

Hans Hinkel

June 19, 1934

Hans Hinkel
Staatskommissar
NSDAP [Nazi Party] *Gau* Hessen-Nassau
District Office, Frankfurt on Main

In reply to your inquiry of June 6, 1934, I wish to state that, for a variety of reasons, it is to be permitted for the Jews to join together in an Organization, the Cultural Association of German Jews (*Kulturbund deutscher Juden*), which will be supervised by the State Police and other Party organizations. The main reasons for this [permission], apart from intentions connected with foreign policy, is the easier supervision and the concentration of the intellectual-artistic Jews in an organization where Jews will "make art" only for Jews. Permission has been given generally for the State of Prussia, because the Secret State Police, which is mainly responsible for the supervision, gave its express approval. The existence of this Jewish organization will depend on its observance of various conditions. One of these conditions is that the gatherings of the Association will not be advertised publicly. Immediately on receipt of your communication I was in touch with Dr. Singer, the head of the local central office of the Association, with the urgent request that he inform the associated organizations and responsible colleagues that in future publicly exhibited posters or announcements in shops would no longer be tolerated and would endanger the whole work of the Association.

Heil Hitler!

Hans Hinkel, "The German Authorities and the Cultural Association of German Jews," Hinkel Files, Wiener Library, Tel Aviv University. From *Documents on the Holocaust: Selected Sources on the Destruction of the Jews of Germany and Austria, Poland, and the Soviet Union,* Yitzhak Arad, Yisrael Gutman, Abraham Margaliot eds. Jerusalem: Yad Vashem, 1981, p. 67.

Activities of the Cultural Association of German Jews

The Cultural Association of German Jews needs you!

The need for the work of the Cultural Association has already been proved in Berlin. Cologne and Munich followed suit with plans and work. Frankfurt on Main, with its significant Jewish tradition and its special Jewish tasks, must also give a lead in these efforts. We have received authority from the State Commissioner for the independent organization of artistic and creative work. Like the centers of the Cultural Association in the main cities, so Frankfurt will be the starting-point for the work done in the District Rhein-Main. The smaller and smallest Jewish communities in cities and the countryside will join in actively and passively.

The creative artists appeal to you! Our program includes music, theater, lectures and art.

Finding work for members of artistic and crafts professions.

Training at all levels for Jewish musicians, painters and sculptors. There is a task here for the Youth Associations that is appropriate to our times.

The aim of our work is the cooperation of all those who take part, actively or passively, in Jewish cultural life, both artists and audience, and this can be achieved only if all Jewish organizations play their part. Every individual is jointly responsible and will decide with us on the success of our work.

Our appeal is addressed to all! We all need contact with elation, consolation, joy!

Therefore: Register as a member of the Cultural Association of German Jews, Frankfurt on Main.

"Activities of the Cultural Association of German Jews," *Frankfurter Israelitisches Gemeindeblatt*, April 1934. From *Documents on the Holocaust: Selected Sources on the Destruction of the Jews of Germany and Austria, Poland, and the Soviet Union,* Yitzhak Arad, Yisrael Gutman, Abraham Margaliot eds. Jerusalem: Yad Vashem, 1981, p. 67.

Activities
of the *Hilfsverein**
in the Field
of Emigration
Urgent Tasks at the Present Time

The *Hilfsverein* has taken on a new task in addition to its former tasks: advice and assistance for those who emigrate from Germany.

The German Jews feel an inner bond with their Fatherland, and they wish to remain in their Homeland, whose fate they see as their own. Where this appears impossible for economic reasons and because of the future of their children, and emigration becomes economically and politically necessary, it becomes the duty of the Aid Association to prepare [emigration] and to help those who have made the grave decision to leave their Fatherland and establish a new life....The *Hilfsverein* advises persons emigrating to all countries with the exception of Palestine. Up to now it has assisted in emigration to 34 countries overseas.

In the course of the year 1933, 60,000 persons received advice and information of all kinds from the *Hilfsverein*. Financial assistance was given to 7,700 persons in the form of subsidies for tickets for railway and ship passage, visas, food, transport of luggage, furniture, machinery and instruments. A voluminous correspondence with authorities, communities, and aid committees has been maintained on behalf of many thousands of persons....

"Activities of the *Hilfsverein* in the Field of Emigration," The Central Archives for the History of the Jewish People, A/176. From *Documents on the Holocaust: Selected Sources on the Destruction of the Jews of Germany and Austria, Poland, and the Soviet Union*, Yitzhak Arad, Yisrael Gutman, Abraham Margaliot eds. Jerusalem: Yad Vashem, 1981, p. 69.
**Hilfsverein der deutschen Juden*—Aid Association of German Jews.

Nuremberg Laws on Reich Citizenship, September 15, 1935
Reich Citizenship Law
September 15, 1935

The Reichstag has unanimously enacted the following law, which is promulgated herewith:

§1

1) A subject of the State is a person who enjoys the protection of the German Reich and who in consequence has specific obligations towards it.
2) The status of subject of the State is acquired in accordance with the provisions of the Reich and State Citizenship Law.

§2

1) A Reich citizen is a subject of the State who is of German or related blood, who proves by his conduct that he is willing and fit faithfully to serve the German people and Reich.
2) Reich citizenship is acquired through the granting of a Reich Citizenship Certificate.
3) The Reich citizen is the sole bearer of full political rights in accordance with the Law.

§3

The Reich Minister of the Interior, in coordination with the Deputy of the Führer, will issue the Legal and Administrative orders required to implement and complete this Law.

Nuremberg, September 15, 1935
at the Reich Party Congress of Freedom

The Führer and Reich Chancellor
Adolf Hitler
The Reich Minister of the Interior
Frick

"Nuremberg Laws on Reich Citizenship, September 15, 1935," *Reichsgesetzblatt*, I, 1935, pp. 1146. From *Documents on the Holocaust: Selected Sources on the Destruction of the Jews of Germany and Austria, Poland, and the Soviet Union,* Yitzhak Arad, Yisrael Gutman, Abraham Margaliot eds. Jerusalem: Yad Vashem, 1981, p. 77.

Nuremberg Law for the Protection of German Blood and German Honor, September 15, 1935

Law for the Protection of German Blood and German Honor September 15, 1935

Moved by the understanding that purity of the German Blood is the essential condition for the continued existence of German people, and inspired by the inflexible determination to ensure the existence of the German Nation for all time, the Reichstag has unanimously adopted the following Law, which is promulgated herewith:

§1

1) Marriages between Jews and subjects of the state of German or related blood are forbidden. Marriages nevertheless concluded are invalid, even if concluded abroad to circumvent this law.
2) Annulment proceedings can be initiated only by the State Prosecutor.

§2

Extramarital intercourse between Jews and subjects of the state of German or related blood is forbidden.

"Nuremberg Law for the Protection of German Blood and German Honor, September 15, 1935," *Reichsgesetzblatt*, I, 1935, pp. 1146–47. From *Documents on the Holocaust: Selected Sources on the Destruction of the Jews of Germany and Austria, Poland, and the Soviet Union*, Yitzhak Arad, Yisrael Gutman, Abraham Margaliot eds. Jerusalem: Yad Vashem, 1981, pp. 78–79.

§3

Jews may not employ in their households female subjects of the state of German or related blood who are under 45 years old.

§4

1) Jews are forbidden to fly the Reich or National flag or to display the Reich colors.
2) They are, on the other hand, permitted to display the Jewish colors. The exercise of this right is protected by the State.

§5

1) Any person who violates the prohibition under §1 will be punished by a prison sentence with hard labor.
2) A male who violates the prohibition under §2 will be punished with a prison sentence with or without hard labor.
3) Any person violating the provisions under §§3 or 4 will be punished with a prison sentence of up to one year and a fine, or with one or the other of these penalties.

§6

The Reich Minister of the Interior, in coordination with the Deputy of the Führer and the Reich Minister of Justice, will issue the Legal and Administrative regulations required to implement and complete this Law.

§7

The Law takes effect on the day following promulgations except for §3, which goes into force on January 1, 1936.

Nuremberg, September 15, 1935
at the Reich Party Congress of Freedom

The Führer and Reich Chancellor
Adolf Hitler
The Reich Minister of the Interior
Frick
The Reich Minister of Justice
Dr. Gürtner
The Deputy of the Führer
R. Hess

Selection from *Mein Kampf*

Adolf Hitler

...

Once, as I was strolling through the Inner City, I suddenly encountered an apparition in a black caftan and black hair locks. Is this a Jew? was my first thought.

For, to be sure, they had not looked like that in Linz. I observed the man furtively and cautiously, but the longer I stared at this foreign face, scrutinizing feature for feature, the more my first question assumed a new form:

Is this a German?

As always in such cases, I now began to try to relieve my doubts by books. For a few hellers I bought the first anti-Semitic pamphlets of my life. Unfortunately, they all proceeded from the supposition that in principle the reader knew or even understood the Jewish question to a certain degree. Besides, the tone for the most part was such that doubts again arose in me, due in part to the dull and amazingly unscientific arguments favoring the thesis.

I relapsed for weeks at a time, once even for months.

The whole thing seemed to me so monstrous, the accusations so boundless, that, tormented by the fear of doing injustice, I again became anxious and uncertain.

Yet I could no longer very well doubt that the objects of my study were not Germans of a special religion, but a people in themselves; for since I had begun to concern myself with this question and to take cognizance of the Jews, Vienna appeared to me in a different light than before. Wherever I went, I began to see Jews, and the more I saw, the more sharply they became distinguished in my eyes from the rest of humanity. Particularly the Inner City and the districts north of the Danube Canal swarmed with a people which even outwardly had lost all resemblance to Germans.

And whatever doubts I may still have nourished were finally dispelled by the attitude of a portion of the Jews themselves.

Among them there was a great movement, quite extensive in Vienna, which came out sharply in confirmation of the national character of the Jews: this was the *Zionists*.

It looked, to be sure, as though only a part of the Jews approved this viewpoint, while the great majority condemned and inwardly rejected such a formulation. But when examined more closely, this appearance dissolved itself into an unsavory vapor of pretexts advanced for mere reasons of expedience, not to say lies. For the so-called liberal Jews did not reject the Zionists as non-Jews, but only as Jews with an impractical, perhaps even dangerous, way of publicly avowing their Jewishness.

Intrinsically they remained unalterably of one piece.

In a short time this apparent struggle between Zionistic and liberal Jews disgusted me; for it was false through and through, founded on lies and scarcely in keeping with the moral elevation and purity always claimed by this people.

The cleanliness of this people, moral and otherwise, I must say, is a point in itself. By their very exterior you could tell that these were no lovers of water, and, to your distress, you often knew it with your eyes closed. Later I often grew sick to my stomach from the smell of these caftan-wearers. Added to this, there was their unclean dress and their generally unheroic appearance.

All this could scarcely be called very attractive; but it became positively repulsive when, in addition to their physical uncleanliness, you discovered the moral stains on this 'chosen people.'

In a short time I was made more thoughtful than ever by my slowly rising insight into the type of activity carried on by the Jews in certain fields.

Was there any form of filth or profligacy, particularly in cultural life, without at least one Jew involved in it?

If you cut even cautiously into such an abscess, you found, like a maggot in a rotting body, often dazzled by the sudden light—a kike![1]

What had to be reckoned heavily against the Jews in my eyes was when I became acquainted with their activity in the press, art, literature, and the theater. All the unctuous reassurances helped little or nothing. It sufficed to look at a billboard, to study the names of the men behind the horrible trash they advertised, to make you hard for a long time to come. This was pestilence, spiritual pestilence, worse than the Black Death of olden times, and the people was being infected with it! It goes without saying that the lower the intellectual level of one of these art manufacturers, the more unlimited his fertility will be, and the scoundrel ends up like a garbage separator, splashing his filth in the face of humanity. And bear in mind that there is no limit to their number; bear in mind that for one Goethe Nature easily can foist on the world ten thousand of these scribblers who poison men's souls like germ-carriers of the worse sort, on their fellow men.

It was terrible, but not to be overlooked, that precisely the Jew, in tremendous numbers, seemed chosen by Nature for this shameful calling.

Is this why the Jews are called the 'chosen people'?

I now began to examine carefully the names of all the creators of unclean products in public artistic life. The result was less and less favorable for my previous attitude toward the Jews. Regardless how my sentiment might resist, my reason was forced to draw its conclusions.

The fact that nine tenths of all literary filth, artistic trash, and theatrical idiocy

---

[1] *Sowie man nur vorsichtig in eine solche Geschwulst hineinschnitt, fand man, wie die Made im faulenden Leibe, oft ganz geblendet vom plötzlichen Lichte, ein Jüdlein.*

can be set to the account of a people, constituting hardly one hundredth of all the country's inhabitants, could simply not be talked away; it was the plain truth.

And I now began to examine my beloved 'world press' from this point of view.

And the deeper I probed, the more the object of my former admiration shriveled. The style became more and more unbearable; I could not help rejecting the content as inwardly shallow and banal; the objectivity of exposition now seemed to me more akin to lies than honest truth; and the writers were—Jews.

A thousand things which I had hardly seen before now struck my notice, and others, which had previously given me food for thought, I now learned to grasp and understand.

I now saw the liberal attitude of this press in a different light; the lofty tone in which it answered attacks and its method of killing them with silence now revealed itself to me as a trick as clever as it was treacherous; the transfigured raptures of their theatrical critics were always directed at Jewish writers, and their disapproval never struck anyone but Germans. The gentle pinpricks against William II revealed its methods by their persistency, and so did its commendation of French culture and civilization. The trashy content of the short story now appeared to me as outright indecency, and in the language I detected the accents of a foreign people; the sense of the whole thing was so obviously hostile to Germanism that this could only have been intentional.

But who had an interest in this?

Was all this a mere accident?

Gradually I became uncertain.

The development was accelerated by insights which I gained into a number of other matters. I am referring to the general view of ethics and morals which was quite openly exhibited by a large part of the Jews, and the practical application of which could be seen.

Here again the streets provided an object lesson of a sort which was sometimes positively evil.

The relation of the Jews to prostitution and, even more, to the white-slave traffic, could be studied in Vienna as perhaps in no other city of Western Europe, with the possible exception of the southern French ports. If you walked at night through the streets and alleys of Leopoldstadt,[2] at every step you witnessed proceedings which remained concealed from the majority of the German people until the War gave the soldiers on the eastern front occasion to see similar things, or, better expressed, forced them to see them.

When thus for the first time I recognized the Jew as the coldhearted, shameless, and calculating director of this revolting vice traffic in the scum of the big city, a cold shudder ran down my back.

But then a flame flared up within me. I no longer avoided discussion of the Jewish question; no, now I sought it. And when I learned to look for the Jew in all

---

[2]Second District of Vienna, separated from the main part of the city by the Danube Canal. Formerly the ghetto, it still has a predominantly Jewish population.

branches of cultural and artistic life and its various manifestations, I suddenly encountered him in a place where I would least have expected to find him.

When I recognized the Jew as the leader of the Social Democracy, the scales dropped from my eyes. A long soul struggle had reached its conclusion.

The Course and Fate of the Jews of Stuttgart
A Memorial Book Issued by the City of Stuttgart

Maria Zelzer

trans. Rita S. Botwinick

The district party leader, Mauer, was ordered by the highest authority in Berlin to hold a meeting in November 1938. Present were the heads of the Stuttgart SA, SS, and SD (Security police). Mauer informed them that during the coming night all the synagogues in the German Reich, including those in Wuerttenberg and Stuttgart, would be burned down. Fire departments were ordered to permit the synagogues to burn but were instructed to protect adjoining buildings. The men present received specific orders and it was also announced that the police had been ordered not to interfere.

The moonlit sky over Stuttgart turned red from the glow of the flames. The synagogue on Hospital Street was ablaze and the fire fighters, with their usual speed, raced from place to place to douse adjoining buildings. At the same time, the synagogue in Bad Cannstatt burnt down. This building was only scantily covered with masonry and was mainly constructed of wood. Consequently, the flames found no resistance and when firemen arrived at 4:30 in the morning to extinguish the fire, they found nothing but a smoking ruin.

In the NS-Kurier [a Nazi newspaper, ed. note] this event made headline news; "THE PEOPLES' RIGHTEOUS FURY EXERTS VENGEANCE." But one could gather from the report that these angry people were in Nazi uniforms or wore party insignia. The NS-Kurier continued: "The night's spectacle understandably had drawn many onlookers. Everywhere they expressed their satisfaction that in this form at

---

Maria Zelzer, *The Course and Fate of the Jews of Stuttgart: A Memorial Book Issued by the City of Stuttgart,* trans. Rita S. Botwinick. Stuttgart, Germany: Ernst Klett Verlag, 1988. Reprinted by permission of Stadtarchiv of the City of Stuttgart, Stuttgart, Germany, 1988.

least a small fraction of the sins committed by the Jews was atoned for....The glow of the fires still hung over the city when here and there the sound of crashing glass could be heard in the streets. Perhaps until yesterday many of our citizens gave no thought to the fact that many Jews were still enjoying the peaceful protection of the National-Socialist state as they carried on their businesses. Today they may realize, with the shards of broken glass glittering in the autumn sun, that the Jews have been hiding behind a facade....Even though the items behind the broken show cases were unprotected, not one piece of merchandise was touched. In light of foreign press reports about plundering, this point needs to be made emphatically. By noon the excited crowd was so large, it was necessary to divert traffic from the Koenigsstrasse. At the entrances to the stores SS troops were posted. The owners of the shops were encouraged to cover the gaping windows with wooden boards."...

The newspaper Schwaebische Merkur treated the events with restraint. To this the NS-Kurier reacted with displeasure: "In the past few days some few people have moaned and groaned about the action against the Jews. They cried over a few window panes that belonged to Jewish speculators and they mourn the synagogues....Is it possible that in this year of 1938 we still have such foolish folk?"...

In Stuttgart the destruction did not spread to private dwellings. Nonetheless, when quiet returned the Jews lived in great agitation. They felt terribly upset because of the wave of arrests which had begun on November 9 and continued for a week. On November 12, 1938, despair resulted in the death of the teacher Felix David (born 1909), his wife Ruth, (born 1911), and their two small sons, Benjamin, (born 1936), and Gideon, born 1938....

The following is an excerpt from the biographical notes of Karl Adler, head of Stuttgart's Jewish Professional Association:

> I received a telephone call that the synagogue was burning on that November night. I raced to the fire but saw at once that there was nothing to be saved. The arsonists actually had poured oil into the flames. I then went to my office at the corner of Garten and Hospital Streets, adjoining the synagogue. I destroyed a number of documents which could not fall into the hands of the Nazis. I did this in the nick of time because I was the first man in Stuttgart to be arrested (this I found out later), by several Gestapo and SS men. No reason for the arrest was given. I was transported by car to a cell in the basement of Gestapo headquarters where I was the only occupant of a totally bare cell. I was dead-tired and stretched out on the floor. I thought I was dreaming when I saw a woman stand before me, a cup of coffee in her hand. She was a secretary for the Gestapo who placed herself in danger with this act. My next stop was at police headquarters on Buechsen Street. Here I came in contact with hundreds of fellow victims and had my first inkling concerning the events which had taken place during the night of the fires. We were told what our prison routine entailed; this lasted until nightfall and then we were were split into groups and transferred. I was pushed into a crammed prison transport and finally we were unloaded at a prison yard. We did not know where we were. In comparison to the Gestapo cell, this overcrowded prison seemed almost like a hotel room. We had straw pallets (not enough), a table, several chairs, and a even a toilet. We finally discovered where we were because I recognized the sound of the church bells. We had to be near the Stiftskirche. Because

most of the prisoners were completely distraught, I organized some activities to distract them. Every one had to relate something from his life's experience. I took on music, English (which I had just begun to study), breathing and exercises. Our writing material consisted of the margins of the newspaper used as toilet paper and a tiny stump of a pencil which had escaped the thorough search of the prisoners. We became aware of the magnitude of the situation when, during roll call, we saw old friends. Of course, we could not speak to them. The ray of sunlight which struck the high, barred window in our cell around noon was longingly awaited. It seemed longer, but after eight days I was released with the understanding that I would promote emigration (except my own) of the Jews by every means possible. Until this point in time I had hardly thought about emigrating. I had been too devoted to my home and my work....

Chapter 7

Hitler's War

INTRODUCTION

The proposition that the German people must expand their territory in order to accommodate a growing population was a leitmotif of Hitler's foreign policy. He contended that the losses imposed by the Treaty of Versailles had made it particularly urgent that Germany acquire increased *Lebensraum*. This theme, first articulated in *Mein Kampf*, was repeated constantly, not as a hope, but as an entitlement. The Reich's new boundaries would be moved eastward to include the farmlands of Poland and part of the agricultural and mineral riches of the Ukraine. The likelihood that such an expansion might lead to war was no deterrent. Certainly, a diplomatic resolution would be preferable, or perhaps a "little war" against an isolated Poland. The specter of a possible two-front war troubled the general staff of the army, but, if called upon, the generals would know their duty.

The theme of *Lebensraum* dovetailed neatly with the Aryan superiority doctrine. The inferior Slavic Poles would be forced to relinquish their land to their Teutonic betters. Himmler and his SS planned in detail the settlement of the master race on the soil of the ousted Poles. Like the helots of ancient Sparta, the wretched Slavs would toil for their German overlords. To implement this design required an army so powerful no nation would dare to defy Germany. By virtue of the "natural superiority" of the Germanic Aryan, this hegemony would be maintained for a thousand years.

Hitler's foreign policy, with all its shifts and reversals, becomes clear when viewed from this perspective. The demands made and met at the Munich conferences, the alliances with non-Aryan Italy and Japan, the short-lived non-aggression treaties with Poland and the Soviet Union, all were targeted toward the same goal. The Vichy French and several Balkan regimes, avaricious and fearful, signed on to the

Fuehrer's dreams. He promised peace when it suited his purpose, usually to gain time, and rattled the saber a few months later. When his aggression led to war in 1939, he welcomed the opportunity to show the world the might of the new Germany. The method was typically Machiavellian; the end always justified the means.

The Germans ruled the defeated nations without a preexisting blueprint. As an area was overrun by the armies, a system of government was devised and installed according to the Fuehrer's will. Of paramount consideration was the compulsion to prevent the subjugated peoples from organizing any resistance to their conquerors. Interference with the exploitation of the region was punishable by death. Both human and economic resources belonged to the victor. No attempt was made to establish even minimally functioning services for the population.

The territories along the German-Polish border were immediately incorporated into the Reich, other areas were slated for future annexation. Several of the defeated states were governed by appointed Nazis, the *Gauleiters*. These men were directly responsible to Hitler, much to the chagrin of the foreign office and the armed services. Several regions were designated as Protectorates, that is dependencies, administered by hated native Nazi puppets. To complete the patchwork, regions designated to be of strategic importance remained under military government.

As there was diversity in the official status of the defeated countries, so the treatment accorded the conquered people differed significantly. German occupation policies evolved from several criteria. Considerable weight was given to the supposed racial quality of the inhabitants; the Nordic people were valued and might be wooed into future cooperation. The need for available resources also affected policy. Slave laborers were needed to support German needs. Everywhere in the Nazi world people lived in fear; even life itself was a gift the conquerors might bestow or take away. From Greece to Denmark, from France to Russia, people worked, suffered, and died in numbers never before recorded in human history.

The Holocaust resulted from the coupling of two of Hitler's obsessions, the drive for *Lebensraum* and his violent anti-Semitism. His early victories and conquests brought him a rich harvest of Jews, particularly in eastern and southeastern Europe. Between 1939 and 1941 it seemed possible that he might win both wars, against the Allies and the Jews. His megalomania served his enemies well, he ignored the advice of his generals and conducted military campaigns with a sense of destiny rather than strategic skill. His "no retreat" order cost the German people millions of lives. All his life Hitler had taken pride in his soldierly qualities, yet he never assumed any responsibility for the disaster he visited upon the German people. In fact, he blamed them for losing the war. Since they had not fought hard enough, they deserved to lose....His patrimony to the men and women who had followed him faithfully was a country without men, cities in rubble, and the shame of genocide that cannot be erased.

Selection from *Mein Kampf*

Adolf Hitler

...

I still wish briefly to take a position on the question as to what extent the demand for soil and territory seems ethically and morally justified. This is necessary, since unfortunately, even in so-called folkish circles, all sorts of unctuous big-mouths step forward, endeavoring to set the rectification of the injustice of 1918 as the aim of the German nation's endeavors in the field of foreign affairs, but at the same time find it necessary to assure the whole world of folkish brotherhood and sympathy.

I should like to make the following preliminary remarks: *The demand for restoration of the frontiers of 1914 is a political absurdity of such proportions and consequences as to make it seem a crime. Quite aside from the fact that the Reich's frontiers in 1914 were anything but logical. For in reality they were neither complete in sense of embracing the people of German nationality, nor sensible with regard to geo-military expediency. They were not the result of a considered political action, but momentary frontiers in a politic struggle that was by no means concluded; partly, in fact, they the results of chance.* With equal right and in many cases with more right, some other sample year of German history could be picked out, and the restoration of the conditions at that time declared to be the aim of an activity in foreign affairs. The above demand is entirely suited to our bourgeois society, which here as elsewhere does not possess a single creative political idea for the future, but lives only in the past, in fact, in the most immediate past; for even their backward gaze does not extend beyond their own times. The law of inertia binds them to a given situation and causes them to resist any change in it, but without ever increasing the activity of this opposition beyond the mere power of perseverance. So it is obvious that the political horizon of these people does not extend beyond the year 1914. By proclaiming the restoration of those borders as the political aim of their activity, they keep mending the crumbling league of our adversaries. Only in this way can it be explained that eight years after a world struggle in which states, some of which had the most heterogeneous desires, took part, the coalition of the victors of those days can still maintain itself in a more or less unbroken form.

All these states were at one time beneficiaries of the German collapse. Fear of our strength caused the greed and envy of the individual great powers among themselves to recede. By grabbing as much of the Reich as they could, they found the best guard against a future uprising. A bad conscience and fear of our people's strength is still the most enduring cement to hold together the various members of this alliance.

And we do not disappoint them. By setting up the restoration of the borders of 1914 as a political program for Germany, our bourgeoisie frighten away every partner who might desire to leave the league of our enemies, since he must inevitably fear to be attacked singly and thereby lose the protection of his individual fellow allies. Each single state feels concerned and threatened by this slogan.

Moreover, it is senseless in two respects:

(1) because the instruments of power are lacking to remove it from the vapors of club evenings into reality; and

(2) because, if it could actually be realized, the outcome would again be so pitiful that, by God, it would not be worth while to risk the blood of our people for *this*.

For it should scarcely seem questionable to anyone that even the restoration of the frontiers of 1914 could be achieved only by blood. Only childish and naive minds can lull themselves in the idea that they can bring about a correction of Versailles by wheedling and begging. Quite aside from the fact that such an attempt would presuppose a man of Talleyrand's talents, which we do not possess. One half of our political figures consist of extremely sly, but equally spineless elements which are hostile toward our nation to begin with, while the other is composed of good-natured, harmless, and easy-going soft-heads. Moreover, the times have changed since the Congress of Vienna: *Today it is not princes and princes' mistresses who haggle and bargain over state borders; it is the inexorable Jew who struggles for his domination over the nations.* No nation can remove this hand from its throat except by the sword. Only the assembled and concentrated might of a national passion rearing up in its strength can defy the international enslavement of peoples. Such a process is and remains a bloody one.

If, however, we harbor the conviction that the German future, regardless what happens, demands the supreme sacrifice, quite aside from all considerations of political expediency as such, we must set up an aim worthy of this sacrifice and fight for it.

The boundaries of the year 1914 mean nothing at all for the German future. Neither did they provide a defense of the past, nor would they contain any strength for the future. Through them the German nation will neither achieve its inner integrity, nor will its sustenance be safeguarded by them, nor do these boundaries, viewed from the military standpoint, seem expedient or even satisfactory, nor finally can they improve the relation in which we at present find ourselves toward the other world powers, or, better expressed, the real world powers. The lag behind England will not be caught up, the magnitude of the Union will not be achieved; not even France would experience a material diminution of her world-political importance.

Only one thing would be certain: even with a favorable outcome, such an attempt to restore the borders of 1914 would lead to a further bleeding of our national body, so much so that there would be no worth-while blood left to stake for the decisions and actions really to secure the nation's future. On the contrary, drunk with such a shallow success, we should renounce any further goals, all the more readily as 'national honor' would be repaired and, for the moment at least, a few doors would have been reopened to commercial development.

As opposed to this, we National Socialists must hold unflinchingly to our aim in foreign policy, namely, *to secure for the German people the land and soil to which they are entitled on this earth.* And this action is the only one which, before God and our German posterity, would make any sacrifice of blood seem justified: before God, since we have been put on this earth with the mission of eternal struggle for our daily bread, beings who receive nothing as a gift, and who owe their position as lords of the earth only to the genius and the courage with which they can conquer and defend it; and before our German posterity in so far as we have shed no citizen's blood out of which a thousand others are not bequeathed to posterity. The soil on which some day German generations of peasants can beget powerful sons will sanction the investment of the sons of today, and will some day acquit the responsible statesmen of blood-guilt and sacrifice of the people, even if they are persecuted by their contemporaries.

And I must sharply attack those folkish pen-pushers who claim to regard such an acquisition of soil as a 'breach of sacred human rights' and attack it as such in their scribblings. One never knows who stands behind these fellows. But one thing is certain, that the confusion they can create is desirable and convenient to our national enemies. By such an attitude they help to weaken and destroy from within our people's will for the only correct way of defending their vital needs. For no people on this earth possesses so much as a square yard of territory on the strength of a higher will or superior right. Just as Germany's frontiers are fortuitous frontiers, momentary frontiers in the current political struggle of any period, so are the boundaries of other nations' living space. And just as the shape of our earth's surface can seem immutable as granite only to the thoughtless soft-head, but in reality only represents at each period an apparent pause in a continuous development, created by the mighty forces of Nature in a process of continuous growth, only to be transformed or destroyed tomorrow by greater forces, likewise the boundaries of living spaces in the life of nations.

State boundaries are made by man and changed by man.

The fact that a nation has succeeded in acquiring an undue amount of soil constitutes no higher obligation that it should be recognized eternally. At most it proves the strength of the conquerors and the weakness of the nations. And in this case, right lies in this strength alone. If the German nation today, penned into an impossible area, faces a lamentable future, this is no more a commandment of Fate than revolt against this state of affairs constitutes an affront to Fate. No more than any higher power has promised another nation more territory than the German nation, or is offended by the fact of this unjust distribution of the soil. Just as our ancestors did not receive the soil on which we live today as a gift from Heaven, but had to fight for it at the risk of their lives, in the future no folkish grace will win soil for us and hence life for our people, but only the might of a victorious sword.

Much as all of us today recognize the necessity of a reckoning with France, it would remain ineffectual in the long run if it represented the whole of our aim in foreign policy. It can and will achieve meaning only if it offers the rear cover for an enlargement of our people's living space in Europe. For it is not in colonial acquisitions that we must see the solution of this problem, but exclusively in the acquisition of a territory for settlement, which will enhance the area of the mother country, and hence not only keep the new settlers in the most intimate community with the land of their origin, but secure for the total area those advantages which lie in its unified magnitude.

The folkish movement must not be the champion of other peoples, but the vanguard fighter of its own. Otherwise it is superfluous and above all has no right to sulk about the past. For in that case it is behaving in exactly the same way. The old German policy was wrongly determined by dynastic considerations, and the future policy must not be directed by cosmopolitan folkish drivel. In particular, we are not constables guarding the well-known 'poor little nations,' but soldiers of our own nation.

But we National Socialists must go further. *The right to possess soil can become a duty if without extension of its soil a great nation seems doomed to destruction.* And most especially when not some little nigger nation or other is involved, but the Germanic mother of life, which has given the present-day world its cultural picture. *Germany will either be a world power or there will be no Germany.* And for world power she needs that magnitude which will give her the position she needs in the present period, and life to her citizens.

...

And so we National Socialists consciously draw a line beneath the foreign policy tendency of our pre-War period. We take up where we broke off six hundred years ago. We stop the endless German movement to the south and west, and turn our gaze toward the land in the east. At long last we break off the colonial and commercial policy of the pre-War period and shift to the soil policy of the future.

If we speak of soil in Europe today, we can primarily have in mind only *Russia* and her vassal border states.

Here Fate itself seems desirous of giving us a sign. By handing Russia to Bolshevism, it robbed the Russian nation of that intelligentsia which previously brought about and guaranteed its existence as a state. For the organization of a Russian state formation was not the result of the political abilities of the Slavs in Russia, but only a wonderful example of the state-forming efficacity of the German element in an inferior race. Numerous mighty empires on earth have been created in this way. Lower nations led by Germanic organizers and overlords have more than once grown to be mighty state formations and have endured as long as the racial nucleus of the creative state race maintained itself. For centuries Russia drew nourishment from this Germanic nucleus of its upper leading strata. Today it can be regarded as almost totally exterminated and extinguished. It has been replaced by the Jew. Impossible as it is for the Russian by himself to shake off the yoke of the Jew by his own resources, it is equally impossible for the Jew to maintain the mighty empire forever. He himself is no element of organization, but a ferment of decomposition. The Persian empire in the east is ripe for collapse. And the end of Jewish rule in Russia will also be the end of Russia as a state. We have been chosen by Fate as witnesses of a catastrophe which will be the mightiest confirmation of the soundness of the folkish theory.

Our task, the mission of the National Socialist movement, is to bring our own people to such political insight that they will not see their goal for the future in the breath-taking sensation of a new Alexander's conquest, but in the industrious work of the German plow, to which the sword need only give soil.

World War Two through German Eyes

James Lucas

The German armed forces at the height of their power, in the summer of 1940, were the mightiest in Europe. On 10 May, they had opened the campaign in the West, Operation 'Gelb' and although fewer in number than their adversaries and less lavishly equipped, had demonstrated a singleness of purpose and a flexibility in action that had brought them victory in fewer than six weeks. Within days of the opening of Operation 'Gelb' the Belgian and Dutch Armies had been so savaged that they posed no threat to the right flank of the German panzer formations as these thrust across northern France. The armies of France and Great Britain, which had been tied to conventional military methods, were outgeneralled by the new tactics of blitzkrieg and were forced back towards the Channel port of Dunkirk. At 0900 hrs on 4 June, General Beaufrere formally surrendered the shattered perimeter around the town. Some thirty to forty thousand, mainly French troops, the last survivors of the allied units which had manned the defence line, marched into captivity. Their staunch defences had allowed the Royal Navy, backed by a mass of little ships, to carry out an enterprise which over the course of a few weeks, had taken off more than 365,000 French and British soldiers.

Those Germans who stood victorious on the beaches of Dunkirk must have been astounded at the scale of destruction which they saw around them. Out to sea, were the wrecks of large ships that had been bombed and sunk during the evacuation. Heavy lorries had been driven into the shallow sea and lined up side by side to form temporary moles from which the lines of patient men had embarked. Field guns stood empty and useless with their breechblocks removed. Light anti-aircraft guns, which had defended the perimeter until ammunition ran out, still pointed their barrels to the sky but they no longer posed a threat. Their muzzles had been shattered to deny the guns to the enemy. Allied prisoners, dejected and exhausted by the fury of the fighting, sat in groups waiting for their captors to march them away. And everywhere were the dead. Some lay in the fields or on the sand, corrupting in the heat of the June day; others bobbed up and down, mingling with the flotsam in the gentle swell of the waves. Strewn across the beaches like discarded toys were rifles and machine-guns in vast numbers. And all that nightmare scene lay darkened, overshadowed by smoke which rose in black rolling clouds from the burning oil tanks.

From James Lucas, *World War Two through German Eyes*, London: Arms and Armour Press, 1987, pp. 122–124, 172–174. Reprinted by permission of Cassell PLC.

German soldiers who had fought their way across Flanders and then through the Dunkirk perimeter to the beaches would have seen, during those weeks of battle, the vast material losses which the Allies had suffered. Those soldiers, remembering the devastation they had witnessed and seeing the shambles of the beaches, knew that their army had gained a great victory. It was unfortunate that the British Expeditionary Force had managed to escape to England, but it had left behind all its heavy equipment and lacking such weapons was almost defenceless.

...

'I can never forget the first mass attack by Russian infantry....I could not believe that in the Second World War the tactics of the First Great War could still be used by any one of the major combatants. The whole assault was so ineptly handled that I found it difficult to believe that it was being carried out by a professional army. That incompetence reinforced the belief held at the time by many German officers, that the Red Army was being handled no differently to the Tsarist army. It was the same old steam-roller.

'The Soviet assaults were carried out by masses of men who made no attempt at concealment but trusted in sheer weight of numbers to overwhelm us...quite a long distance from our positions there were lines of brown-uniformed men tramping forward. The first of these...was followed at about 200 metres distance by a second line. Then there rose out of the grass a third wave, then a fourth and then a fifth. The lines of men stretched to the right and left of our regimental front overlapping it completely and the whole mass of Russian troops came trampling stolidly and relentlessly forward. It was an unbelievable sight, a machine-gunner's dream target....At 600 metres we opened fire and whole sections of the first wave just vanished, leaving here and there an odd survivor still walking stolidly forward. The second wave had also taken losses but closed up towards the centre, marched round and across the bodies of their comrades who had fallen. Then as if on a signal the lines of men began running forward. As they advanced there was a low rumbling "Hooooraaaay."...

'The first three waves had been destroyed by our fire but not all of the men in them had been killed. Some who dropped were snipers who worked their way forward through the grass to open fire upon our officers and machine-gun posts. The rush by the fourth wave came on more slowly for the men had to pick their way through a great carpet of bodies....The great mass of Soviet troops was now storming up the slope towards us but our fire was too great and they broke. About an hour later a further five lines of men came on in a second attack. We smashed this and then crushed a third and fourth assault. The numbers of the enemy seemed endless and the new waves of men advanced across their own dead without hesitation....The Ivans kept up their attacks for three days and even during the nights....The number and fury of those attacks exhausted and numbed us...not to hide the truth, they had frightened us....I think that on that day in 1941, some of us began to realize for the first time that the war against the Soviet Union was going to be bigger than we had thought it would be and a sense of depression, brought about by a fear of the unknown, settled upon us. That we would win we had no doubt, but what we were now engaged in would be a long, bitter and hard-fought war.'

...

Winter came early, lasted long and was terrible in ferocity. When the battle for Moscow ended in December 1941, more than half a million German soldiers had become casualties. Another 100,000 had to be taken out of the line suffering from frost bite.

The German planners had underestimated the size of the Red Army, had been ignorant of the strategic reserve armies that could be put fresh into battle and whose numbers turned the tide. German Intelligence had been unaware of the relocation of Russian industry and the Nazi authorities had rejected contemptuously the offers of help in the fight against the Soviets which had been made by the peoples of the Baltic republics, the Ukrainians and by the nations of southern Russia. The political perspective of the Slav as an Untermensch—less than human—was a part of the Party philosophy. It was into the hands of men who believed fervently in that dogma that the administration of occupied Russia was placed and the brutality of the regimes they set up alienated the ordinary Russian and made him an enemy instead of the ally against the Soviets that he might have become.

In 1942, a new German summer offensive opened and thrust in a blitzkrieg campaign southwards into the Caucasus and eastwards to Stalingrad. These were offensives without purpose. By 1942 there were no circumstances under which the Germans could defeat the Red Army and win the war in Russia. German formations might still win encirclement victories, they might still conquer vast areas of steppe land—but the decisive victory could no longer be gained.

It is unlikely that the Germans could ever have won the war against Russia—a country which Hitler and his Generals had declared could be defeated within five months. The million German soldiers who fell between 22 June and 31 December 1941, proved that the perspective of the the German Führer and his military subordinates had been a tragically distorted one.

Lost Victories

Erich von Manstein

SIXTH ARMY'S LAST BATTLE

The death-struggle of Sixth Army, which began around the turn of the year, is a tale of indescribable suffering. It was marked not only by the despair and justified bitterness of the men who had been deceived in their trust, but even more by the steadfastness they displayed in the face of an undeserved but inexorable fate, by their high degree of bravery, comradeship and devotion to duty, and by their calm resignation and humble faith in God.

If I refrain from dwelling on these things here, it is certainly not because we at Army Group Headquarters were not intensely affected by them. Respect for a heroism which may never find its equal renders me incapable of doing full justice to these happenings at Stalingrad.

There is one question, however, which I feel both impelled and qualified to answer as the former commander of Don Army Group. Was it justifiable or necessary—and if so, for how long—to demand this sacrifice of our soldiers? In other words, did Sixth Army's final battle serve any useful purpose? To answer the question properly, one must examine it against the background of the current situation, and the stern exigencies this imposed, rather than in the light of Germany's ultimate defeat.

On 26th December the commander of Sixth Army sent us the message reproduced below. We passed it straight on to O.K.H., our policy all along having been to present the Army's position in a quite unembellished form. (From this moment onwards the only reports we received on the position inside the pocket came by radio or from officers flown out as couriers. We had been unable to maintain the ultra-high-frequency radio link by which it was possible to hold teleprinter conversations over a brief period.)

The message from Colonel-General Paulus ran as follows:

Bloody losses, cold, and inadequate supplies have recently made serious inroads on divisions' fighting strength. I must therefore report the following:

1. Army can continue to beat off small-scale attacks and deal with local crises for some time yet, always providing that supply improves and replacements are flown in at earliest possible moment.

From Erich von Manstein, *Lost Victories,* Ed. and trans. Anthony G. Powell. Novato, CA: Presidio Press, 1982, pp. 350–357.

2. If enemy draws off forces in any strength from Hoth's* front and uses these or any other troops to launch mass attacks on Stalingrad fortress, latter cannot hold out for long.

3. No longer possible to execute break-out unless corridor is cut in advance and Army replenished with men and supplies.

I therefore request representations at highest level to ensure energetic measures for speedy relief, unless overall situation compels sacrifice of army. Army will naturally do everything in its power to hold out till last possible moment.

I have also to report that only 70 tons were flown in today. Some of the corps will exhaust bread supplies tomorrow, fats this evening, evening fare tomorrow. Radical measures now urgent.

The contents of this message confirmed how wrong Paulus's Chief-of-Staff had been only a week before when he asserted that the army could hold out till Easter if properly supplied.

The message also showed that when the Army Group had ordered Sixth Army to break out of the pocket one week previously, this—in view of the approach of Fourth Panzer Army—had not only been its *first* chance of being rescued but—as could be seen from the state the army was in—its *last* one, too.

Otherwise, except for local attacks, there was relative calm on the Sixth Army fronts around the end of December and beginning of January. This was either because the enemy wished to munition his artillery for a grand assault or because he was putting all the forces he could spare into an attempt to destroy Fourth Panzer Army and to score the success he was after in the large bend of the Don.

On 8th January General Hube appeared at Army Group Headquarters on his way back from seeing Hitler. The latter had had Hube flown out of Stalingrad to Lötzen to brief him on the situation of Sixth Army. Hube told me that he had given Hitler a completely unvarnished picture of things in the pocket. (This cannot, in fact, have differed in any respect from the one already available to Hitler from the Army Group's daily situation reports, but presumably he was not prepared to credit our own version without further evidence.)

Nevertheless, it was remarkable how Hube's stay in Lötzen had impressed him and to what extent he had been influenced by Hitler's display of confidence—genuine or otherwise. Hitler had declared that everything would be done to *supply Sixth Army for a long time to come* and had drawn attention to the plan for its relief at a later date. With his confidence thus restored, Hube returned into the pocket, only to be flown out again on instructions from Hitler to take over the running of the airlift from outside. Not even he was able to improve it, however, its low efficiency being due to the prevailing weather and the inadequate resources of the Luftwaffe and not to any shortcomings in the actual organization. One statement of Hube's which touched me personally concerned a rumour circulating in Sixth Army that I had sent them the

*I.e. Colonel-General Hoth, commanding Fourth Panzer Army. *Tr.*

signal: 'Hang on—I'll get you out: Manstein.' While I left no stone unturned to extricate Sixth Army from Stalingrad, it has never been my custom to promise the troops anything which I was not certain of fulfilling and did not rest with me alone.

General Hube, who was a fearless man, had tried to bring home to Hitler how damaging such events as the encirclement of Sixth Army must be to his prestige as Head of State. By this means he wished to suggest that Hitler should hand over command—at least on the Eastern Front—to a soldier. In view of the fact that Hube had called in to see us on his way to Lötzen, Hitler doubtless supposed that Hube's *démarche* had been inspired by me. This was in fact not the case.

When, after the fall of Stalingrad, I myself proposed a change in the supreme military command to Hitler, he was already forewarned and flatly refused to consider such a thing. Otherwise—especially as he was then still under the impression of his responsibility for the loss of Sixth Army—he might have proved more receptive to my ideas.

On 9th January the enemy called upon Sixth Army to capitulate. On Hitler's orders, the demand was rejected.

I do not think I can be reproached with ever having taken an uncritical view of Hitler's decisions or actions in the military sphere. Yet I entirely support the decision he made in this instance, for however harsh it may have been from the humanitarian point of view, it was still necessary at the time.

I do not propose to deal here with the purely soldierly viewpoint that no army may capitulate as long as it still has any strength left to fight. To abandon it would mean the very end of soldiering. Until we reach the happy era when states can do without armed might and soldiers no longer exist, this conception of soldierly honour will have to be maintained. Even the apparent hopelessness of a battle that can be avoided by capitulation does not in itself justify a surrender. If every Commander-in-Chief were to capitulate as soon as he considered his position hopeless, no one would ever win a war. Even in situations apparently quite bereft of hope it has often been possible to find a way out in the end. From General Paulus's point of view, at all events, it was his soldierly duty to refuse to capitulate. An exception could only have been made if the army had had no further role to play and could serve no useful purpose in prolonging its struggle. And this in turn brings us to the crucial point which justifies Hitler's order to refuse to capitulate and also barred the Army Group from intervening in favour of such action at that particular time. No matter how futile Sixth Army's continued resistance might be in the long run, it still had—as long as it could conceivably go on fighting—a decisive role to fulfill in the overall strategic situation. It had to try to tie down the enemy forces opposing it for the longest possible space of time.

At the beginning of December an approximate total of sixty formations (i.e. rifle divisions, armoured and mechanized brigades etc.) had been identified in the siege ring around the army. Some of them had doubtless been temporarily drawn off by the attack of Fourth Panzer Army, but new ones had been brought up to replace them. By 19th January, ninety of the 259 formations reported to be facing Don Army Group were committed around Sixth Army. What would have happened if the bulk of these ninety formations had been released through a capitulation of Sixth Army on 9th January is plain enough in the light of what has already been said about the Army Group's position and the consequent threat to the southern wing as a whole.

The army was still capable of fighting, even though this was ultimately futile from its own point of view. Yet its ability to hold out was of decisive importance for the situation on the southern wing. Every extra day Sixth Army could continue to tie down the enemy forces surrounding it was vital as far as the fate of the entire Eastern Front was concerned. It is idle to point out today that we still lost the war in the end and that its early termination would have spared us infinite misery. That is merely being wise after the event. In those days it was by no means certain that Germany was bound to lose the war in the military sense. A military stalemate, which might in turn have led to a similar state of affairs in the political field, would have been entirely within the bounds of possibility if the situation on the southern wing of the German armies could in some way have been restored. This, however, depended first and foremost on Sixth Army's continuing the struggle and holding down the enemy siege forces for as long as it possessed the slightest capacity to resist. It was the cruel necessity of war which compelled the Supreme Command to demand that one last sacrifice of the brave troops at Stalingrad. The fact that the self-same Supreme Command was responsible for the army's plight is beside the point in this context.

Following Sixth Army's refusal to capitulate on 9th January, the Soviet attack, preceded by intensive artillery preparation and supported by a large number of tanks, broke loose on all fronts. The main pressure was directed against the salient which protruded furthest west by Marinovka, and the enemy was able to break in at several points.

On 11th January the situation became even more critical, and because of the lack of ammunition and fuel the army could no longer restore it to any appreciable extent. The loss of the positions in the Karpovka Valley—and in particular of the inhabited localities there—deprived the troops on the western front of what protection they had hitherto enjoyed against the cold. Furthermore, the state of the weather ruled out any hope of an airlift.

This aggravation of Sixth Army's plight was made clear in a special report of 12th January which the Army Group immediately forwarded to O.K.H.

'Despite the troops' heroic resistance,' the army stated, 'the heavy fighting of the last few days has resulted in deep enemy penetrations which could so far be contained only with difficulty. Reserves are no longer available; nor can any be formed. Heavy weapons now immobilised. Severe losses and inadequate supplies, together with cold, have also considerably reduced troops' powers of resistance. If enemy maintains attacks in present strength, fortress front unlikely to hold more than a few days longer. Resistance will then resolve itself into localised actions.'

On 12th January weather again stopped the airlift and also prevented the Luftwaffe from flying any sorties in support of the army's hard defensive battles.

That evening General Pickert, the man responsible for controlling the Luftwaffe's side of the airlift, came out of the pocket. He painted a shocking picture of the position and set a limit of two to four days on the army's capacity for continued resistance—an estimate that was to prove inaccurate by reason of the bravery and self-sacrifice of the troops. In Pickert's opinion not even an improvement of the airlift could make much difference from now on, as the army's resources no longer sufficed to patch up the points where the enemy had broken in.

The following information on the tactical situation inside the pocket emerged from a report brought out to us by Pickert from Paulus (who had meanwhile been promoted Colonel-General):

On the north-western front the enemy had attacked with a force of between ten and twelve divisions. Parts of 3 and 29 Motorized Infantry Divisions had been outflanked from the north and smashed, with the result that it no longer seemed possible to rebuild a defence line here. The two gallant divisions had knocked out 100 tanks between them, but the enemy still appeared to have fifty intact.

On the southern front of the pocket, in spite of heroic resistance by 297 Infantry Division, the enemy had succeeded in breaking in after two days of intensive artillery bombardment. Here, too, there were no more forces available to close the gap. Of over 100 Soviet tanks taking part in this assault, forty had been knocked out.

The eastern front of the pocket was still holding at present, though here, too, heavy enemy pressure was being exerted.

On the north-eastern front the enemy had penetrated deeply in several places. 16 Panzer Division's fighting strength was exhausted.

Paulus further stated that the army would stand and fight to the last round. Any reduction in the size of the pocket as now suggested by Hitler to General Hube* would only serve to hasten the collapse, as no heavy weapons could now be moved. Since the airlift had been inadequate all along, no improvement could help matters now. The length of time the army could continue to resist depended entirely on the intensity of the enemy's attacks.

That same day the Pitomnik airfield was lost. Henceforth the only one left to us in the Stalingrad pocket was that at Gumrak.

During the night, however, Paulus reported that there might still be some prospect of continuing to defend the city if several battalions of troops were flown in forthwith with their full scale of weapons. He had already asked us repeatedly to fly in several thousand men to make good his losses, but the Army Group had been unable to comply because it possessed neither the necessary replacements nor, indeed, a single uncommitted battalion. Nor would it in any case have acceded to these requests from Sixth Army once Fourth Panzer Army's rescue drive had become bogged down, if only because there could be no justification for dispatching any reinforcements or replacements into the pocket from then on. It was already quite bad enough to have to fly unit commanders and General Staff officers back into the pocket on their return from leave. But apart from the fact that the army urgently needed them, these officers—some of whom bore such old military names as Bismarck and

---

*At the time when it was vitally necessary to accumulate forces for the break-out Hitler had issued an order expressly forbidding such action. *Author.*

Below—themselves insisted on returning to their troops, thereby proving that the tradition of self-denial and comradeship could withstand the hardest of tests.

On 13th January Colonel-General Paulus's senior aide, Captain Behr, an exemplary young officer who had already won the Knight's Cross, flew out to see us, bringing the army's war diary with him. He told us how bravely the troops were still fighting and what fortitude all ranks had shown in coming to terms with the cruelty of their fate.

Chapter 8

The Ghettos

INTRODUCTION

When Himmler became the chief of the SS it consisted of three divisions. At the height of his power he commanded thirty-five units. Of these, the Waffen SS made up the largest branch; they consisted of military troops who fought in the Russian and French campaigns. To wage the ideological/racial crusade against the Jews, Himmler organized special units. The *Einsatzgruppen* or Mobile Task Forces were directed to find, round up, and shoot their victims. The *Totenkopfverbaende* or Death Head Formations provided the manpower for the concentration and death camps. Preparatory to the final solution, however, was the formation of ghettos, also under the direction of the SS.

To save manpower and to shift the onus of cruel measures from the SS onto fellow Jews, the day-by-day affairs of the ghettos were run by the *Judenraete,* Councils of Jewish Elders. These Elders were forced to carry out Nazi demands while, at the same time, they tried to alleviate the suffering of their people. They directed the economic life and provided the essential public services to the community. They distributed the food allotments, instructed the work forces, collected taxes and, of course, enforced the decrees of their German masters. Some historians have pronounced harsh judgments upon the *Raete,* but we would do well to consider them carefully. Members and leaders of the councils faced an impossible quandary, working for the survival of the Jews while facilitating their transport to the death camps. Let it suffice to emphasize the following points:

1. Motivation to participate on a Council varied greatly, from self-aggrandizement to the desire to ease the misery of the ghetto population.

2. Members of ghetto administration were promised by the SS that they and their families would be immune from expulsion and would survive.
3. Conditions within the various ghettos differed according to circumstances such as the momentary political climate within a locality and the dispositions of the Germans in charge.

Life behind the barbed wire or stone walls of the Polish ghettos was not a dirge of unrelieved misery. Wherever Jews gathered, hungry or cold or terror-stricken, cultural activity continued. While veritable horror scenes were enacted in the streets, people found solace and moments of forgetfulness in learning, in theater, in music, and even dance. The chroniclers of ghettos described how the hunger in the belly was sometimes allayed by satisfying the hunger of the soul.

While some ghetto leaders complied quickly and mechanically to Nazi directives, others encouraged resistance. One common denominator was their desire to buy time—time to save some of their people for the day of liberation. If that meant that the Jews would work for their tormentors, they must work. When the Germans ordered that the old and the young had to be given up, ghetto police tore apart screaming families. If a few could survive, Jewish existence could recover, that was the hope.

In the end the stratagem did not work. When the Soviet armies moved west into Poland, they found no living Jews in the ghettos.

Establishment of Judenräte (Jewish Councils) in the Occupied Territories, November 28, 1939

REGULATION FOR THE ESTABLISHMENT OF THE JUDENRÄTE, NOVEMBER 28, 1939

1. In each community a body representing the Jews will be formed.
2. This representation of the Jews, known as the Judenrat, will consist of 12 Jews in communities with up to 10,000 inhabitants, and in communities with more than 10,000 inhabitants, of 24 Jews, drawn from the locally resident population. The Judenrat will be elected by the Jews of the community. If a member of the Judenrat leaves, a new member is to be elected immediately.
3. The Judenrat will elect a chairman and a deputy from among its members.
4. 1) After these elections, which must be completed not later than December 31, 1939, the membership of the Judenrat is to be reported to the responsible sub-district Commander (*Kreishauptmann*), in urban districts to the City Commander (*Stadhauptmann*).
   2) The sub-district Commander (City Commander) will decide whether the Judenrat membership submitted to him should be approved. He may order changes in the membership.
5. It is the duty of the Judenrat through its chairman or his deputy to receive the orders of the German Administration. It is responsible for the conscientious carrying out of orders to their full extent. The directives it issues to carry out these German decrees must be obeyed by all Jews and Jewesses.

Cracow, November 28, 1939

The Governor General
for the Occupied Polish Territories
Frank

"Establishment of Judenräte (Jewish Councils) in the Occupied Territories, November 28, 1939," *Documents on the Holocaust: Selected Sources on the Destruction of the Jews of Germany and Austria, Poland, and the Soviet Union,* Yitzhak Arad, Yisrael Gutman, Abraham Margaliot eds. Jerusalem: Yad Vashem, 1981, pp. 191–192.
VBIGG, 1939, pp. 72–73.

Report by Uebelhoer on the Establishment of the Ghetto in Lodz, December 10, 1939

Top secret !

Establishment of a Ghetto in the City of Lodz

In Greater Lodz there are today 320,000 Jews* according to my estimate. Their immediate evacuation is not possible. Thorough investigations by all offices concerned indicate that it is possible to collect all the Jews in a closed ghetto. The Jewish question in the city of Lodz must be solved in the following manner for the time being:

1. The Jews living north of the line formed by Listopada Street...will be collected in a closed ghetto. Firstly, an area around the *Freiheitsplatz,* required for the establishment of a German power center, will be cleansed of Jews; and, secondly, the northern part of the city, which is inhabited almost exclusively by Jews, will be included in the ghetto.
2. Jews fit for work living in other parts of the city of Lodz will be collected for labor battalions, housed in barracks and guarded.

Preparations and execution of this plan will be carried out by a staff which will include representatives of the following authorities and offices:

1. N.S.D.A.P. (Nazi Party)
2. The [branch] office in Lodz of the Local Governor in Kalisch.
3. The City Administration of Lodz (Departments of Housing, Building, Health, Nutrition, etc.)
4. Order Police

"Report by Uebelhoer on the Establishment of the Ghetto in Lodz, December 10, 1939," *Documents on the Holocaust: Selected Sources on the Destruction of the Jews of Germany and Austria, Poland, and the Soviet Union,* Yitzhak Arad, Yisrael Gutman, Abraham Margaliot eds. Jerusalem: Yad Vashem, 1981, pp. 192–194.

Eksterminacja, pp. 77–81.

*The City of Lodz, which housed the second largest Jewish population in Poland, was included in the areas annexed to the Reich. According to the Record of *Pinkas ha-Kehillot Polin,* I., *Lodz ve-ha-Galil* ("Encyclopedia of Jewish Communities, Poland, I, The Communities of Lodz and its region"), Jerusalem, 1976, p. 24, the estimated number of Jews in Lodz in 1939 was 219,866.

5. Security Police
6. Death's Head Unit *(Totenkopfverband)* [of the SS]
7. Chamber of Trade and Industry
8. Finance Department

I shall serve as Chairman of the Staff for this operation....The first task of the Staff will be to decide on the borders of the ghetto that is to be established, and the settling of problems that will arise, such as the re-aligning of thoroughfares, tramway lines, etc. Further, it is to be ascertained immediately how many Germans and Poles still live in the area of the future ghetto, and will have to be resettled. At the same time, new apartments must be found for this group of persons and made available in order to ensure that the resettlement can be carried out without friction. As far as Germans are concerned, this will be done by the Party and the City Administration; as regards the Poles, it will be done by the City Administration alone....

After the preparations have been completed and sufficient guard personnel has been made available, the establishment of the ghetto will be carried out all at once, on a date to be decided by myself; this means that at a certain hour the intended border line of the ghetto will be manned by the guards provided for this purpose, and the streets closed by means of barbed-wire barriers and other measures. At the same time a start will be made on the blocking-up and sealing of the fronts of houses at the edge of the ghetto by Jewish labor to be taken from the ghetto. A Jewish autonomous administration will be set up immediately in the ghetto, consisting of the Jewish Elder *(Judenältester)* and a much enlarged Community Council. This Council of the ghetto must carry out the following tasks:

1. Department of Nutrition...
2. Department of Health...
3. Department of Finance...
4. Department of Security...
5. Department of Housing...
6. Department of Registration...

The Nutrition Department of the city of Lodz will deliver the required foodstuffs and fuel at locations in the ghetto still to be decided, and hand these over to the representative of the Jewish administration for distribution. The principle must be that foodstuffs and fuel can be paid for only by means of an exchange of materials, such as textiles, etc. In this way we should succeed in getting from the Jews all their hoarded and hidden items of value....

At the same time, i.e., shortly after the establishment of the ghetto, Jews living outside the ghetto who are unfit for work are to be moved off into the ghetto (Security Police, Order Police, City Administration). The apartments vacated in other parts of the city as a result of the removal of the Jews must be guarded against illegitimate interference. The strongest measures are to be taken against Jews who carry out malicious damage when they are forcibly moved from their apartments....

The creation of the ghetto is, of course, only a temporary measure. I reserve to myself the decision concerning the times and the means by which the ghetto and with it the city of Lodz will be cleansed of Jews. The final aim (*Endziel*) must in any case bring about the total cauterization of this plague spot.

Signed Uebelhoer

Rumkowski's Address at the Time of the Deportation of the Children from the Lodz Ghetto, September 4, 1942

...The ghetto has been struck a hard blow. They demand what is most dear to it—children and old people. I was not privileged to have a child of my own and therefore devoted my best years to children. I lived and breathed together with children. I never imagined that my own hands would be forced to make this sacrifice on the altar. In my old age I am forced to stretch out my hands and to beg: "Brothers and sisters, give them to me! —Fathers and mothers, give me your children...." (Bitter weeping shakes the assembled public)....Yesterday, in the course of the day, I was given the order to send away more than 20,000 Jews from the ghetto, and if I did not—"we will do it ourselves." The question arose: "Should we have accepted this and carried it out ourselves, or left it to others?" But as we were guided not by the thought: "how many will be lost?" but "how many can be saved?" we arrived at the conclusion—those closest to me at work, that is, and myself—that however difficult it was going to be, we must take upon ourselves the carrying out of this decree. I must carry out this difficult and bloody operation, I must cut off limbs in order to save the body! I must take away children, and if I do not, others too will be taken, God forbid...(terrible wailing).

I cannot give you comfort today. Nor did I come to calm you today, but to reveal all your pain and all your sorrow. I have come like a robber, to take from you what is dearest to your heart. I tried everything I knew to get the bitter sentence can-

---

"Rumkowski's Address at the Time of the Deportation of the Children from the Lodz Ghetto, September 4, 1942," *Documents on the Holocaust: Selected Sources on the Destruction of the Jews of Germany and Austria, Poland, and the Soviet Union*, Yitzhak Arad, Yisrael Gutman, Abraham Maraliot eds. Jerusalem: Yad Vashem, 1981, pp. 283–284.

I. Trunk, *Lodzsher Geto* ("Lodz Ghetto"), New York, 1962, pp. 311–312.

celled. When it could not be cancelled, I tried to lessen the sentence. Only yesterday I ordered the registration of nine-year-old children. I wanted to save at least one year—children from nine to ten. But they would not yield. I succeeded in one thing—to save the children over ten. Let that be our consolation in our great sorrow.

There are many people in this ghetto who suffer tuberculosis, whose days or perhaps weeks are numbered. I do not know, perhaps this is a satanic plan, and perhaps not, but I cannot stop myself from proposing it: "Give me these sick people, and perhaps it will be possible to save the healthy in their place." I know how precious each one of the sick is in his home, and particularly among Jews. But at a time of such decrees one must weigh up and measure who should be saved, who can be saved and who may be saved.

Common sense requires us to know that those must be saved who can be saved and who have a chance of being saved and not those whom there is no chance to save in any case....

Notes by a Jewish Observer in the Lodz Ghetto following the Deportation of the Children*

Lodz Ghetto   September 16, 1942

On September 5 the situation became clearer, and the frightening whispers of the past days became terrifying fact. The evacuation of children and old people took on the shape of reality. A small piece of paper on the wall in a busy part of the city announced an address by the President in an urgent matter. A huge crowd in Fire Brigade Square. The "Jewish Elder" will reveal the truth in the rumors. For it concerns the young, for whom he has great love, and the aged, for whom he has much respect. "It cannot be that they will tear the babes from their mothers' breasts, and drag old fathers and old mothers to some unknown place. The German is without mercy, he wages a terrible war,

"Notes by a Jewish Observer in the Lodz Ghetto Following the Deportation of the Children," *Documents on the Holocaust: Selected Sources on the Destruction of the Jews of Germany and Austria, Poland, and the Soviet Union*, Yitzhak Arad, Yisrael Gutman, Abraham Margaliot eds. Jerusalem: Yad Vashem, 1981, pp. 284–286.

Dokumenty i materialy, II, *Akcje i wysiedlenia* ("Documents and Records, II, *Aktionen* and Deportations", Warsaw..., 1946, pp. 243–246.
*From the description written by O. S. (Oscar Singer), a Czechoslovakian refugee and journalist who managed the Jewish archives in Lodz at the time of the Occupation.

but he will not go as far as that in cruelty." Everybody has faith in the President [Rumkowski] and hopes for words of comfort from him.

The representative of the ghetto is speaking. His voice fails him, the words stick in his throat. His personal appearance also mirrors the tragedy. One thing was understood by everybody: 20,000 persons must leave the ghetto, children under 10 and old people over 65....

Everybody is convinced that the Jews who are deported are taken to destruction....People ran here and there, crazed by the desire to hide the beloved victims. But nobody knew who would direct the *Aktion*: the Jewish Police, the Gestapo in the ghetto, or a mobile unit of the SS. The President, in coordination with the German authorities (Biebow) decided in his area of responsibility to carry out the deportation (with his own forces). It was the Jewish Police that had to tear the children from the mothers, to take the parents from their children....It was to be expected that parents and relatives would try in this situation to make changes and corrections in registered ages. Errors and inaccuracies that had not been corrected up to now did exist. Something that gives you the right to live today may well decide your fate tomorrow. There was a tendency to raise the age of the children, because a child from the age of 10 up could go to work and so be entitled to a portion of soup. Other parents lowered the age, because a younger child had a prospect of getting milk. Yesterday the milk and the soup were the most important things, today there is literally a question of staying alive. The age of the people also moved up and down for various reasons.

An unprecedented migration began to the Registration Office. The officials tried to manage the situation. They worked without stopping, day and night. The pressure of the people at the office windows increased all the time. The applicants yelled and wept and went wild. Every second could bring the death sentence, and hours passed in the struggle to restrain their passion....On Saturday the Gestapo already began on the operation [deportation], without paying any attention to the feverish work of registration that had been going on at No. 4 Church Square. Everyone had supposed that the Order Police [Jewish Police] would not stand the test. It could not itself carry out the work of the hangmen....

The little ones who were loaded on the cart behaved quietly, in submission, or yelling, according to their ages. The children of the ghetto, boys and girls less than 10 years old, are already mature and familiar with poverty and suffering. The young look around them with wide-open eyes and do not know what to do. They are on a cart for the first time in their lives, a cart that will be pulled by a real horse, a proper horse. They are looking forward to a gay ride. More than one of the little ones jumps for joy on the floor of the wagon as long as there is enough space. And at the same time his mother has almost gone out of her mind, twisting about on the ground and tearing the hair from her head in despair. It is difficult to overcome several thousand mothers. It is difficult to persuade them to give their children up willingly to death, as a sacrifice. It is difficult to take out the old people who hide in the smallest and most hidden corners.

All this was to be expected. The President imposed a general curfew which came into force at 5 o'clock on Sunday afternoon. Anyone who broke it was threatened with deportation.

Call to Resistance by the Jewish Fighting Organization in the Warsaw Ghetto, January 1943

TO THE JEWISH MASSES IN THE GHETTO

On January 22, 1943, six months will have passed since the deportations from Warsaw began. We all remember well the days of terror during which 300,000 of our brothers and sisters were cruelly put to death in the death camp of Treblinka. Six months have passed of life in constant fear of death, not knowing what the next day may bring. We have received information from all sides about the destruction of the Jews in the Government-General, in Germany, in the occupied territories. When we listen to this bitter news we wait for our own hour to come, every day and every moment. Today we must understand that the Nazi murderers have let us live only because they want to make use of our capacity to work to our last drop of blood and sweat, to our last breath. We are slaves. And when the slaves are no longer profitable, they are killed. Everyone among us must understand that, and everyone among us must remember it always.

During the past few weeks certain people have spread stories about letters that were said to have been received from Jews deported from Warsaw, who were said to be in labor camps near Minsk or Bobruisk. *Jews in your masses, do not believe these tales. They are spread by Jews who are working for the Gestapo.* The blood-stained murderers have a particular aim in doing this: to reassure the Jewish population in order that later the next deportation can be carried out without difficulty, with a minimum of force and without losses to the Germans. They want the Jews not to prepare hiding-places and not to resist. Jews, do not repeat these lying tales.

"Call to Resistance by the Jewish Fighting Organization in the Warsaw Ghetto, January 1943," *Documents on the Holocaust: Selected Sources on the Destruction of the Jews of Germany and Austria, Poland, and the Soviet Union,* Yitzhak Arad, Yisrael Gutman, Abraham Margaliot eds. Jerusalem: Yad Vashem, 1981, pp. 301–302.

Archiwum Zydowskiego Instytutu Historycznego w Polsce (Archives of the Jewish Historical Institute in Poland), ARII/333.

Do not help the [Nazi] agents. The Gestapo's dastardly people will get their just desserts. *Jews in your masses,* the hour is near. You must be prepared to resist, not to give yourselves up like sheep to slaughter. *Not even one Jew must go to the train. People who cannot resist actively must offer passive resistance, that is, by hiding.* We have now received information from Lvov that the Jewish Police there itself carried out the deportation of 3,000 Jews. Such things will not happen again in Warsaw. The killing of Lejkin proves it. Now our slogan must be:

Let everyone be ready to die like a man!

January 1943

Behind the Walls

Alexander Donat

The ordeal began on the sixth day of the war. On the evening of September 6, 1939, the government radio made an urgent appeal: German panzers had broken through Polish defenses and were headed for Warsaw; all able-bodied men were ordered to leave the capital immediately and assemble to the east, across the Bug River. A new army would be formed there to stand against the invaders.

My name was Michal Berg. My family had lived in Poland for generations and my father had settled down in Warsaw around the turn of the century. I was thirty-four years old then, publisher of the morning daily newspaper *Ostatnie Wiadomosci (Latest News),* a Warsaw tabloid. Hasty preparations, hurried farewells. With the paper's entire staff I joined the exodus, leaving behind my wife, Lena, and our twenty-one-month-old son, Wlodek.

Hundreds of thousands left Warsaw that night. In the pale twilight dawn, a torrent of people with knapsacks headed eastward on foot, bicycles, motorcycles, carts, carriages, automobiles, trucks, and buses. Through the golden shine of the Polish autumn the stream flowed east, or rather crawled. It was our first meeting with war's disorganization: burning towns, outbreaks of spy and paratroop manias, the despair of unbelievably swift defeat, and the incessant dive-bombing by Nazi Stukas.

Who can describe that fateful Polish September of 1939? In vain all Poland prayed for the miracle of rain, rain which would turn the notoriously bad Polish roads into swamps impassable to German tanks. But the sun shone with merciless brightness in a flawless sky. The army was on the run, the government was on the run, we were

Alexander Donat. "Behind the Walls" *The Holocaust Kingdom: A Memoir.* New York: Holocaust Library, 1978, pp. 3–12. Reprinted by permission of the Estate of Alexander Donat.

all on the run. In Lutsk, in southeastern Poland, we watched Soviet tanks rolling in. Allies, we thought at first.

The war ended for Poland on September 27. After a bitter battle Warsaw surrendered, and there seemed no further point in staying in Lutsk. Jews had to face the decision: to return to Nazi-occupied Warsaw to join their families, or to remain under Soviet rule. The new Nazi-Soviet border was not too difficult or too dangerous to cross. Wave after wave of refugees from Nazi-held Poland brought terrifying reports of what was happening there. From that side thousands fled Nazi persecution; from the other, thousands returned, overwhelmed by family attachments or possessions. How many lives might have been saved then, at the very beginning of the war, when the Soviet Union opened its gates to refugees from Nazism.

At the beginning of November I returned to Warsaw to take my wife and child to the security of the Soviet Union. But Lena refused to go. She took me on a tour of our beautiful seven-room apartment and talked about how miserable life was in Russia. It was November, already turning cold, and how could we expect to sneak across the frontier with a baby not yet two years old? And what about the seventy-two-year-old aunt who lived with us? And the rest of our family? Lena was sure the Germans would be vicious, but what could happen to women and children? She was a licensed pharmacist, and war or no war they would need her. She could support herself and our son. But I was in danger. Hadn't I published the *Brown Book* and other exposés of the Nazis? The sensible thing was for me to return to the Soviet-held sector of Poland. The war wouldn't last long and we'd be reunited then. In the meantime, they'd make out somehow.

She persuaded me and I went back via the well-known escape route Malkinia-Bialystok. But not for long. Rumors grew more persistent that the borders were going to be closed and all contact with the Nazi-held area cut off, that refugees would be registered and have to opt for Soviet citizenship. This meant separation from my family, perhaps for a lifetime. I knew it was a fateful decision and I made it. At the end of December 1939, I set out for Warsaw once more, but now it wasn't easy. The frontier was well guarded, and the trip in temperatures of forty below was not uneventful. Finally, on January 2, 1940, I did succeed in rejoining my family in Warsaw, to share with them whatever fate had in store for all of us. I was there to stand and fall with them, to shield and protect. We knew we faced dreadful anguish, but never in our wildest dreams did we anticipate the ultimate holocaust. On this road to calvary I entered in love and humility, even with a drop of pride.

One of the results of the September exodus and the subsequent migrations to the East was that Warsaw Jewry was a body without a head. Leaders in every walk of life had left. We needed heroes and were left with mediocrities. To these the Nazis handed the tragic scepter of a spurious "Jewish autonomy," and these men were to lead us along the tortuous road to disaster. An early decree (October 4, 1939) appointed a Jewish Council, the *Judenrat,* as the supreme authority of the Jewish community of Warsaw. Its head was to be titled *Obmann,* or "Elder of the Jews," and an engineer named Adam Czerniakow was appointed to the job. He in turn co-opted twenty-four councilors to serve with him. So was born the monstrous organization which came to be so bitterly hated by Jews. Czerniakow and the Council members—many of whom I knew personally—were in the main decent men who honestly hoped to serve the Jewish community. The theory was that it was desirable to have a buffer between the Jewish population at large and the Nazi occupation authorities, and the *Judenrat* would be that buffer.

Warsaw Jews had never paid much attention or given much respect to their community leaders and therefore the appointment of the *Judenrat* made little stir. No one was eager to serve on it. Because Jews had been excluded from civil service in pre-war Poland, the *Judenrat*'s aides and staff workers were men without skill or experience, inefficient and time-serving, prone to nepotism and corruption.

After I returned from Lutsk our apartment in Orla Street was jampacked, sufficiently crowded to suit even the taste of the *Judenrat*'s housing authority. In addition to my wife and my son, there was our elderly Aunt Sarah Eisner, who kept house for us; Stefa, a Gentile governess, indispensable since my wife was now the breadwinner of the family; Miriam Orleska, a well-known Jewish actress; Rudolf Langer, a lawyer, and his wife; Ignacy Moskowicz, a former Lodz textile manufacturer, and his wife; and Slawka Szenwic, an office girl whose mother later joined her after being deported from Plock.

The Jewish intelligentsia was the first target in the Nazi process of pauperizing the Jews. Lawyers were no longer permitted to appear in court; doctors were forbidden to have non-Jewish patients; journalists, writers, artists, musicians, and teachers were now all superfluous because practicing their professions had been declared illegal. Their very existence was an anachronism. Without practical skills or experience, such people were ill adapted to survive in the jungle Warsaw was swiftly becoming.

It is not easy to declass oneself, even if one is willing, but the most energetic intellectuals got into trade in the early stages of the German occupation. They became dealers in foreign currencies, gold, dry goods, wrist watches, flour, anything they could lay their hands on that could be sold or traded. Unfortunately many discovered that trade is no occupation for normal people in abnormal times, I was one of those.

Nothing had prepared me for such a life. After a very few attempts, it was clear I would never be a success as a businessman. A cousin of mine phrased it succinctly: "As a businessman, you're a good carpenter." When I bought anything, prices instantly sank; when I sold, prices doubled the next day. I still knew how to operate a linotype, a skill learned in my student days, but such skill was as much in demand as the ability to teach classical philology.

Not only intellectuals suffered under the Nazis; all Jews were fair game for persecution. Beginning in December, 1939, every Jew over twelve was required to wear the Jewish arm band. Quite an industry sprang up to produce these arm bands; some were made of finest linen, with or without embroidery, but there were paper and celluloid ones, too. For the first few weeks arm band peddlers loudly hawked their wares and except for a few rare rebels, Jews accepted the arm bands and wore them with dignity, feeling that to do so disgraced not us but those who imposed them on us.

No Jew was permitted to have more than 2,000 zlotys in cash either on his person or in his home. The remainder of his money had to be deposited in a bank from which be was permitted to withdraw no more than 500 zlotys a month. When currency-control measures were invoked, everyone had to have his paper money validated at a bank. Long queues lined up at bank windows, but Jews were forcibly thrown out and subjected to other indignities. Jews also had to file special returns detailing all their wealth. Synagogues were closed down and Jews prohibited from assembling for religious services as an antityphus measure. Jews who wanted to travel needed special passes, presumably a precaution against "the spreading of typhus by Jewish black marketeers." In sections of the city where many Jews lived posters in the streets warned passersby: "This is a quarantined zone."

Nazi commissars (*Treuhänder*) were put in charge of every branch of Jewish business and property. These so-called trustees had orders never to pay bills owed to Jewish firms or individuals, but to collect all debts Jews owed. No Jewish creditor was permitted to collect a debt, but every Jewish debtor bad to pay up all his own debts and, in some cases, the debts of others as well. Tax officials began to force payments of every conceivable kind of tax, legitimately owed or not. The moment a German trustee took charge, all Jewish employees were dismissed from their jobs and all contracts with Jewish suppliers were canceled. In this manner the very roots of Jewish economic life were sapped.

The most unmistakable indication of Nazi intentions concerning the Jews was the food ration. Germans in Warsaw were allotted 2,500 calories a day and could obtain a wide variety of goods at fixed prices in special stores. The Jewish ration came to less than 200 calories a day for which Jews paid twenty times the price Germans did.

Jews resisted as best they could. They tried to arrange for trustees over their affairs who came from among their Polish or *Volksdeutsch* (ethnic German) friends. They could then continue business on a "partnership" basis by sharing the profits with the trustee. Others managed to make deals with the trustees who were imposed on them. When the Postal Savings Bank (P.K.O.) blocked all Jewish accounts, German acquaintances could be persuaded to make false claims against the accounts of Jews alleged to owe them money. The German acquaintances would then share the money received with the owners of the accounts.

There was a stubborn, unending, continuous battle to survive. In view of the unequal forces, it was a labor of Sisyphus. Jewish resistance was the resistance of a fish caught in a net, a mouse in a trap, an animal at bay. It is pure myth that the Jews were merely "passive," that they did not put up resistance to the Nazis who had decreed their destruction. The Jews fought back against their enemies to a degree no other community anywhere in the world would have been capable of were it to find itself similarly beleaguered. They fought against hunger and starvation, against disease, against a deadly Nazi economic blockade. They fought against murderers and against traitors within their own ranks, and they were utterly alone in their fight. They were forsaken by God and by man, surrounded by hatred or indifference. Ours was not a romantic war.

Although there was much heroism, there was little beauty; much toil and suffering, but no glamour. We fought back on every front where the enemy attacked—the biological front, the economic front, the propaganda front, the cultural front—with every weapon we possessed.

In the end, it was ruse, deception, cunning beyond anything the world had ever before seen, which accomplished what hunger and disease, terror and treachery could not achieve. What defeated us, was Jewry's unconquerable optimism, our eternal faith in the goodness of man, our faith that even a German, even a Nazi, could never have so far renounced his own humanity as to murder women and children coldly and systematically. And when, finally, we saw how we had been deceived, and resorted to the weapon which we were least well prepared to use—historically, ideologically, and psychologically—that is, when we finally took up arms, we inscribed in the book of history the unforgettable epic of the Ghetto Uprising.

One of the most powerful instruments of Jewish self-defense sprang up spontaneously during the first weeks of the war. Tenants' Committees (so-called House Committees) were organized in every apartment house. Where the *Judenrat* was an institution created by the Nazi occupiers to transmit their decrees to the Jewish population, the Tenants' Committees were created by the Jews themselves to defend their own interests. The man who promoted them in Warsaw was generally believed to be the eminent historian, Emanuel Ringelblum. Eventually the individual house committees were grouped into a federation, the Z.T.O.S. (*Zydowskie Towarzystwo Opieki Spolecznej*), the Jewish Society of Social Welfare, and what remained of active social and intellectual leadership in Warsaw gravitated toward this organization. As the *Judenrat* became increasingly remote from the people, the Z.T.O.S. became more closely identified with them. These committees resisted all efforts by the *Judenrat* to make them its tools and they also served as the core of opposition to it. Small wonder, then, that the Z.T.O.S. was unpopular with the *Judenrat* and later also with the Jewish police.

The Tenants' Committees were democratically elected and served as the real authority in each apartment house. At first they confined themselves to helping poor tenants, especially poor children. Gradually their activities were extended to health and hygiene, education and entertainment. In some buildings they organized communal kitchens and coordinated fuel and food purchases. At one stage a certificate issued by any Tenants' Committee was a document respected and honored by all Jewish authorities. The first big campaign the Committees organized was a clothing collection for Jewish prisoners of war who came back to Warsaw in large numbers in March, 1940. Forbidden to wear their uniforms and without any civilian clothes, these men were helped by the Tenants' Committees.

But even the Tenants' Committees were helpless against the mounting plague of looting. Any German, in uniform or not, could rob a Jewish house or individual with impunity. Many highly placed occupation authorities, including all ranks in the *Wehrmacht* and *Schutzstaffel* (SS) as well as German and *Volksdeutsch* civilians, were officially and unofficially involved in looting. So were some Jewish criminals who tipped Germans off about the best places to plunder, or threatened Jews that they would do so in order to blackmail them. The Germans stole goods off the shelves of stores; furniture from private homes; bed linen, silver, glassware, rugs, paintings, china, cameras. They even stole food—coffee, tea, and cocoa being most popular.

To carry off what they wanted, the Germans would stop Jews in the streets and force them to help move the heavier things. Victims of the robbery themselves were also "persuaded" to help. Such situations gave rise to all kinds of abuse. But in time the German thieves lost confidence in the reliability of these Jewish "assistants," because pieces of furniture that came down one flight of stairs mysteriously mounted another flight, and somehow found their way back to where they had been in the first place.

In the early days of the occupation, many Jews, especially those who lived in predominantly non-Jewish neighborhoods, were simply dispossessed by Germans who took their apartments and everything in them. Victims were permitted to take no more than a small valise at the time of eviction and were frequently beaten up as well if they did not seem sufficiently delighted with what was being done to them. I know of one elderly couple who, in anticipation of being robbed, had carefully buried their valuables in the walls or under the floors of their apartment. When they were suddenly evicted, they lost not only their home and furniture, but also all their buried treasure.

Persecution of Jews was not at first well organized. A German would simply attack a Jew in the street, and there were many who obviously enjoyed that kind of thing. A speeding car might swerve to the curb, Germans jump out of it and set on the first Jew they met. Anything might serve as a pretext. Some Jews were beaten for not having taken off their hats, others for having done so—"You don't know me. I'm no friend of yours."—and some for politely stepping off the sidewalk when they saw Germans coming. Still others for having failed to do so. Arm-band etiquette might also serve as an excuse: arm bands were being worn too high or too low, were dirty or torn, or were too elegant and expensive-looking.

Assaults in the street became more and more frequent. A few Germans would stop some decently dressed Jews and order them to sweep the street, abusing them for the amusement of passersby. Later such incidents became more serious. One lady walking in the street wearing a Persian lamb coat was dragged to Gestapo headquarters. There she was ordered to take off her underwear and scrub the floor with it. Then, made to put the dirty, wet underwear back on, she was thrown into the street without her coat. It was a very cold day and she caught pneumonia and died.

The main centers of Nazi terror were in three places: Gestapo headquarters in Szuch Avenue; a building in Wiejska Street where the Polish parliament had formerly been housed; and Blanks Palace in Senatorska Street. All three became notorious as torture chambers in the first months of the occupation.

Hunger, filth, and disease increased by leaps and bounds because the Germans were herding thousands of Jews into Warsaw daily. Most were penniless and only a handful could look after themselves; the bulk succumbed to the dreadful conditions of the refugee reception centers. The threat of typhus was everywhere. It was a feat to move through the crowded streets without coming into contact with lice-infested individuals. I knew people who stayed in their apartments for months to avoid contacts of that kind and yet, in the end, found that they too had lice. Lice were so ubiquitous that people began to tell each other quite seriously that typhus was not only a lice-borne disease but also airborne.

On the floor above our Orla Street apartment there lived Dr. lzrael Milejkowski, the *Judenrat* member in charge of public health. In the evenings after curfew he often dropped by for a cup of tea and we either played cards or talked politics late into the night. Small, with a Mephistophelian smile, he was an ardent Zionist, had a fine sense of humor, and always knew the latest jokes. Milejkowski took his work very seriously and often discussed it with us. For hours on end he described the unequal struggle against hunger and typhus which was decimating the Jewish population. Worst of all were the conditions in the reception centers for recent Jewish refugees from other parts of Poland. The mortality rate was climbing appallingly swiftly and in his judgment our survival depended on checking the typhus epidemic.

Though Milejkowski was a dedicated physician, he could do almost nothing in the face of the conditions decreed by the authorities of the Third Reich. And his German counterpart and superior, Dr. Wilhelm Hagen, treated him and his efforts with contempt, and gave him no co-operation. Milejkowski and his aide Dr. Antoni Wortman, honest men with the best of intentions, could not even control their own employees. The *Judenrat* disinfection squads were composed of hungry people concerned with the fate of their own families. A few zlotys were enough to bribe them. The rich therefore bribed their way out of the fumigation proceedings, which they thought would damage their properties, and only the poor people were induced to follow the prescribed delousing procedure. This made the entire elaborate public health program a farce. No matter how rigorous the rules, doctors could be persuaded not to report cases of typhus so that the patient might remain in an overcrowded apartment where he would certainly infect others. Besides, there never was enough room in the hospitals. In addition, fumigation equipment was of the poorest quality and the "soul snatchers," as those fumigation squads were called, never sealed the rooms as hermetically as they should have; nor was there ever enough coal to provide hot water and steam in the delousing baths.

One day Dr. Milejkowski came home visibly shaken. His face was ashen and he seemed to have aged immeasurably. At one of the refugee reception centers an eight-year-old child had gone out of his mind with hunger, and begun to scream, "I want to rob and steal. I want to eat. I want to be a German!" Milejkowski also told us that at the funeral of some children who had died of hunger, the children in the orphans' home in Wolska Street had sent a wreath inscribed, "From children who are starving to children who have died of starvation." Milejkowski wept as he told me this, and we cried with him. We felt powerless. The same thing would be happening tomorrow and the day after that and the day after that.

Destitute former musicians wandered the streets and in the courtyards all day long, turning Warsaw into a city of song. It was enough to drive one mad. They were, of course, trying to earn a living and, after a month or two of this, they would be forced to sell their instruments and be standing at the street corners with outstretched palms. A little later their bodies and those of their families would be found in the streets one morning covered with newspapers—a common enough sight—which no one got used to.

Chapter 9

The Genocide

INTRODUCTION

Survivors of the Holocaust have given personal history a new legitimacy. Their memoirs summon up their own experiences while they also speak for the millions who died at the hands of the Nazis. We, who did not share their past, cannot imagine the extent of their suffering. We can only marvel at their courage to relive their pain a second time in the process of remembering and committing words to paper.

The number of Holocaust autobiographies has not abated. The deniers of the Holocaust compel some survivors, silent for more than fifty years, to finally record their stories. If they do not do so now, then when? They are aging and dying and soon none will be left. Every detail they recall adds a fragment to the picture of an alien world; a world where women and children were slain first, where lies became truth and the truth a lie. Technocrats devised murder on the assembly line and men with college degrees supervised the slaughter. The entire procedure of annihilation was based on the falsehood that Jews were genetically programed to be the mortal enemy of everything German. It is this irrationality which places the Holocaust beyond our common sense understanding. How tempting it is to argue that because such an event *could* not happen, it *did* not happen.

Although the details of survivors' experiences differ according to particular circumstances, there are several recurring threads. Almost universal is the need to summon to mind the people who were killed. The closer the kinship, the greater the urgency to remember them. Parents, brothers and sisters, and particularly the children who were murdered are lovingly recalled. Remembrance of the touch of a hand, the sweetness of a smile, the sound of a voice, gives a moment of life to the dead. There is pain in memory but also comfort. The words on a page acknowledge the fact that even though there is no picture, no grave, the loved ones are mourned and never forgotten.

162

Many Holocaust survivors visit classrooms. Students invariably ask them how they account for their own survival when so many others died. What did you do? How were you different? Younger? Stronger? Smarter? The answers are rarely what the students expected to hear. "No, I was no better than six million others, many of the dead were probably stronger than I and wiser, but luck was with me. Mainly, survival was a matter of luck. By chance I was pushed onto a train that went to a slave labor and not a death camp. By accident, not by my design, was I assigned to work which did not kill me in a matter of weeks. When I was ill and we stood for hours in the freezing rain, it was my good fortune that friends held me up. Many times the issue of my life or death was decided by events over which I had no control. Credit my preservation to God if you wish, or fate, or friends, but not to any qualities within me."

A theme that echoes in many of the memoirs concerns the ignorance of the Eastern Jews concerning the fate that awaited them. No information about Nazi intentions had reached them. They knew of pogroms of the past, but total genocide was without precedent and certainly would not be carried out by such a highly civilized people as the Germans. That was quite unthinkable. Thus, many victims, Jews and Gentiles as well, were unprepared to resist or escape the mobile killing squads that followed Hitler's armies. When the fine looking officers and men of the *Einsatzgruppen* ordered Jews to assemble, they assembled. Whole villages and towns were emptied of their Jewish population before the unbelievable was believed: the Germans meant to kill them all.

The executions by the *Einsatzgruppen* were followed by the construction of mass killing centers. Trains from all the conquered lands rolled into the death camps. Eventually rumors circulated that "resettlement" was a euphemism for wholesale killings. But even then it was impossible for many people to accept the truth. As the memoirs of the survivors testify, such reports were rarely believed. Hope was the last refuge of a people abandoned by the rest of mankind. Even when standing in the line before the deadly showers, many of the victims denied the terrifying reality. The Germans, wanting an orderly procedure, maintained the fiction of the "delousing bath" to the very door of the gas chambers.

Survivors frequently express the fear that when the living corroborators of the Holocaust are gone, the murder of the six million will be forgotten. They need not worry. Not as long as the students like you relive their experiences through words and pictures.

Protocol of the Wannsee Conference, January 20, 1942

Reich Secret Document
30 copies

PROTOCOL OF CONFERENCE

I. The following took part in the conference on the final solution (*Endlösung*) of the Jewish question held on January 20, 1942, in Berlin, Am Grossen Wannsee No. 56-58:

Gauleiter Dr. Meyer and Reich, Office Director Dr. Leibbrandt	Reich Ministry for the Occupied Eastern Territories
Secretary of State Dr. Stuckart	Reich Ministry of the Interior
Secretary of State Neumann	Plenipotentiary for the Four Year Plan
Secretary of State Dr. Freisler	Reich Ministry of Justice
Secretary of State Dr. Bühler	Office of the Governor General
Undersecretary of State Dr. Luther	Foreign Ministry
SS *Oberführer* Klopfer	Party Chancellery
Ministerial Director Kritzinger	Reich Chancellery
SS *Gruppenführer* Hofmann	Race and Settlement Main Office
SS *Gruppenführer* Müller	Reich Security Main Office
SS *Obersturmbaniführer* Eichmann	Reich Security Main Office
SS *Oberführer* Dr. Schöngarth, Commander of the Security Police and the SD in the Government-General	Security Police and SD

"Protocol of the Wannsee Conference, January 20, 1942," *Documents on the Holocaust: Selected Sources on the Destruction of the Jews of Germany and Austria, Poland, and the Soviet Union,* Yitzhak Arad, Yisrael Gutman, Abraham Margaliot eds. Jerusalem: Yad Vashem, 1981, pp. 249–261.

SS *Sturmbannführer* Dr. Lange,   Security Police and SD
   Commander of the Security
   Police and the SD in the
   Generalbezirk Latvia as
   Representative of the Commander
   of the Security Police and the SD
   for the *Reichskommissariat*
   for the *Ostland*

II. The meeting opened with the announcement by the Chief of the Security Police and the SD, SS *Obergruppenführer* Heydrich, of his appointment by the Reich Marshal[1] as Plenipotentiary for the Preparation of the Final Solution of the European Jewish Question.[2] He noted that this Conference had been called in order to obtain clarity on questions of principle. The Reich Marshal's request for a draft plan concerning the organizational, practical and economic aspects of the final solution of the European Jewish question required prior joint consideration by all central agencies directly involved in these questions, with a view to maintaining parallel policy lines.

Responsibility for the handling of the final solution of the Jewish question, he said, would lie centrally with the *Reichsführer* SS and the Chief of the German Police (Chief of the Security Police and the SD), without regard to geographic boundaries.

The Chief of the Security Police and the SD then gave brief review of the struggle conducted up to now against this foe.

The most important elements are:

a) Forcing the Jews out of the various areas of life (*Lebensgebiete*) of the German people.
b) Forcing the Jews out of the living space (*Lebensraum*) of the German people.

In pursuit of these aims, the accelerated emigration of the Jews from the area of the Reich, as the only possible provisional solution, was pressed forward and carried out according to plan.

On instructions by the Reich Marshal, a Reich Central Office for Jewish Emigration[3] was set up in January 1939, and its direction entrusted to the Chief of the Security Police and the SD. Its tasks were, in particular:

a) To take all measures for the *preparation* of increased emigration of the Jews;
b) To *direct* the flow of emigration;
c) To speed up emigration in *individual* cases.

The aim of this task was to cleanse the German living space of Jews in a legal manner.

The disadvantages engendered by such forced pressing of emigration were clear to all the authorities. But in the absence of other possible solutions, they had to be accepted for the time being.

In the period that followed, the handling of emigration was not a German problem alone, but one with which the authorities of the countries of destination or immigration also had to deal. Financial difficulties—such as increases ordered by the various foreign governments in the sums of money that immigrants were required to have and in landing fees—as well as lack of berths on ships and continually tightening restrictions or bans on immigration, hampered emigration efforts very greatly. Despite these difficulties a total of approximately 537,000 Jews were caused to emigrate between the [Nazi] assumption of power and up to October 31, 1941.

These consisted of the following:

From January 30, 1933:	from the *Altreich* [Germany before 1938]	Approx. 360,000
From March 15, 1938:	from the *Ostmark* [Austria]	Approx. 147,000
From March 15, 1939:	from the Protectorate of Bohemia and Moravia	Approx. 30,000

The financing of the emigration was carried out by the Jews or Jewish political organizations themselves. To prevent the remaining behind of proletarianized Jews, the principle was observed that wealthy Jews must finance the emigration of the Jews without means; to this end, a special assessment or emigration levy, in accordance with wealth owned, was imposed, the proceeds being used to meet the financial obligations of the emigration of destitute Jews.

In addition to the funds raised in German marks, foreign currency was needed for the monies which emigrants were required to show on arrival abroad and for landing fees. To conserve the German holdings of foreign currency, Jewish financial institutions abroad were persuaded by Jewish organizations in this country to make themselves responsible for finding the required sums in foreign currency. A total of about $9,500,000 was provided by these foreign Jews as gifts up to October 30, 1941.

In the meantime, in view of the dangers of emigration in war-time, and the possibilities in the East, the *Reichsführer* SS and Chief of the German Police has forbidden the emigration of Jews.[4]

III. Emigration has now been replaced by evacuation of the Jews to the East, as a further possible solution, with the appropriate prior authorization by the Führer.

However, this operation should be regarded only as a provisional option; but it is already supplying practical experience of great significance in view of the coming final solution of the Jewish question.

In the course of this final solution of the European Jewish question approximately 11 million Jews may be taken into consideration, distributed over the individual countries as follows:

Country	Number
A. *Altreich*	131,800
Ostmark	43,700
Eastern Territories[5]	420,000
Government-General	2,284,000
Bialystok	400,000
Protectorate of Bohemia and Moravia	74,200
Estonia—free of Jews	
Latvia	3,500
Lithuania	34,000
Belgium	43,000
Denmark	5,600
France: Occupied territory	165,000
France: Unoccupied territory	700,000
Greece	69,600
Netherlands	160,800
Norway	1,300
B. Bulgaria	48,000
England	330,000
Finland	2,300
Ireland	4,000
Italy, including Sardinia	58,000
Albania	200
Croatia	40,000
Portugal	3,000
Rumania, including Bessarabia	342,000
Sweden	8,000
Switzerland	18,000
Serbia	10,000
Slovakia	88,000
Spain	6,000
Turkey (in Europe)	55,000
Hungary	742,800
U.S.S.R.	5,000,000
Ukraine	2,994,684
Byelorussia, without Bialystok	446,484
Total:	over 11,000,000

As far as the figures for Jews of the various foreign countries are concerned, the numbers given include only Jews by religion (*Glaubensjuden*), since the definition of Jews according to racial principles is in part still lacking there. Owing to the prevailing attitudes and concepts, the handling of this problem in the individual countries will encounter certain difficulties, especially in Hungary and Rumania. For instance, in Rumania the Jew can still obtain, for money, documents officially certifying that he holds foreign citizenship.

The influence of the Jews in all spheres of life in the U.S.S.R. is well known. There are about 5 million Jews in European Russia, and barely another 250,000 in Asiatic Russia.

...

Under appropriate direction the Jews are to be utilized for work in the East in an expedient manner in the course final solution. In large (labor) columns, with the sexes separated, Jews capable of work will be moved into these areas as they build roads, during which a large proportion will no doubt drop out through natural reduction. The remnant that eventually remains will require suitable treatment; because it will without doubt represent the most [physically] resistant part, it consists of a natural selection that could, on its release, become the germ cell of a new Jewish revival. (Witness the experience of history.)

Europe is to be combed through from West to East in the course of the practical implementation of the final solution. The area of the Reich, including the Protectorate of Bohemia and Moravia, will have to be handled in advance, if only because of the housing problem and other socio-political needs.

The evacuated Jews will first be taken, group by group, to so-called transit ghettos, in order to be transported further east from there.

An important precondition, SS *Obergruppenführer* Heydrich noted further, for the carrying out of the evacuation in general is the precise determination of the groups of persons involved. It is intended not to evacuate Jews over 65 years old, but to place them in an old-age ghetto—Theresienstadt is being considered.

In addition to these age groups—about 30% of the 280,000 Jews who were present in the *Altreich* and the *Ostmark* October 31, 1941, were over 65 years old— Jews with severe war injuries and Jews with war decorations (Iron Cross, First Class) will be admitted to the Jewish old-age ghetto. This suitable solution will eliminate at one blow the many applications for exceptions.

The start of the individual major evacuation *Aktionen* will depend largely on military developments. With regard to the handling of the final solution in the European areas occupied by us and under our influence, it was proposed that the officials dealing with this subject in the Foreign Ministry should confer with the appropriate experts in the Security Police and the SD.

In Slovakia and Croatia the matter is no longer too difficult, as the most essential, central problems in this respect have already been brought to a solution there. In Rumania the government has in the meantime also appointed a Plenipotentiary for Jewish Affairs. In order to settle the problem in Hungary, it will be necessary in the near future to impose an adviser for Jewish questions on the Hungarian Government.

With regard to setting in motion preparations for the settling of the problem in Italy, SS *Obergruppenführer* Heydrich considers liaison with the Police Chief in these matters would be in place.

In occupied and unoccupied France the rounding-up of the Jews for evacuation will, in all probability, be carried out without great difficulties.

On this point, Undersecretary of State Luther stated that far-reaching treatment of this problem would meet with difficulties in some countries, such as the Nordic States, and that it was therefore advisable to postpone action in these countries for the present. In view of the small number of Jews involved there, the postponement will in any case not occasion any significant curtailment. On the other hand, the Foreign Ministry foresees no great difficulties for the south-east and west of Europe.

SS *Gruppenführer* Hofmann intends to send a specialist from the Main Office for Race and Settlement to Hungary for general orientation when the subject is taken in hand there by the Chief of the Security Police and the SD. It was decided that this specialist from the Race and Settlement Main Office, who is not to take an active part, will temporarily be designated officially as Assistant to the Police Attaché.

IV. In the implementation of the plan for the final solution, the Nuremberg Laws are to form the basis,[6] as it were; a precondition for the total clearing up of the problem will also require solutions for the question of mixed marriages and *Mischlinge*.

…

SS *Gruppenführer* Hofmann is of the opinion that extensive use must be made of sterilization, as the *Mischling,* given the choice of evacuation or sterilization, would prefer to accept sterilization.

Secretary of State Dr. Stuckart noted that in this form the practical aspects of the possible solutions proposed above for the settling of the problems of mixed marriages and *Mischlinge* would entail endless administrative work. In order to take the biological realities into account, at any rate, Secretary of State Dr. Stuckart proposed a move in the direction of compulsory sterilization.

To simplify the problem of the *Mischlinge* further possibilities should be considered, with the aim that the Legislator should rule something like: "These marriages are dissolved."

As to the question of the effect of the evacuation of the Jews on the economy, Secretary of State Neumann stated that Jews employed in essential war industries could not be evacuated for the present, as long as no replacements were available.

SS *Obergruppenführer* Heydrich pointed out that those Jews would not be evacuated in any case, in accordance with the directives approved by him for the implementation of the current evacuation *Aktion.*

Secretary of State Dr. Bühler put on record that the Government-General would welcome it if the final solution of this problem *was begun in the Government-General,* as, on the one hand, the question of transport there played no major role and considerations of labor supply would not hinder the course of this *Aktion.* Jews must be removed as fast as possible from the Government-General, because it was there in particular that the Jew as carrier of epidemics spelled a great danger, and, at the same time, he caused constant disorder in the economic structure of the country by his continuous black-market dealings. Furthermore, of the approximately 2½ million Jews under consideration, the majority were in any case *unfit for work.*

Secretary of State Dr. Bühler further states that the solution of the Jewish question in the Government-General was primarily the responsibility of the Chief of the Security Police and the SD and that his work would have the support of the authorities of the Government-General. He had only one request: that the Jewish question in this area be solved as quickly as possible.

In conclusion, there was a discussion of the various possible forms which the solution might take, and here both *Gauleiter* Dr. Meyer and Secretary of State Dr. Bühler were of the opinion that certain preparatory work for the final solution should be carried out locally in the area concerned, but that in doing so, alarm among the population must be avoided.

The conference concluded with the request of the Chief of the Security Police and the SD to the participants at the conference to give him the necessary support in carrying out the tasks of the [final] solution.

NOTES

[1]Reich Marshal Hermann Göring.
[2]See Document 106.
[3]See Document 57.
[4]See Document 68.
[5]The reference is to the districts of western Poland annexed to the Reich.
[6]See Documents 32, 33, 34.

The Survivor in Us All
Four Young Sisters
in the Holocaust

Erna F. Rubinstein

The fire did not consume us physically, yet something had happened to me. I felt as if the whole inside of my body was taken out and the remainder—that is, the outer body, the legs and the eyes—were marching on.

I could not feel anything. I tried to tell myself that my mother had just been taken from me, yet I didn't feel the loss. I tried to tell myself that Tola, Henia, and Renia, my very best friends, had been taken away, segregated, and were probably burning in that fire, yet I still had no feeling of loss. All I could feel was the discomfort of the wooden Dutch shoes on my feet and the cold air on my exposed breasts.

I must also add that as I looked around at my sisters and the others and saw the funny clothes they were wearing, I couldn't help but laugh. Somebody pointed out: "Hanka, that evening dress fits you beautifully." I looked at her and began to laugh hysterically. Hanka was short and the dress was long; she had to hold it up to avoid tripping over it. The funniest part was that with our hair shaven completely, we looked rather like little hairless monkeys.

I shall never forget the way my sister Anna looked. She had been handsome. Her features were strong but not coarse, her nose straight, her mouth well shaped and not too small. Her great beauty lay in her eyes. They were exceedingly clear, the black and white pure and separate. When I looked at her now, all I could see were the white and black of her eyes. They looked like two large balls attached to a bony face with long legs. With her dark hair shaven, her scalp was very white. The striped pajama top she had been given scarcely covered her buttocks, and her long legs wobbled in wooden shoes of two different sizes. I cursed the Dutch for making them. They added considerably to our misery. When we put them on at night, our feet were wet and cold. By the time we had taken a few steps, the skin of our feet was rubbed off, and we could hardly walk. Yet we marched, we marched to the beat of the SS men's boots. We arrived in Birkenau, Lager B2B.

I didn't know how long we marched or where or how far. I had no feelings, no desire to live, or to die. I was just numb.

When I found myself lying down, I went to sleep. I think I could have slept forever if it hadn't been for the whistles blowing, noises, and shouts all around me.

From Erna F. Rubinstein, *The Survivor in Us All: Four Young Sisters in the Holocaust*. North Haven, CT: Archon Books, 1983, pp 123–128. © 1983 by Erna Rubinstein. Reprinted by permission of Archon Books, North Haven, CT.

When I came to, I was told that it was four o'clock in the morning and we had to go outside.

My sister Pola took my hand and pulled me along with her. In no time, we were standing in fives. A young girl who couldn't have been more than fifteen, chubby with red cheeks and her hair combed neatly, blew the whistle. "Undress!" she shouted.

She was what we called a "Capo." The Germans didn't want to waste their manpower in small positions, so they trained the prisoners to do the dirty work for them. Most of the inmates of Auschwitz were dehumanized to such an extent that it didn't matter what kind of work they did, as long as they could get a little more food and a bed they didn't have to share with twelve other people. At a time when nothing else mattered and the chance for survival was becoming less and less, the job of being a Capo was the last straw. Not everybody could stomach behaving like a monster, punishing their own people and, as at Auschwitz, quite often sending them to the gas chambers. But there were those who did take the job—some by choice, and many others selected by the Germans.

In seconds we had freed ourselves of our clothing—there were no undergarments, of course—and stood naked. We had stood like that the first day and would for many days to come. When nobody was watching us, we would sit down for a moment. But no sooner had we begun to rest when the voice of the Devil behind that angelic face screamed; "Get up! stand up!"

The Capo had a whip in her hand and always let us know she meant business. The whip would flick our naked bodies and burn like hell. We couldn't figure her out. She spoke Czech, so she must have been from Czechoslovakia. She was very young, and at first we couldn't understand what made her so vicious toward us. Every now and then I would try to talk to her, and she would look at me, seemingly friendly, but just when I thought she was ready to say something to me, she would shout: "Go away, go away, before I punch you!"

Later we learned that she had been one of the early comers to Auschwitz and had been chosen to dig a grave for her parents and her sisters. For a while, she had worked in the crematorium. She had been educated to be tough. The poor soul didn't even know why she did what she did.

At noon, we were given a bowl of soup. At first, we were reluctant to drink it because we were told that it had some medication in it to stop us from menstruating. Some said that we would lose our womanhood completely. We didn't understand what that meant, but we knew it was bad. The first day I wouldn't touch the soup, but the next day my stomach was cramping so terribly that I swallowed the soup with delight. We didn't menstruate, and what a blessing it was under those circumstances.

When evening came, we were allowed to go into the barracks. The barracks were located in Birkenau, which was a suburb of Auschwitz and its actual transit camp. The barracks were very long and filled with beds, one three-decker close to another. Each bed was the size of a regular double bed, and on each slept twelve people. When night came, we tried to find a comfortable position, which was quite a chore. If we lay next to one another, we had no room to breathe. If we lay alternating head down and feet up, we were kicked continuously. If we had to turn at night, we had to do it simultaneously.

Eventually we developed a routine. Everybody was dead tired at night, and we just slept, if they let us. Unfortunately, they decided that the best time for us to stand outside was at four o'clock in the morning, and when the whistle blew, we had to line up in fives outside.

This gave some kind of added pleasure to our Capo, and she practiced it every night. When a prisoner was too slow in getting into her row, she was forced to stand all day or had her bowl of soup taken away from her.

I began to have nightmares and was obsessed with the thought that I might not get my bowl of soup, that my stomach would begin to cramp again; I knew I couldn't stand it anymore. I was so possessed by hunger and my own feelings that I didn't even think about my sisters. At times I realized that I didn't care whether anyone was dead or alive, just as long as I could get the bowl of soup to keep me going.

"Ruth, Ruth, I know you aren't asleep. Why can't you talk to me?" Anna whispered, but I wouldn't answer her. I felt numb.

Slowly, however, the daily routine got under my skin, and I began to feel things. When Mania was punished, I realized that I cared. I didn't speak to her, but I tried to find a way of letting her know that I cared. She wasn't to have anything to eat for twenty-four hours. She had been separated from us all day, but when evening came, she was already on the bed waiting for us. "I have to tell you something," she said in a low voice. "The Devil (as we all called the Capo by now) wants me to sew something for her. When she punished me, I managed to talk to her. I told her I could sew, and she will have something for me tomorrow."

"You are kidding," Pola murmured. She never believed anything good could happen to us.

Sure enough, the next morning my sister was standing naked outside and sewing a dress for the Devil. Every time an inspection was made, we had to hide it, but as it didn't belong to us, we weren't too concerned. We knew the Devil would cover for it.

Since our routine was to stand outside all day and wait for segregations, we stood that day and helped Mania sew. In the evening, the dress was ready and, after delivery, Mania came back with a huge slice of bread. What a feast! We each had a bite. We were beginning to live.

The next day the Devil brought another piece of material, with white and blue checks for a blouse. Of course, she had to supply us with scissors, needles, and thread, which she did. We sewed again, and again we had a slice of bread. This time it was an even greater joy. Besides getting a piece of bread, Mania was able to cut a piece of material and fill in the cut-out of my dress where my breasts were showing. In spite of everything, I felt much better at not being so exposed.

Next to our camp, separated by heavy barbed wire, was a camp of men. They must have been hungry, hungry for food and women. They stood there and stared at us all day. There was nothing else they could do. We were there, and they were right next to us. They had to look. Strangely enough, we didn't mind. We were all women from fourteen to about forty, yet we didn't mind having the men look at our naked bodies day in and day out because we didn't feel like women. What could they possibly see in a skeleton-like body without hair? Also, the fact that we didn't know any of them made a difference.

One day I learned that Mark, my dear friend who had been taken out of the ghetto with his father, was in Auschwitz. I wondered if he had heard of his mother's suicide, but I wasn't going to mention it. He was an electrician and was coming to our camp. "How am I going to face him?" I asked my sisters. "I can't let him see me like this!"

"What is all this talk? For months you have been standing out here, showing off to all the men, and now that Mark is coming you make such a fuss," Pola snapped.

"Pola, please stop it. These men don't mean anything to me. Mark is different."

"Don't worry, darling, we'll make you look beautiful," Mania added. Her sewing came in handy again. She was making a skirt for another Capo, and she cut a piece of material to make a scarf for me. With my dress patched and the blue scarf covering my bald head, I looked like a girl again.

Suddenly I wanted to look attractive and act human, mainly, I think, because Mark had known me when I was young and pretty, and I wanted to look the same to him. He loved me, he had said so many times. The night we went to the concert in the ghetto, he had held my hand and kissed me. I could still feel it. What does he look like after two years in Auschwitz? Does he still have any feelings, especially for a girl, for me? So many thoughts went through my mind.

Morning came, and again we all had to stand outside naked and shivering. It was the end of October, and the air was very cold and windy.

Finally, the day of Mark's visit arrived. He was coming to repair the electric wiring in one of the barracks, and I was to meet him there. Mania tied the little blue square over my bald head, and one could hardly see that I had no hair. "You look beautiful," my sister Anna said. "He loves you anyhow," Pola added.

My heart beat fast as I walked into the barrack. I saw him; it was easy to spot a man among hundreds of women. He came towards me. He recognized me. My knees trembled; for a moment, I was ready to turn back and run.

"Hello, Ruth," he said slowly, looking at me intensely. He can see through me, I thought. It seemed as if he would eat me up with his eyes. He stared at me without saying a word. I moved towards him and kissed him on the cheek. He touched my face like a blind person. He couldn't believe it was really I.

"Your father, your sister," I managed to say. He glared up into the skies. I understood.

"I brought you a toothbrush," he whispered and handed it to me.

"Mark, how much longer can this last? What do you think?" I asked.

"Not much longer. The Russians are coming, for sure," he answered quickly and took me in his arms, hugging me and kissing my forehead. "Ruth, listen, it won't be long. You must be strong. Try not to register for any outside commandos. The Russians are not far; we can even hear them. A Capo told me it won't be long. Please, Ruth, you must live," he said, holding me so tightly I ached. But I didn't mind that it hurt. He cared for me. And he had even offered me hope. I hadn't thought of that word for ages. As a matter of fact, I didn't even think about the future anymore. It was meaningless when all I cared about was surviving the tortures of each day.

I soon left Mark, afraid that someone might discover me. I joined my row of fives, took the scarf off my head, and once again stood naked. But deep inside, something that I had thought was dead was being born again—the will to live.

Commandant of Auschwitz
The Autobiography
of Rudolf Hoess

Rudolf Hoess

...

The women's camp, tightly crammed from the very beginning, meant psychological destruction for the mass of the female prisoners, and this led sooner or later to their physical collapse.

From every point of view, and at all times, the worst conditions prevailed in the women's camp. This was so even at the very beginning, when it still formed part of the base camp. Once the Jewish transports from Slovakia began to arrive, it was crammed to the roof within a matter of days. Washhouses and latrines were sufficient, at the most, for a third of the number of inmates that the camp contained.

To have put these swarming ant hills into proper order would have required more than the few female supervisors allotted me from Ravensbrück. And I must emphasize once again that the women I was sent were not the best.

These supervisors had been thoroughly spoiled at Ravensbrück. Everything had been done for them to persuade them to remain in the women's concentration camp, and by offering them extremely good living conditions it was hoped to attract new recruits. They were given the best of accommodation, and were paid a salary they could never have earned elsewhere. Their work was not particularly onerous. In short, the Reichsführer SS, and Pohl in particular, wished to see the female supervisors treated with the utmost consideration.

Up to that time conditions in Ravensbrück had been normal, and there was no question of overcrowding.

These supervisors were now posted to Auschwitz—none came voluntarily—and had the job of getting the women's camp started in the most difficult conditions.

From the very beginning most of them wanted to run away and return to the quiet comforts and the easy life at Ravensbrück.

From Rudolf Hoess, *Commandant of Auschwitz: The Autobiography of Rudolf Hoess*, trans. Constantine FitzGibbon. Cleveland, OH: World Publ. Co., 1959, pp. 151–154.

The chief female supervisor of the period, Frau Langefeldt, was in no way capable of coping with the situation, yet she refused to accept any instructions given her by the commander of the protective custody camp. Acting on my own initiative, I simply put the women's camp under his jurisdiction, since this seemed the only method of ending the disorderly way in which it was being run. Hardly a day passed without discrepancies appearing in the numbers of inmates shown on the strength returns. The supervisors ran hither and thither in all this confusion like a lot of flustered hens, and had no idea what to do. The three or four good ones among them were driven crazy by the rest. The chief supervisor regarded herself as an independent camp commander, and consequently objected to being placed under a man of the same rank as herself. In the end I actually had to cancel her subordination to him. When the Reichsführer SS visited the camp in July 1942 I reported all this to him, in the presence of the chief female supervisor, and I told him that Frau Langefeldt was and always would be completely incapable of commanding and organizing the women's camp at Auschwitz as this should be done. I requested that she be once again subordinated to the first commander of the protective custody camp.

The Reichsführer SS absolutely refused to allow this, despite the striking proofs he was given of the inadequacy of the chief supervisor and of the female supervisors in general. He wished a women's camp to be commanded by a woman, and I was to detail an SS officer to act as her assistant.

But which of my officers would be willing to take his orders from a woman? Every officer whom I had to appoint to this post begged to be released as soon as possible. When the really large numbers of prisoners began to arrive, I myself devoted as much time as I could to helping in the running of this camp.

Thus from the very beginning the women's camp was run by the prisoners themselves. The larger the camp became, the more difficult it was for the supervisors to exercise control, and self-rule by the prisoners became more and more apparent. Since it was the "greens" who had the supremacy, and who therefore ran the camp by reason of their greater slyness and unscrupulousness, it was they who were the real masters in the women's camp, despite the fact that the camp senior and other key officials were "red." The women controllers, as the female Capos were called, were mostly "green" or "black." It was thus inevitable that the most wretched conditions prevailed in the women's camp.

The original female supervisors were, even so, far and away superior to those we got later. In spite of keen recruiting by the National Socialist women's organizations, very few candidates volunteered for concentration camp service, and compulsion had to be used to obtain the ever-increasing numbers required.

Each armaments firm to which female prisoners were allotted for work had in exchange to surrender a certain percentage of their other female employees to act as supervisors. It will be understood that, in view of the general wartime shortage of efficient female labor, these firms did not give us their best workers.

These supervisors were now given a few weeks "training" in Ravensbrück and then let loose on the prisoners. Since the selection and allocation took place at Ravensbrück, Auschwitz was once again at the end of the line. Obviously Ravensbrück kept what seemed the best ones for employment in the new women's labor camp which was being set up there.

Such was the position regarding the supervisory staff in the women's camp at Auschwitz.

As was only to be expected, the morals of these women were, almost without exception, extremely low. Many of them appeared before the SS tribunal charged with theft in connection with the Reinhardt Action.[1] But these were only the few who happened to be caught. In spite of the most fearful punishments, stealing went on, and the supervisors continued to use the prisoners as go-betweens for this purpose.

[1]*Aktion Reinhardt* was the code name give to the operation of collection and marketing the clothing, valuables, and other belongings, including gold fillings from teeth, and women's hair, taken from the slaughtered Jews.

The March

Henry Orenstein

We were on a road leading north, in a column of five prisoners to a row, half a mile long. The SS guards were walking on both sides of the column, fingers on the triggers of their machine guns. Two or three were marching ahead of the column and a few behind it. An officer on a motorcycle was riding up and down the road making sure everything was in order. Many military vehicles of all kinds were driving past. Some of the German formations seemed still intact, while others looked like the remains of a fighting force that had taken a bad beating. There were many stalled or abandoned vehicles lying on the shoulder of the road. Civilians were walking along carrying bundles; some had horse carts packed with their belongings. Allied planes and a few Russian ones flew continuously over our heads, but we didn't see a single German plane. From time to time, when one of the Allied planes spotted a group of German military vehicles, the pilot would dive down and strafe them. It did my heart good to see Germans jump and dive for cover. Somehow we weren't much concerned for our own safety; our column was very visible from the air, and our striped uniforms made it obvious that we were prisoners. Whenever the planes flew low over us, the guards stepped up to the column, feeling safer from air attack when closer to us.

After a while they led us onto a secondary road parallel to the main one, where things were much quieter. The peasants in the fields, almost all of them old men,

Henry Orenstein. "The March," *I Shall Live: Surviving Against All Odds, 1939-1945.* New York; Beaufort Books, Publ., 1987, pp. 240–253. Reprinted by permission of Henry Orenstein.

women, and children, looked with curiosity but no surprise at the endless column of prisoners in their striped uniforms. I now weighed less than a hundred pounds, Sam, about eighty-five or ninety, and most of the others were in a similar state. But the guards kept us marching at a brisk pace.

It was not yet noon when an elderly Pole marching a couple of rows ahead of us suddenly tripped and fell. He got up again with the help of the others around him, but he must have sprained or twisted an ankle, because he continued walking only with great difficulty, heavily favoring one leg. For a mile or so his neighbors on both sides supported him, but he was in constant pain and after a while couldn't walk at all—he had to be literally carried. An SS guard saw that he was holding up the column, and with his gun motioned to him to step out of the ranks. When one of the prisoners who was carrying him wanted to stay with him, the guard pointed his machine gun at him in turn, and ordered him to keep moving. The guard then pushed the man over to the side of the road and raised his machine gun. Realizing that he was going to be killed, the man fell on his knees and joined his hands together in a gesture of prayer. The SS guard, his gun about two feet from the man's head, let loose with a burst of fire, and the Pole keeled over and lay still on the ground. Seeing that the other prisoners were slowing down, their heads turning to look at the man lying on the ground, the guard ran back to the column and started hitting the marchers within his reach to hurry them along.

Our mood changed abruptly. Conversation stopped, and all of us walked carefully, making sure not to stumble. Sam and I took turns holding each other's arm. The incident had driven home to us that we were all still in mortal danger. Even though the war was in its last days, the SS obviously had orders not to let a single prisoner out of their control. The rules for this march were: Walk or die.

We continued walking nonstop for several more hours. Some of the weaker prisoners, unable to keep up the pace, began to fall back toward the end of the column. This, we knew, meant a bullet in the head. The stragglers at the end of the column were using their last drop of strength in a desperate effort not to get separated from the rest. Some were wheezing, gasping for air; others stumbled on until finally, all strength gone, they fell one by one to their knees, or simply dropped. Like angels of death the SS men at the rear of the column were looking for stragglers and shot them where they fell as if it were the most routine thing in the world. Their faces were blank. There was no hate in them, no pity, just business as usual. By the time they ordered us to stop for our first break, five or six prisoners from our column were gone, their bodies left behind on the side of the road, riddled with bullets.

Strangely, even though it was now clear that the march was going to be a murderous affair, I still felt far safer than I ever had in the camp. Here they didn't know I was a Jew, and if they were going to kill me it would be only because I couldn't walk, not simply because I was a Jew. To my mind, killing a man because he could not keep up the pace in a forced march somehow wasn't as bad as killing him because he had been born a Jew. Such reasoning may seem lunatic, but under the circumstances it made perfect sense to me. Having lived for so many years under the gun, when any one of the guards had the clear and unquestioned right to murder me at any moment,

at a whim, even for fun, even though I had done nothing to provoke it, for the sole reason that I was born a Jew, I had grown to yearn to have my right to live judged by some
other criterion, any other—even by whether or not I was able to walk.

Sam and I divided our food rations carefully into twelve portions, and we ate one
portion during our brief rest. We knew that our lives depended on making it last as long
as possible, on conserving every last bit of energy. However, we saw many other
prisoners, no hungrier than we, consume their entire three or four days' ration in a few
minutes.

There was another Jewish prisoner in our column, Warshawski, and when the
guards ordered us to resume our march, Warshawski walked alongside Sam and me.
Despite the shooting of the stragglers, I was more optimistic than ever about our
chances to make it. The odds seemed good that the SS would not kill so many people,
especially since as far as they knew there were no Jews among us. Besides, even if they
had planned to execute us all, it would have been almost impossible for them to manage it. They couldn't mow us all down at once out there in the open; thousands would
escape, and their own lives would be greatly endangered. I even overheard some of the
Poles discussing the possibility of suddenly jumping the guards, but they had their
machine guns at the ready; whoever attacked them first would surely be killed, and no
one was willing to die moments before liberation, to save the others. Besides, even if
a substantial number of prisoners managed to escape, the SS might still have time to
hunt down many of them.

As the sun began to sink slowly in the west, the guards led us off the road to a
large farm, which was to be our resting place for the night. They pushed perhaps a thousand of us into a large barn. There wasn't enough room for all of us to lie down, and
some had to lay their legs over others' bodies. Sam and I were especially cautious with
our food, waiting until it was completely dark before we ate our next portion, and being
very quiet about it. We were afraid that some of the prisoners who had no food left might
jump us and take ours by force.

The hay in the barn smelled good, and even though we were packed in so tight,
I had a good night's sleep. Early in the morning the guards ordered us out, and we were
once more on the march. Fortunately, it wasn't raining and the weather was mild.
We turned into another road, on which we could tell another column was marching
ahead of us; every few hundred feet we saw bullet-ridden bodies of prisoners lying at
the side of the road.

All day long the SS played their deadly game of march or die, with the killings
increasing every hour. Some of the prisoners' shoes were either too big for them or too
small, and they were beginning to develop painful blisters; many walked barefoot, carrying their shoes tied together around their necks. Occasionally we heard the rumble
of artillery, but now it seemed more remote and sporadic than it had just before we left
the camp. I didn't feel as hungry as I had in the camp either, perhaps because I was so
absorbed in the life-and-death game with the SS. We were marching now on winding
country roads; evidently the SS wanted to stay away from the highways. I felt good,
and Sam was holding up fairly well too. We were on the north German plain, which
was sparsely populated, and, luckily for us, very flat. The roads would have been

much more thickly strewn with our bodies had the terrain been hilly. That night the guards again brought us to a large farm, but this time they let all of us sleep outside, so at least we had plenty of room to stretch our legs.

This went on day after day, except that the number of victims kept increasing hourly. Sam and I had enough food for four days, but many of the others had had nothing to eat since the first rest stop, and more and more were unable to continue the march. The pace was slowing, which helped a little, but still many prisoners, especially the older ones, were unable to keep up and were shot down in cold blood. The lack of any visible emotion in the killers continued to amaze me. Many of the victims fought for their lives until the very last minute, pleading in vain with their executioners for mercy, while others, having witnessed too many earlier killings with no mercy shown, accepted their deaths with resignation. Some prisoners were so hungry they started eating roots and even grass, which caused many of them to develop dysentery, weakening them still further. Most had started the march in fairly good spirits, but now many were losing hope. The battlefront seemed more remote, and we had no idea whatever as to what was going on.

By the sixth or seventh day, Sam was weakening; he had to hold on to my arm most of the time. If we didn't get some food very soon, we wouldn't be able to make it. We were marching in a heavily wooded area, and at night the guards were letting us rest on the edge of these woods.

The killings became very frequent now, as more and more people were collapsing from exhaustion. At least seven hundred in our column were shot to death in two days. We could see hundreds of other corpses alongside the road, left by columns marching ahead of us. The countryside was beautiful, spring was in full bloom. The incongruity between the radiance of the nature around us and the slaughter of innocent people was hard to reconcile.

It was still broad daylight at the end of the seventh day, April 26, and we were lying on the ground, exhausted and hungry, in a corner formed by the country road and a narrow cow path, when suddenly a small white truck appeared and turned into the path. More trucks just like it, perhaps eight or nine in all, followed and stopped, lined up next to each other. They all had red crosses painted on their sides. It seemed like a mirage. A wild thought struck me; maybe they had brought food for us! But that could only be my hunger talking. It was too incredible even to contemplate. Why would the Germans want to feed us now? It was totally inconsistent with all their other actions, and, anyway, they themselves were short of food. Besides, why white trucks with red crosses? We saw a few civilians from the convoy talking to the SS officer in charge. Then the guards ordered some of the stronger prisoners to open the back doors of the trucks, and to my astonishment they started unloading corrugated white boxes marked with red crosses.*

*As I found out after the liberation, it was the Swedish Red Cross that delivered the food packages to us. The Swedish Count Folke Bernadotte, who organized the delivery, and a few others, were able to get approval for this mission of mercy from Himmler, who was trying to ingratiate himself to the Western powers, hoping that his cooperation would somehow save his

A surge of joy rushed through our ranks. Food! It looked like food! And in seconds we heard that it was, as the prisoners unloading the trucks passed the word along to the others. Most of us had risen to our feet. They were piling the boxes up. Hundreds of them were being unloaded, so it couldn't all be for just the SS; it had to be for us!

The guards ordered us to line up, and soon the prisoners at the head of the line were receiving one box for every four people. The guards warned us that the prisoners themselves were responsible for dividing the food evenly, and that anyone who started a fight would be immediately shot. Sam and I were standing far down the line, but it was moving fast. We heard shouts of joy from the prisoners as they tore the boxes open, and cries of "Chocolate! Cheese! Meat!"

I was dizzy from excitement. It was a miracle, a real miracle was happening before our eyes. Someone wanted to save us! Having known for so long nothing but brutality, hardened by the daily inhumanity of the camps, the thousands of deaths, it was hard to take it in, this evidence of some good in man. What did it mean? Who had sent this food? How had they found us in the middle of nowhere? Warshawski, Sam, a friendly Pole, and I received our box, and when we opened it we saw that it came from America. It was neatly packed with two different kinds of cheese, a can of sardines, three or four packages of crackers, including Ritz, a bar of Hershey's chocolate, a can of Spam, a can of powdered milk, and a long package of small, square slices of pumpernickel. We could not believe our eyes. I suggested that I divide everything in the box into four parts, and we would then alternate choosing our shares. Everyone agreed, and so I set to work, conscious of my heavy responsibility to make sure each share was exactly even.

I divided the crackers first, so we could get something inside us immediately. Next came the sardines, because we had no way to store them. We tried not to cram the food into our months, but it was hard to hold back. Our bodies were starved, every cell aching for nourishment. The sardines tasted fantastically good. Each morsel was a little piece of heaven, and every part of my body was crying out, "Thank you! Thank you!" to the food as it traveled through.

I used a spoon which I sharpened on a stone to divide the cheese and the Spam. We had never heard of Spam. It was delicious. How clever of the Americans to invent such a wonderful new kind of food! The chocolate was difficult to divide because it was very hard and crumbly, but I finally managed to cut it up into four equal parts. The powdered milk presented a storage problem, but we had some of it mixed with water, and saved the rest. I kept the chocolate for last. It was so good I was longing to eat my whole share at once, but Sam and I had decided that this food had to last us at least three days, and we each divided our share into little bits.

life. Himmler was captured at the end of the war, and realizing that nothing would save him, committed suicide by crushing a cyanide pill in his mouth. A note of interest: there are several eyewitness stories about Himmler personally observing, through a small window, the suffocation of hundreds of Jews in a gas chamber during his visit to the Auschwitz extermination camp.

Since I was stronger than Sam at this point, when the march resumed the following morning I offered to carry his food as well as my own. As we walked along we could talk of nothing but the "miracle." No one told us how the food had got to us, so we could only speculate. Something very unusual must be going on; never before had the SS permitted anything like it. Maybe Hitler was dead; were he still alive, he would never permit anything like that. Or perhaps the war was over. But if so, why were the guards still here? Perhaps the International Red Cross had arranged this, and if so it was a sign that a crack had appeared in the wall with which the SS had isolated us from the rest of the world. Whatever its source, the food not only fed our starving bodies, it gave a lift to our spirits as well. We had not yet reached the end of the road, but at least there was someone out there who cared. Knowing this, I felt more at peace than I had in a long time, and I fell sound asleep.

···

The march continued, and so did the killings. The distribution of the Red Cross boxes evidently hadn't changed the SS's standing order: Any prisoner who couldn't keep up with the pace was to be shot to death. They were not letting anyone out of their hands alive. However, the shootings weren't quite as frequent now as they had been the day before the food arrived. Those parcels had given us a life-saving infusion of energy and hope. Now once more, as at the beginning, it was legs giving out or injuries to them rather than failing strength that were the main cause of the killings. The column was moving more slowly now, too, and the guards were not hurrying us so much.

Again we stopped for the night at the edge of a forest. The moment of liberation was very close, and we had some food again. If only our legs would hold up, we had a good chance of making it. I slept well that night, and the next morning, April 28, I felt better than I had in a long time. That day went by uneventfully. Sam, Warshawski, and I stayed close together. We ate a little more of the food from the Red Cross, and it was heavenly.

The next morning, after we had marched for an hour or so, we saw a number of dead horses lying on the road, evidently victims of Allied strafing. Frenziedly the prisoners ahead of us were throwing themselves on the carcasses and cutting off hunks of flesh with their stone-sharpened spoons. Some were even trying to tear off pieces with their fingers and teeth. As long as the prisoners stayed on the road, the guards didn't interfere. When the crowd around the carcasses had thinned out a little, Sam and I and some of the other prisoners toward the end of the column cut off some meat for ourselves. It was a grisly business and our spoons weren't sharp enough, but we persisted and got at least a couple of pounds. None of us had anything to put it in, so we stuffed our jackets inside our pants, tightened the pants, and carried the meat inside the jackets above the waist. The meat was bloody, and soon our jackets were soaked with blood. The column looked like a bunch of butchers on the march.

Still there was no relief from the killings; prisoner after prisoner was shot down. It seemed utterly senseless. By now we couldn't be far from the North Sea, and a mad thought struck me: Perhaps the Red Cross had boats waiting to take us to Sweden.

That night we stopped near another forest. A few of the prisoners had brought matches with them from Sachsenhausen, and soon there were hundreds of little fires going. We all sat around them cooking our horsemeat, using the sharpened ends of wooden sticks to hold chunks of it over the flames. This was the first meat I had tasted in almost two years. It was very tough, but I kept at it doggedly chewing each piece as long as I could, knowing that this extra energy could mean the difference between life and death. We ate only part of the meat, saving the rest, for it was still impossible even to guess how much longer we would have to hold out. Why was it taking the Allies so long to reach us? Most of the prisoners were very subdued, as if the long march had dulled our senses; the last few days we had been shuffling along in a sort of stupor.

On the morning of April 30, we were about to resume our march when the little white Red Cross trucks appeared again on the road. Sam and I still had some food left from the first parcel, but many of the others had long since eaten all their share. We greeted the trucks with cheers, not only because of the food, but also because their arrival meant that someone on the outside knew we were alive, cared about us, and was in touch with the SS on our behalf. This time each box had to be shared among five prisoners, so the portions were a little smaller. But with the horsemeat and what was left over from the first box, our food reserve was building up and Sam an I could afford the luxury of eating a larger part of our portion.

Once again Allied planes appeared, in large numbers and flying very low. We could see them diving in and out over a wide road not far from us that had on it a heavy concentration of German tanks, armored cars, and trucks. They could see us very well, and were clearly taking pains not to hit the column—which was no help to the unfortunate ones who couldn't keep up, and who were still being executed with the same cold, mechanical ruthlessness as before.

When we stopped again for the night, fires soon started up again to cook more of the horsemeat. I didn't eat much of it this time, since I preferred the food from the Red Cross box. Again I slept well in the open air; it was quite warm for that time of year. When the morning of May 1 came, someone suggested that maybe the Russians had been holding off until today, their big national holiday, to liberate us. We marched off once again, still surrounded by the guards. This evacuation, if it could still be called that, was taking much longer than anyone had anticipated. Prisoner after prisoner was killed, the bodies still littering the road. I knew that if it hadn't been for the Red Cross food, it would have been far worse; many more prisoners would have been dead by now.

I looked around. We were all filthy, unshaven, our striped suits soaked with blood from the horsemeat. Many were stumbling along, unable to walk. I occupied my mind with wondering how those food parcels had reached us, but could arrive at no explanation. We came upon more dead horses lying on the road and replenished our supply of meat, throwing away what had been left from before; it had started to go bad.

In the evening we stopped at the edge of another forest, and the SS guards stationed themselves as usual around us to make sure no one escaped. Now that we had a fresh supply of meat, hundreds of fires started again. A Pole who had been walking along with Sam, Warshawski, and me during the last few days, who had been a truck driver before the war, ate prodigious quantities of the horsemeat with relish, but I had to force myself. That truck driver was a good-natured fellow who probably suspected that we were Jews but never asked outright, and we of course volunteered nothing. For dessert I ate a little more of the chocolate I had left, promising myself that if I survived, I would eat nothing else for the rest of my life.

Night fell, the fires were extinguished, and we went to sleep. From time to time I woke up at the noise from the military vehicles moving along the road. Early next morning, before we had to set out on the march again, the fires were started up to cook some more of the horsemeat. We were all sitting around our fires, holding chunks of the meat on sticks over the flames, when a voice came from the edge of the forest: "The guards are gone."

Extract from Evidence Given at the Nuremberg Trials on the Auschwitz Extermination Camp*

M. DUBOST: What do you know about the Jewish transport that arrived from Romainville about the same time as you?

VAILLANT-COUTURIER: When we left Romainville the Jewish women who were together with us remained behind. They were sent to Drancy, and finally arrived in Auschwitz, where we saw them again three weeks later. Of 1,200 who left, only 125 arrived in the camp. The rest were taken to the gas chambers immediately, and of the 125 not a single one was left by the end of a month.

The transports were carried out as follows: at the beginning, when we arrived, when a Jewish transport came there was a "selection." First the old

"Extract from Evidence Given at the Nuremberg Trials on the Auschwitz Extermination Camp," *Documents on the Holocaust: Selected Sources on the Destruction of the Jews of Germany and Austria, Poland, and the Soviet Union,* Yitzhak Arad, Yisrael Gutman, Abraham Margaliot eds. Jerusalem: Yad Vashem, 1981, pp. 358–361.

Trial of the Major War Criminals before the International Military Tribunal, Nuremberg 14 November 1945–1 October 1946, VI, Nuremberg, 1947, pp. 214–216.

*From the evidence of a Freedwoman, Marie-Claude Vaillany-Couturier, who was a prisoner in the Auschwitz concentration camp, where she arrived on January 1, 1943.

women, the mothers and the children. They were told to get on trucks, together with the sick and people who looked weak. They kept only young girls, young women and young men; the latter were sent to the men's camp. In general, it was rare for more than 250 out of a transport of 1,000 to 1,500 to reach the camp, and that was the maximum; the others were sent to the gas chambers straight away.

At this "selection" healthy women between 20 and 30 years old were also chosen, and sent to the Experimental Block. Girls and women, who were a little older or not chosen for this purpose, were sent to the camp and, like us, had their heads shaved and they were tattooed.

In the spring of 1944 there was also a block for twins. That was at the time of the immense transport of Hungarian Jews, about 700,000* persons. Dr. Mengele, who was carrying out the experiments, kept back the twin children from all transports, as well as twins of any age, so long as both twins were there. Both children and adults slept on the floor in this block. I don't know what experiments were made apart from blood tests and measurements.

M. DUBOST: Did you actually see the "selection" when transports arrived?

VAILLANT-COUTURIER: Yes, because when we were working in the Sewing Block in 1944, the block in which we lived was situated just opposite the place where the trains arrived. The whole process had been improved: Instead of carrying out the "selection" where the trains arrived, a siding took the carriages practically to the gas chamber, and the train stopped about 100 m. from the gas chamber. That was right in front of our block, but of course there were two rows of barbed wire between.

Then we saw how the seals were taken off the trucks and how women, men and children were pulled out of the trucks by soldiers. We were present at the most terrible scenes when old couples were separated. Mothers had to leave their daughters because they were taken to the camp, while the mothers and children went to the gas chambers. All these people knew nothing of the fate that awaited them. They were only confused because they were being separated from each other, but they did not know that they were going to their death.

To make the reception pleasanter there was then—in June and July 1944, that is—an orchestra made up of prisoners, girls in white blouses and dark blue skirts, all of them pretty and young, who played gay tunes when the trains arrived, the "Merry Widow," the Barcarolle from the "Tales of Hoffmann," etc. They were told it was a labor camp, and as they never entered the camp they saw nothing but the small platform decorated with greenery, where the orchestra played. They could not know what awaited them.

Those who were taken to the gas chambers—that is, the old people, children and others—were taken to a red brick building.

M. DUBOST: Then they were not registered?

*The correct number of Hungarian Jews sent to Auschwitz was about 430,000.

VAILLANT-COUTURIER: No.

DUBOST: They were not tattooed?

VAILLANT-COUTURIER: No, they were not even counted.

DUBOST: Were you yourself tattooed?

VAILLANT-COUTURIER: Yes.

(The witness shows her arm)

They were taken to a red brick building with a sign that said Baths. There they were told to get undressed and given a towel before they were taken to the so-called shower room. Later, at the time of the large transports from Hungary, there was no time left for any degree of concealment. They were undressed brutally. I know of these particulars because I was acquainted with a little Jewess from France, who had lived on the Place de la Republique....

DUBOST: In Paris?

VAILLANT-COUTURIER: In Paris, she was known as "little Marie" and was the only survivor of a family of nine. Her mother and her seven sisters and brothers had been taken to the gas chambers as soon as they arrived. When I got to know her she worked on undressing the small children before they were taken into the gas chamber.

After the people were undressed they were taken into a room that looked like a shower room, and the capsules were thrown down into the room through a hole in the ceiling. An SS man observed the effect through a spy-hole. After about 5 to 7 minutes, when the gas had done its job, be gave a signal for the opening of the doors. Men with gas-masks, these were prisoners too, came in and took the bodies out. They told us that the prisoners must have suffered before they died, because they clung together in bunches like grapes so that it was difficult to separate them....

Chapter 10

Resistance and Rescue

INTRODUCTION

The once prevalent image of Jews going to their death like lambs to their slaughter continues to be revised. Worldwide Yom Hashoah ceremonies which commemorate the Holocaust are observed during the week of the Warsaw ghetto revolt. Thus, remembrance of those who died is linked with the symbol of resistance to the Nazis.

We define resistance as organized, armed opposition. It is true that this was the response of only a few thousand of the Holocaust victims. Nonetheless, the men and women who fought the Germans against impossible odds comprise a meaningful part of Holocaust history. They challenged their oppressors with a courage born of desperation. They joined partisans in the forests, organized attacks from ghetto hideouts, planned and executed assaults in death camps. They had few and outdated weapons, were nearly always on the verge of starvation and were able to secure little help from the world outside. Despite all their sacrifices, they probably did not shorten the war by any measurable extent. Still, this does not invalidate their heroic efforts.

From the safety of our lives in the United States, it is arrogant and simplistic to fault the millions who complied quietly with Nazi directives. Jewish resistance faced conditions far more difficult than those of other anti-German underground movements in the occupied nations. Although the context of time and place created varying conditions, some general comments can provide an overview of the enormous obstacles the Jews had to overcome.

That German military power was vastly superior is a given. Also, there was no doubt that the Nazis were totally committed to the destruction of the Jews. Beyond these obstacles, there were historic and psychological problems that undermined the Jews' ability to fight and favored German counter attacks. For example:

1. Hitler's aim to eradicate the Jews of Europe was so irrational, it was widely disbelieved. Even in the face of evidence to the contrary, such information was often rejected as illogical and untrustworthy.
2. The will to live, particularly the hope of parents for the survival of their children, resulted in the denial of the truth even when contrary to the facts.
3. Jews had survived their two thousand years of Diaspora by reliance on such methods as bribery, pleas and petitions. Often, their economic value to the ruling classes had resulted in protection. When all efforts failed and pogroms killed a portion of their people, the remnant rebuilt the community. The elders of the *Judenraete* generally clung to the old formulas and did not comprehend that Hitler was a completely different foe.
4. The Nazis used the concept of collective guilt to punish even the slightest resistance. Dozens, even hundreds of innocent prisoners in ghettos or camps were killed for the action of one or a few. The families of the men and women involved in opposition were the first to be executed. The effect of such measures was at least heart-wrenching, at most, paralyzed possible action.
5. Even if an uprising or escape was initially successful, Jews got little or no support from the native population. Thus survival after flight was the exception rather than the rule, particularly in Poland.

The following selection of readings can be understood only in light of the nearly insurmountable difficulties which confronted the martyrs and heroes of Jewish resistance.

Concerning rescue: Six million Jews died. This does not speak well for the Christian world. The complaint that *no one* cared about the fate of the Jews oversimplifies a complicated issue. The best opportunity to save Jews had been missed during the period between 1933 and 1939. But the Western world was still recovering from the aftermath of the First World War and immigration quotas were too small to allow large numbers to escape.   Such emigration, however, would have related mainly to German and Austrian Jews. Hitler's assurances that he sought peace were widely believed, and Jews outside the Third Reich did not understand the imminent peril. Once the war began, the opportunities for rescue became minimal. The Nazis shut the doors when they enacted laws which forbade emigration. The Final Solution was no longer interpreted as an effort to make Europe *Judenrein* by forcing Jews to leave; the new interpretation called for genocide. Supporters of the idea that it might have been possible to "buy" Jewish lives from the Nazis do not grasp Hitler's obsession: a Europe without Jews.

Rescue took several forms. The greatest number of survivors rescued themselves by escaping from eastern Poland deeper into Russian territories. Jews also saved other Jews by smuggling them into Palestine and neutral countries, particularly Spain. The funds to undertake these very dangerous missions usually were donated by the American Jewish community.

Christians, now designated as Righteous Gentiles, kept Jews alive by hiding them, feeding them, and, sometimes, nursing them. These were acts of uncommon courage which sometimes failed (Anne Frank), and sometimes succeeded (Cardinal Lustiger of France was a Jewish orphan hidden by French nuns). *Schindler's List* recounts how the owner of a small factory used the antagonism between German military and civilian authorities in Poland to safeguard hundreds of men and women. The people of Denmark spirited their Jews away to Sweden under the noses of the Nazis.

Could more lives have been saved if the will to do so had been stronger? The most telling case in point for an affirmative answer comes from the remarkable accomplishment of Raoul Wallenberg. In 1944 Franklin D. Roosevelt established the War Refugee Board in order to save Jews still remaining in Hungary. Wallenberg, a Swede, undertook the mission. His energy and ingenuity resulted in the largest number of Jews rescued; some 100,000 escaped Eichmann's grasp. Inevitably the question arises: were there other opportunities which were allowed to slip by? The answer is: possibly. Perhaps it would be wiser to ask instead: how many heroes does any generation produce?

Call for Resistance by the Jewish Military Organization in the Warsaw Ghetto, January 1943*

We are rising up for war!

We are of those who have set themselves the aim of awakening the people. Our wish is to take this watchword to our people:

Awake and fight!

Do not despair of the road to escape!

Know that escape is not to be found by walking to your death passively, like sheep to the slaughter. It is to be found in something much greater: in war!

Whoever defends himself has a chance of being saved! Whoever gives up self-defense from the outset—he has lost already! Nothing awaits him except only a hideous death in the suffocation-machine of Treblinka.

Let the people awaken to war!

Find the courage in your soul for desperate action!

Put an end to our terrible acceptance of such phrases as: We are all under sentence of death!

It is a lie! ! !

We also were destined to live! We too have a right to life!

One only needs to know how to fight for it!

It is no great art to live when life is given to you *willingly*!

But there is an art to life just when they are trying to rob you of this life.

Let the people awaken and fight for its life!

Let every mother be a lioness defending her young!

Let no father stand by and see the blood of his children in silence!

Let not the first act of our destruction be repeated!

An end to despair and lack of faith!

An end to the spirit of slavery amongst us!

"Call for Resistance by the Jewish Military Organization in the Warsaw Ghetto, January 1943," *Documents on the Holocaust: Selected Sources on the Destruction of the Jews of Germany and Austria, Poland, and the Soviet Union*, Yitzhak Arad, Yisrael Gutman, Abraham Margaliot eds. Jerusalem: Yad Vashem, 1981, pp. 303–304.

Archiwum Zydowskiego Instytutu Historycznego w Polsce (Archives of the Jewish Historical Institute in Poland), ARII/333.

*The appeal is attributed to the Jewish Military Organization (*Zydowski Zwiazek Wojskowy—ZZW*).

Let the tyrant pay with the blood of his body for every soul in Israel!
Let every house become a fortress for us!
Let the people awaken to war!
In war lies your salvation!
Whoever defends himself has a hope of escape!
We are rising in the name of the war for the lives of the helpless masses whom we seek to save, whom we must arouse to action. It is not for ourselves alone that we wish to fight. We will be entitled to save ourselves only when we have completed our duty! *As long as the life a Jew is still in danger, even one, single, life, we have to be ready to fight! ! !*
Our watchword is:
Not even one more Jew is to find his end in Treblinka!
Out with the traitors to the people!
War for life or death on the conqueror to our last breath!
Be prepared to act!
Be ready!

The Last Letter from Mordecai Anielewicz, Warsaw Ghetto Revolt Commander, April 23, 1943*

It is impossible to put into words what we have been through. One thing is clear, what happened exceeded our boldest dreams. The Germans ran twice from the ghetto. One of our companies held out for 40 minutes and another—for more than 6 hours. The mine set in the "brushmakers" area exploded. Several of our companies attacked the dispersing Germans. Our losses in manpower are minimal. That is also an achievement. Y [Yechiel] fell. He fell a hero, at the machine-gun. *I feel that great things are happening and what we dared do is of great, enormous importance....*

"The Last Letter from Mordecai Anielewicz, Warsaw Ghetto Revolt Commander, April 23, 1943," *Documents on the Holocaust: Selected Sources on the Destruction of the Jews of Germany and Austria, Poland and the Soviet Union,* Yitzhak Arad, Yisrael Gutman, Abraham Margaliot eds, Jerusalem: Yad Vashem, 1981, pp. 315–316.

[M. Kann], *Na oczach swiata* ("In the Eyes of the World"), Zamosc, 1932, [i.e. Warsaw, 1943]. pp. 33–34.

*Written to Yitzhak Cukierman.

Beginning from today we shall shift over to the partisan tactic. Three battle companies will move out tonight, with two tasks: reconnaissance and obtaining arms. Do you remember, short-range weapons are of no use to us. We use such weapons only rarely. What we need urgently: grenades, rifles, machine-guns and explosives.

It is impossible to describe the conditions under which the Jews of the ghetto are now living. Only a few will be able to hold out. The remainder will die sooner or later. Their fate is decided. In almost all the hiding places in which thousands are concealing themselves it is not possible to light a candle for lack of air.

With the aid of our transmitter we heard a marvelous report on our fighting by the "Shavit" radio station. The fact that we are remembered beyond the ghetto walls encourages us in our struggle. Peace go with you, my friend! Perhaps we may still meet again! *The dream of my life has risen to become fact. Self-defense in the ghetto will have been a reality. Jewish armed resistance and revenge are facts. I have been a witness to the magnificent, heroic fighting of Jewish men of battle.*

M. Anielewicz

Ghetto, April 23, 1943

The Helplessness of Dutch Jewry

B. A. Sijes

I have referred to the helplessness of Dutch Jewry during World War II. In many respects this description is accurate, and I would like to add a few remarks on this subject. It should be remembered that about 24,000 persons did have the presence of mind to try and hide. In addition, another 3,000 people escaped from Holland during the war. All these people manifested resistance of some sort. There were also many Jews who were active in the resistance movement in Holland. It is difficult to express all this in figures. It can, however, be safely assumed that more than 27,000 Jews actively resisted the German measures, but at the same time, it is also a fact that the great majority of the Jewish population, which numbered approximately 100,000 persons, did not see any possibilities of escape nor did they make any attempts in this direction. In order to gain a better understanding of the helplessness of this large group of ordinary Dutch Jews, the actions of the Secretaries-General and of the Jewish Council have to be stressed time and again. The Secretaries-General abandoned the Jewish citizens, and

From B.A. Sijes, "The Helplessness of Dutch Jewry," *Rescue Attempts During the Holocaust: Proceedings of the Second Yad Vashem International Historical Conference,* Jerusalem, April 8–11, 1974, pp. 542–548.

by not stopping the government agencies under their control from assisting in one way or another in the deportations, they in fact delivered the Jews into the hands of the Germans. The leaders of the Jewish Council assisted the Germans in the execution of the deportation orders. Was it surprising that under these circumstances the ordinary Jewish citizen felt deserted and isolated? This is especially true when one recalls that from May 1942 the Jews had to wear the Yellow Star. Was it not Dutch policemen, i.e., Dutch officials, who assisted in collecting the Jews from their homes? Were not the municipal streetcars of the capital of Holland, often referred to as the "Jerusalem of the North," used to bring the Jews to the train stations? Weren't Dutch trains, conducted by Dutch engineers, used to transport them to Westerbork, the point of departure for the *Arbeitseinsatz,* in "the East"?

One of the factors which played a role in the lack of resistance on the part of Dutch Jewry was the fact that the Jews were the first group against whom the German propaganda apparatus was directed with full force. The Jews were abused, slandered, and threatened. There were also severe special decrees; Jews were no longer allowed to change their place of residence, travel, walk in parks, swim, and buy in non-Jewish shops. Special schools were opened for Jewish children, bicycles were confiscated and all telephones were cut off. These and many other anti-Jewish measures were announced between September 1941 and the end of July 1942. The Jews received blow after blow in order to soften them up for deportation to break any willingness they might have had to resist the "authorities" and to strengthen their feeling that evading the measures decreed by the occupying authorities, and by the body which the Germans had invested with "authority" (the Jewish Council), was strictly forbidden.

Another reason why so few Dutch Jews survived the war was that the *Sperren*** created a false illusion of security. As a result of the existence of various select groups, each of whose members possessed an exemption which was valid up to a certain date, it was possible to deport one group after the other. One stayed at home, blindly believing in the power of the *Sperre* (there was after all nothing else to cling to!), until it "blew" (*platzte*). Every Jew hoped for a speedy victory by the Allies, but their invasion came too late for anyone who did not use the time granted by the temporary "exemption," in order to find a good hiding place. The Germans also provided exemptions for the leaders of the Jewish Council and for those who were in any way connected with it. The Council had asked for a total of 35,000 exemptions; the Germans issued half that number. The Jewish Council's acceptance of exemptions granted by the Germans was the natural result of their policy. The Council, however, was unable, lest it undermine its own position, to advise people to go into hiding. Furthermore, by accepting the *Sperren* they automatically doomed those Jews who did not possess these documents. On February 8, 1966, Dr. W. Harster, Commander of the German

---

*Various types of *Sperren* (exemptions) were issued, i.e., to "Protestant Jews," foreign Jews, Jews who worked in industries and in other branches of the economy who were indispensable to the Germans, Jews with non-Jewish spouses. Some Jews were exempt from deportation due to the personal intervention of Dr. H. G. Calmeyer, an official of the German *Generalkommissariat* for Administration and Justice in Holland.

Security Police in Holland openly declared during an interrogation by the Attorney-General of the Munich District Court:

> "In view of the general plan for the deportations, the large number of temporary exemptions could in no way be seen as final. Moreover, it had already been decided in advance, that these exempt groups would eventually be done away with."

The work of the Jewish Council was based on dialogue and loyal cooperation—otherwise the Germans would not have permitted its existence—and in the end it dragged thousands to their ruin. In this context, it should be noted that in his above mentioned interrogation, Harster mentioned that the leaders of the Jewish Council had requested permission to visit the work camps in the East (*Arbeitseinsatzmatten im Osten*). The Reich Security Main Office (RSHA), however, refused this request. The Jewish Council also made no serious attempt to check the reports broadcast by Radio Oranje concerning the murder of Jews in Poland, nor did they make their cooperation in the deportation dependent upon their being allowed to go to Poland to check the veracity of the reports broadcast by Radio Oranje.

On July 29, 1942 Radio Oranje reported:

> "...How is the German war effort being served by the murder of large groups of thousands of Polish Jews in the gas chambers? Which German effort is advanced by the fact that thousands of Dutch Jews are presently being deported?"

On July 30, 1942 Radio Oranje reported:

> "...what is happening now is no longer robbery and plunder, it can no longer be called deportation in order to make room for Germans in Holland. It cannot even be termed as a forced resettlement of Jews in Eastern Europe. It is a conscious extermination attempt, a conscious effort to murder helpless people."

On August 5, 1942 Prof. P. S. Gerbrandy, Prime Minister of the Netherlands, declared on Radio Oranje:

> "Cardinal Hinsley, who is usually well informed, has confirmed the reports that 700,000 Jews have been killed in Poland."

By July and August 1942, there were already numerous warnings in the illegal press concerning the murder of Jews. The leaders of the Jewish Council, however, went their own way and did not take the trouble to check whether these reports were true. The members of the Jewish Council, like the Secretaries-General, probably had serious reservations about, if not aversion for, the "reckless people" of the resistance movement.

Yet despite the attitude of the Secretaries-General, the Jewish Council, the Church, and the Dutch Government-in-Exile in London (and much criticism can be voiced against the latter two as well), the ultimate responsibility whether to obey the "authorities"—German or Dutch—rested with the Dutch Jews. They, however, were not always able to act according to their own free will in this matter. While the courage to attempt to evade orders is indeed closely connected with the ideological and social attitude of the individual, or of the group to which he belongs or of which he considers himself a member, it also depends on the direct force used by the authorities to assert their domination. Under such circumstances, the revision of existing ideas—which are determined by previous education and other traditional factors—is a very slow process. Motivated by the desire to remain alive, the individual begins to search for new ways to evade persecution. For the Jewish citizen, the period of the attempts to adjust to the new circumstances and to resist was extremely short. The social factor cannot be overlooked in determining why so few survived and why so many people simply waited until they were "picked up."

Furthermore, there were practical difficulties. The Jews, as a group, were marked not only by the Yellow Star, but also by their names and/or appearances. The majority of the Jews were poor and therefore lacked "connections." Their relationships with non-Jews were generally not such that as a matter of course the Jew could turn to the Gentile for support and help. "The majority of our people were never expressly pro-Jewish...." (*Oranjekrant*, end of July 1942). In The Netherlands, the Jews were the first large group who, as a group, faced the problem of "going into hiding." At this time there was no trained resistance movement which could provide the Jews with addresses, forged identity and ration cards, or even with money. The Jews were the first group on which those extremely small first bands of resistance fighters had to practice their illegal work. All these obstacles made it difficult for Jews to escape and this was also true as far as intellectuals and wealthy people were concerned. It is amazing though to what extent these illegal groups were able to improvise.

All of the above demonstrates that the circumstances had altered so drastically, that any form of organized resistance by the Jews as a group could hardly have been expected. In February 1941, the young Jewish men who took the initiative to resist in the streets of Amsterdam were not sufficiently intimidated by the Germans to prevent them from acting. However after the raids of February 1941 and the reports of the deaths in Mauthausen, the Jews began to be afraid, and this fear took its toll. When the deportations started in July 1942, there was still resistance, but it did not last long (as explained above). It should be noted, however, that the Jews' reaction to the German measures was not in any way exceptional. In spite of the fact that the non-Jewish population had more possibilities for evasion, as well as for resistance (they were not as isolated as the Jews, nor were they as easily recognizable), they too were soon forced to yield to the pressure of the Germans and the Dutch collaborators. A few examples will suffice to illustrate this point. In March 1942, the Germans announced that Dutch workers would be taken for forced labor in Germany. About a year later, 187,000 of the 254,000 workers (74%) demanded by the Germans had already been deported. Another example—when a strike broke out in Eastern Holland in April 1943 in response to the Germans' order that the Dutch prisoners of war who had been released by the Germans in 1940 return to German prison camps, the inhabitants of Western Holland, and especially the city of Amsterdam, who still remembered the brutal way in which the February strike of 1941 had been broken, did not participate. In those days, I heard workers call upon the populace to strike using the slogan, "Now our own men are at stake," but to no avail. Only a few factories stopped work for several hours.

Another example—in July 1944, shortly after the Allies invaded Normandy, Allied planes began bombing the railways in Holland. Soon the Dutch railroad workers lost their desire to continue working. Illegal newspapers urged the workers to strike, but for several reasons their call remained unanswered; at most, several workers were replaced.

In September 1944, however, when the Dutch Government in London and the management of the Dutch Railways called upon the railroad workers to strike in order to ensure the success of the landing of airborne Allied troops in Arnhem, the appeals were successful chiefly because the Allied troops were fighting on Dutch soil, the liberation was in sight, the order to strike came from an authority which was generally recognized by the Dutch population, and the workers knew that those who continued to work for the Germans would be punished.

One final example—when heavily armed German troops marched into many towns in October and November 1944 and announced by loudspeaker that all men between 18 and 40 years of age were to pack some clothing and food and report in order to be sent to work in Germany, an estimated 80,000 to 90,000 men answered this call. The illegal press called this "readiness to report" (*Meldungsfreudigkeit*) a scandal, but this denunciation does not help explain the reasons for this phenomenon.

By presenting these examples, I merely want to show how extremely difficult it was in July 1942 for the ordinary Jewish citizen to find an adequate answer for the awkward position in which he found himself. Moreover, the same applies for the period afterwards, since the fewer Jews that remained in Holland the more noticeable the remnants became and the more intense were the Germans' efforts to find them. They were placed in a position from which it became more and more difficult to escape, both practically and psychologically.

Rescue or Resistance

Nachama Tec

Tuvia was not interested in military glory. To live, to keep his people alive, to bring more Jews into the otriad, these were his goals.[1]

He would avoid talking to the non-Jewish partisans about his main preoccupation: the saving of lives. To them he presented himself as a guerilla fighter and continually repeated that he had come to the forest to wage war against the enemies of the Soviet Union, the Germans. And when Panchenko suggested that they cooperate in anti-Nazi moves he readily agreed.

Their joint military ventures began in the last quarter of 1942 and continued into the second half of 1943. Although such anti-German moves were initiated by Panchenko, the two otriads each carried the same burden. Publicly Tuvia continued to emphasize his personal commitment to anti-German activities. In reality he and his group were under pressure to participate. A refusal could have endangered the very existence of the Bielski otriad. Russian partisans would not have tolerated an unwillingness to fight, especially not from Jews whom they suspected of cowardice.

At this early stage, all forest dwellers were united in their hatred toward the Germans and their collaborators. These feelings of hostility were supported by equally strong ideas that it was important to fight their common enemy, the Germans.

Russian partisans were very belligerent when they talked about their enemy—killing Germans was equated with patriotism. Hero worship was common. How much of a hero a person was depended on how daring and life-threatening the person's opposition was to the Nazis. But this high value placed on fighting the enemy did not correspond to actual combat; their belligerence was merely verbal.

Inevitably, however, these favorable ideas about guerilla fighting came with a devaluation of those who could not wage war. Non-fighters were subjected to ridicule and contempt. The disheveled and hungry ghetto runaways in particular were sometimes greeted by Russian partisans with a sneering, "Why did you work for the Germans instead of fighting?"[2]

The forest was pervaded with ideas that fighting and causing damage to the Germans and their collaborators was good. Even young ghetto runaways after they were accepted into a Russian otriad would soon become strong advocates of the "wage a war ethic." In their case, as with others, the admiration of anti-German fighters came with a disapproval of non-fighters.

One of these young Jewish partisans admits, "I looked at the Bielski otriad with its 1000 Jews, most of whom could not fight, and thought: 'So what? But they do not fight!' I believed that they should have fought the Germans. As a Russian partisan I felt self-important."[3]

The idea that waging war against the Germans was more important than saving lives was implicitly accepted by many others. And while the degree of such acceptance varied, to some extent it was always there. Indirectly, support for this ideology some-times had tragic consequences.

The actions of known Jewish partisan fighters reflect this attitude. Dr. Icheskel Atlas, Alter Dworecki, and Hirsz Kaplinski each distinguished himself as an out-standing partisan leader. Each courageously battled the enemy. By the end of Decem-ber 1942, they had all been killed in action.[4]

During their short careers as partisan leaders, the three operated in and around the huge Lipiczańska forest. With its jungle-like growths, islands of swampy terrain, and irregular, poorly built country roads, this forest promised safety to many of the per-secuted. Lipiczańska forest became home for both Jewish and Russian partisans. It also became a haven for ghetto runaways, many of whom were older people, women, and children. Small family clusters or units of unattached fugitives were scattered all over this forest. Disorganized and unprotected, these groups lived in primitive bunkers. Some would beg for food from surrounding farms; the few who had guns would get their provisions by using force. Still, the very few who brought some money or valu-ables with them would exchange these for food. Unaccustomed to life in the forest, many fugitives were attacked by unruly partisan bands and robbed of their meager belongings and some were murdered in the process. Without the support of a large group like the Bielski otriad many died from cold, starvation, and epidemics.[5]

A survivor of a family camp tells how Russian partisans robbed them of their few weapons. For them, no arms meant no food. They lived in a poorly constructed bunker, with water seeping through every corner. The few children with them were barely dressed, ravaged by hunger and fever. The adults helplessly awaited the children's and their own deaths. Only a fraction survived.

The three Jewish partisan leaders, Atlas, Dworecki, and Kaplinski, had wit-nessed the plight of these Jewish civilians. Concerned, each in a different way tried to help these poor defenseless people—with warnings about danger, with food supplies and moral support.

Dr. Atlas became very depressed during one of his visits to such a half-starved and defenseless family camp. He told the people he could take ten of them with him, but they all had to be fit for combat. He explained that all his men were fighters and were taking revenge for the suffering of the Jewish people. He is quoted as saying, "We are lost, but we must fight."[6]

Like so many other Jewish leaders who fought the Germans, Dr. Atlas identified with the Jewish plight. Yet, hardly any of these leaders devoted themselves to saving Jews. The help they offered was sporadic, not organized, and hence not very effective.

Their commitment to wage war interfered with their desire to curtail Jewish destruction. It was as if their preoccupation with fighting the enemy made no room for saving Jewish lives. They might also have thought that in the long run fighting would save more people. In comparing Tuvia Bielski and Dr. Icheskel Atlas, Hersh Smolar believes that they are the two most important symbols of Jewish resistance: the Jewish fight for existence and the Jewish fight for revenge. Atlas stood for revenge and Bielski for life, for the biological existence of the Jews. Faced with a choice between saving and fighting—a choice that seemed clearer in hindsight—Atlas and others like him opted for the latter.[7]

The great value placed on fighting the Germans appeared under different guises and penetrated the most unexpected places. In some ways it reached even the Bielski otriad. It was in part expressed in the relatively high prestige enjoyed by those who had arms. The bulk of the otriad, the unarmed, were placed into a less valued category disdainfully called "malbush." Malbush is a Hebrew term for clothes. No one seems to know how the term acquired its negative meaning. Of course this did not necessarily mean that in the Bielski otriad fighting took precedence over saving lives. It only meant that fighting carried with it prestige and status.

An astute leader, Tuvia had to be aware of the value most others place on fighting. And so, only in the privacy of his inner circle, he would repeat "Don't rush to fight and die. So few of us are left, we have to save lives. To save a Jew is much more important than to kill Germans."[8]

In the Bielski otriad saving lives became intricately connected to moderate involvement with fighting. As one young partisan from the Bielski otriad asked, "If we perished, who would protect our families?"[9]

Disputes over the relative value of saving a life or fighting the enemy have continued until this day. Raja, who is convinced that saving lives was more important, tells of her exchange with a Jewish partisan who accusingly said, "You in the Bielski otriad sat in the forest without fighting!"

I asked, 'Tell me how many Germans did you kill?' 'Two.' Then I asked, 'How many Jews did you save?'"

This last question was met with silence. Raja continues, "They have been writing about Jewish resistance, uprisings of different kinds, but not about Jewish rescue by Jews. All the time I have been arguing about why no one writes about the heroism that was involved in the rescue of Jews. As far as I am concerned this is a holy thing."[10]

Only recently have others come to similar conclusions. One former forest fighter told me, "For forty years we had discussions about what was more important, fighting the Germans or saving Jews. We came to the conclusion that our heroism was not heroism. When I was fighting with guns together with other partisans, this was not heroism. Heroism was to save a child, a woman, a human being. To keep Jews in the forest for two years and save them, this was heroism."[11]

Among all partisans a discrepancy existed between the value placed on fighting and the actual number of attacks on the Germans. It was as if the pressure to oppose the Germans lost its momentum somewhere on the way to the real strikes. This lack of correspondence between ideas and actions was probably responsible for some of the exaggerated claims about extraordinary anti-Nazi escapades.

Until 1943, in Western Belorussia, attacks on the Germans by Russian partisans were rare. The few anti-enemy moves that did occur were in the form of sabotage that included the destruction of trains, bridges, telephone lines, and other installations.

At first infrequent and sporadic, such ventures became more coordinated and more common after the arrival of specially trained men from the USSR. With time, more partisans were parachuted into the area. Others had come in planes that landed at secretly constructed airports, close to the forests. Before 1943, however, only a handful of this new breed of partisans reached the forest.

On balance, throughout their entire history, partisan combat activities have been "highly exaggerated. Many of the anti-German expeditions that were planned and discussed by Russian partisans never materialized."[12]

Whatever military encounters between the partisans and the enemy did take place, they reflect the overall characteristics of guerilla warfare, particularly its avoidance of direct enemy confrontations.

And so, even when attacked, partisans preferred not to fight. Instead, they tried to disperse, thinking they would regroup later. Only when these tactics were not possible, only when the partisans had no choice, did they fight. As in Western Belorussia, so in other places, moves initiated by guerilla fighters were usually in the form of sabotage. On rare occasions, and not by design, sabotage did lead to direct confrontation.[13]

Tuvia had a particularly warm feeling for the youthful Jews who fought within the Russian otriads. Moreover, the Bielski otriad participated in armed resistance to the Germans. The joint military moves of the Bielski and Octiaber otriads might have satisfied Tuvia's need to stand up to the Germans; in some way, Tuvia's armed resistance supported his sense of freedom and independence.

One important anti-German move happened shortly after the 1942 harvest. The German law required each peasant to deliver a portion of his farm products to the authorities. In contrast to the treatment of the farmers, estate owners were divested of their entire holdings. Some estate owners were murdered; the rest were banished or sent to concentration camps. Confiscated estates were then run with cheaply paid or unpaid slave labor. What an estate produced went directly to the authorities.

The 1942 harvest was rich and the granaries were filled with wheat. Unable to confiscate this large amount of food, Victor and Tuvia, in a jointly planned operation, decided to burn the fruits of the harvest. The plan was to set fire to all the estates at once, under the cover of darkness. At each location partisans were posted to prevent people from extinguishing the flames.

The authorities and the local population knew that the partisans were responsible for the job.

But then something surprising happened.

"Just as the fires were at their peak planes flew over the area and bombed the flames. Evidently these were Russian planes that were on their way back from an enemy attack. The pilots probably understood the meaning of the fires and decided to 'lend a hand.' The Germans were overcome with horror. It looked like there was a link between the partisans and the Russian Command."[14] In reality this partisan-army cooperation happened by chance.

Convinced that the Bielski otriad had had a hand in these fires, the Germans were even more determined to eliminate the three brothers, particularly Tuvia. They promised a substantial reward for Tuvia's capture or for information leading to his arrest. Depending on who tells the story, the sum offered differs, ranging from 50,000 to a million rubles. A realistic figure probably comes closer to the 50,000 level.[15]

This eagerness to catch Tuvia only underlined his importance. The local people got the message. Their fear and respect grew as did their contempt for the "ineffectual" enemy.

Now that the partisans had destroyed an important food supply, they wanted to prevent the Germans from recuperating their losses and collecting food from the farmers. Consequently, the purpose of their next operation was to hurt the enemy and silence the peasants who grumbled, "You take, the Germans take, how shall we survive?" The partisans decided to deprive the Germans rather than the natives.

The plan was to lie in ambush, wait for cars filled with provisions, and attack. They selected the road leading from Nowogródek to Nowojelnie.

Loyal natives supplied the partisans with information about the enemy's whereabouts. Although they saw it coming, the partisans missed the first small vehicle. Success came only with the appearance of bigger trucks and much more important loot. Tuvia remembers. "Boom! Boom! The first vehicle stopped. We had hit the wheels and the driver. From our side came a hailstorm of bullets. Eight German and White Russian police jumped from the vehicle, fell to the ground and began to return machine-gun fire. Suddenly a 'Hurray!' from Panchenko's people. The enemy is overwhelmed. I don't know how many of them were running away screaming and shooting....The enemy was retreating. We got up and pursued them, but most of them disappeared among the trees in the forest....We decided not to miss the opportunity to gather the loot. We swooped down on the machine guns, the boots and the fowl as well as on the boxes of ammunition. All this took only a few minutes. Our booty on hand: two machine guns, four rifles and thousands of bullets. Trembling with excitement we left the area and went into the forest. The first armed victory and it was ours!"[16]

A less successful move is remembered by the Bielski partisan, Pinchas Boldo. Initiated by Victor, the idea was to destroy the Yatzuki train station and kill the Germans who guarded the place.

"We arrived at the rails in the dark. There was a small building in which there were Germans. From our positions we could see them well. We even had a machine gun. Actually it was in our way and it contributed to our defeat. Instead of going into the rooms of the Germans' house all bullets went over the roof. The enemy had realized that they were being attacked and they opened fire on us...not one German was killed and neither were any of us. Somehow they did not imagine that we were so close to them. Their bullets went far past us into the forest. They thought that we were in the forest, some distance away from them. None of us died. But we did not succeed."[17]

On balance, the Bielski-Panchenko cooperation gave a measure of security to the Bielski otriad and led to its expansion. But expansion also meant older people, women, and children and eventually resulted in a curtailment of movement. Tuvia felt that by dividing his people into coordinated subgroups he would improve the otriad's mobility. And so, he created subunits of twenty to twenty-five people.

Usually a person's group affiliation was based on family relations and friendships. People were free to choose those they wanted to join. Tuvia stepped in when these preferences violated the principle of safety or denied a place to those who were alone and whom no one wanted.[18]

Each group had to be properly balanced. It had to include young armed men, older people, women, and children. The correct mix was determined by the commander. Because each person belonged to a group, evacuation could be more efficiently accomplished. Each group had a leader and several other positions with specially designed functions. For example, Tuvia insisted that military protection and food distribution not be in the same hands. He felt the separation of these two basic functions would avoid abuses.[19]

Each unit was assigned to a particular space. Each had a special pot in which to cook its meals. Similarly, provisions were assigned to each group. The expansion of the otriad required more frequent food expeditions, which meant more danger. The authorities were eager to cut off all partisan supplies and especially those of the Bielski otriad.

Partisan food collections, known as "bambioshka," took place at night. From the Bielski otriad, "Every night one or two groups were sent out to bring food. A group consisted of ten to twelve armed men. One of these men acted as the leader. Some of the participants had to be familiar with the side roads and the particular villages. Of course, one had to select people that first of all were not afraid and second of all to whom the peasants would give food."[20]

When a group reached a village it would first collect provisions from the richest farms. As one partisan explains, this was possible because "In each village we had a peasant, usually himself poor, he would give us information about the other peasants. This way we knew what each had, how many horses, cows, etc. Such a peasant we called 'legalshchyk.' We took nothing from him. Sometimes we would give him some of the booty. Some of the rich peasants tried to hide their products . . . we would search and if this was the case, we took more from them."[21]

Toward the end of 1942 horse-drawn wagons, confiscated from farmers, were used for food expeditions. When a group left a village, it had to subdivide and prepare the goods on the way back to the camp. For example, cows had to be killed and cut into manageable portions. All this had to be done quickly. At dawn a group was expected to be back at the base—daylight was the partisans' enemy.

Food expeditions were both risky and unpredictable. One never knew if all those who set out would return. Nor did one know what they would bring back. Some items were chronically in short supply, especially bread. It was impossible to find enough; people longed for bread and continuously talked about it.

When a bambioshka was about to return, "people would run out to see what it brought...they would touch the goods and if they came upon bread they would not leave. They would form a line. Those at the head would get some bread, but those behind would not get any."[22] This would lead to resentment and envy.

By October 1942, the Bielski otriad, which by that time numbered about 200 people, established a base in the two connecting forests, Perełaz and Zabiełowo. Because of cold weather and the threat of snow they decided to build more permanent quarters. The otriad tried to collect more food to last for part of the winter.

A more permanent forest home or bunker was called a "ziemlanka," a name derived from the word soil. In part it was a dug-up rectangular space. When finished, two-thirds of the bunker was in the ground and one-third above. The upper part consisted of wooden sticks or branches that touched each other, forming a pyramid. These were in turn covered by sheets of bark, leafy branches, or other materials that kept out extreme temperatures and helped camouflage the place.

If constructed properly, the inside walls of such a ziemlanka were lined with wood. This in turn prevented the soil from crumbling. Instead of beds, around the walls were wooden bunks covered with straw or leaves and, if available, flour sacks.

In the middle, between the two rows of bunks, there was an iron stove, with a pipe leading to the ceiling and outside. In the winter months this stove would cook the food and heat the place. Depending on size and need, a ziemlanka could accommodate up to forty people.

In preparation for their first winter, 1942–1943, Tuvia wanted these ziemlankas to cover a wide area. He felt that by scattering them he would be spreading the risks. If the enemy discovered one bunker, the rest had a chance to remain unnoticed. Each bunker was large, accommodating thirty to forty people. One was to serve as a hospital.

For most of the people this was their first forest winter. This alone created anxieties and fears. People were highstrung, and emotional imbalance led to much grumbling. Complaints were frequently directed at the most vulnerable among them: the newcomers.

A few made arrangements to stay in more protected places, with peasants. This method was used by part of the Boldo family. The Bielski brothers and their families could have found more comfortable quarters with some of their Belorussian and Polish friends, but they did not. They would not abandon the people. Not only did they themselves stay in the forest, but they insisted that those close to them should do the same. Others, the majority, had no choice and remained in the forest.

NOTES

[1] Pinchas Boldo, Personal Interview, Haifa, Israel, 1990.

[2] The literature is filled with descriptions of abusive behavior toward the Jews by Russian and other partisans. For a few examples see Reuben Ainsztein, *Jewish Resistance in Occupied Eastern Europe* (New York: Barnes & Noble, 1974), pp. 307–308; Nachum Alpert, *The Destruction of Slonim Jewry* (New York: Holocaust Library, 1989), pp. 290–298; Shalom Cholawsky, "Jewish Partisans—Objective and Subjective Difficulties," *Jewish Resistance During the Holocaust,* Proceedings of the Conference on Manifestations of Jewish Resistance (Jerusalem: Yad Vashem, 1971), pp. 323–334; Shumel Krakowski, *The War of the Doomed: Jewish Armed Resistance in Poland, 1942–1944* (New York: Holmes & Meier Publishers, Inc., 1984), pp.

28–58; Dov Levin, "Baltic Jewry's Armed Resistance to the Nazis," in Issac Kowalski (ed.) *Anthology of Armed Resistance to the Nazis, 1939–1945* (New York: Jewish Combatants Publishing House, 1986), Vol. 3, pp. 42–48; Dov Levin, *Fighting Back: Lithuanian Jewry's Armed Resistant to the Nazis, 1941–1945* (New York: Holmes & Meier, Publishers, Inc. 1985), pp. 206–227; J. Tennenbaum, *Underground: The Story of a People* (New York: Philosophical Society, 1952), p. 292.

[3] Jashke Mazowi, Personal Interview, Tel Aviv, Israel, 1989.

[4] For activities of these leaders see *Sefer Hapartisanim Hajehudim (The Jewish Partisan Book)* (Merchavia: Sifriath Paolim Hashomer Hatzair, 1958), Vol. 1, pp. 375–382, 337–343; Samuel Bornstein, "The Platoon of Dr. Atlas," pp. 217–240, in Meyer Barkai (ed.), *The Fighting Ghettos* (New York: J. B. Lippincott Company, 1962); Lester Eckman and Chaim Lazar, *The Jewish Resistance* New York: Shengold Publishers, Inc., 1977), pp. 51–58; Leonard Tushnet, "The Little Doctor—A Resistance Hero," pp. 253–259 in Yuri Suhl (ed.), *They Fought Back, The Story of the Jewish Resistance in Nazi Europe* (New York: Schocken Books, 1975); *Pinkas Zetel (A Memorial to the Jewish Community of Zdzienciól*, Baruch Kaplinski (ed.) (Tel Aviv: Zetel Association in Israel, 1957) contains several articles about Lipiczanska and other forests and talks about the two leaders Dworecki and Kaplinski.

[5] Family camps varied in size, ranging from a handful of individuals to the largest single group, the Bielski otriad, that grew to more than 1200 individuals. For a discussion of the instability and precarious position of these different camps, see Yitzhak Arad, "Jewish Family camps in the Forests: An Original Means of Rescue," pp. 333–353 in *Rescue Attempts During the Holocaust,* Proceedings of the Second Yad Vashem International Historical Conference (Jerusalem: Yad Vashem, 1977); Eckman and Lazar, *The Jewish Resistance,* pp. 83–99; Tennenbaum, *Underground,* p. 404; Lea Garber Kowenska, a member of a small family group in the Lipiczanska forest, touchingly describes how great suffering and mutual caring intermingled in the lives of this group. See Lea Garber Kowenska "Dos Fos Hot Sich Fargidenk of Aibik" (What is Remembered Forever) *Journal Fu Sovietisher Heimland (Journal of the Soviet Homeland)*, No. 4, 1971, pp. 92–102; Lea Garber Kowenska also describes her life in the forest, in Yiddish, in an unpublished memoir. In her group of fifteen there were seven children. Some were orphans whom she and others picked up on the way to and inside the forest.

[6] *Jewish Partisan Book,* pp. 346–394.

[7] Hersh Smolar, Personal Interview, Tel Aviv, Israel, 1989–1990.

[8] Raja Kaplinski, Personal Interview, Tel Aviv, Israel, 1987–1989.

[9] Pinchas Boldo, Personal Interview.

[10] Raja Kaplinski, Personal Interview.

[11] Jacov Greenstein, Personal Interview, Tel Aviv, Israel, 1984–1990.

[12] Even after the Russian-German war turned in favor of the USSR, it took quite a while before Soviet partisans became an effective force. Some are convinced that the partisan fighting was much less extensive than officially claimed. Pinchas Boldo, Personal Interview, Oswald Rufeisen, a member of the Ponomarenko otriad, is convinced that the partisan battles and heroism have been highly exaggerated. See Nechama Tec, *In the Lion's Den: The Life of Oswald Rufeisen* (New York: Oxford University Press, 1990), pp. 201–202.

[13] Henri Michel, *The Shadow War: European Resistance, 1939–1945* (New York: Harper & Row Publishers, 1972), pp. 278–279; Jack N. Porter (ed.), *Jewish Partisans, A Documentary of Jewish Resistance in the Soviet Union During World War II* (New York: University Press of Amer-

ica, 1982), p. 9; J. K. Zawodny, "Guerrilla and Sabotage: Organization, Operations, Motivations, Escalations," *The Annals of the Academy of Political Science,* Vol. 341 (May 1962), pp. 8–18.

[14]Tuvia Bielski, in *Yehudei Yaar (Forest Jews)* (Tel Aviv: Am Oved, 1946).

[15]Chaja Bielski, Personal Interview, Haifa, Israel, 1987–1991; Raja Kaplinski, Personal Interview. At one point, at the start of 1943, German planes dropped leaflets announcing monetary rewards for information leading to Tuvia Bielski's capture. This leaflet, aimed at reaching the Christian population, claimed that whoever would give the Nazis information leading to the capture of Tuvia Bielski would receive a reward of 50,000 marks. This figure was later doubled. Because of these leaflets many Jews learned about the existence of the Bielski otriad. This information, in turn, gave them courage to escape and search for the camp. See *Sefer Lida (Lida Book)* (Tel Aviv: Published by the Association of Lida Jews, 1970), p. xv. The official currency exchange rate at the time was 2.5 marks per $1. For this and other exchange rates see Leni Yahil, *The Holocaust: The Fate of European Jewry* (New York: Oxford University Press, 1990), pp. 661–662.

[16]This anti-German move is described by several Bielski partisans. Chaja Bielski, Personal Interview; Tuvia Bielski, *Forest Jews*; Pinchas Boldo, Personal Interview; Zus Bielski, Personal Interview, Brooklyn, New York, 1989; Raja Kaplinski, Personal Interview. Boldo and the Bielski brothers participated in the move.

[17]This is a quote from a personal interview with Pinchas Boldo. He used this case as an example of a failed anti-German move. While Tuvia admits that the incident was not a great success, he is less critical. Tuvia says that this "combined attack on the Germans by the Jewish partisans and Panchenko's group brought us no loot, but we killed seven to eight Germans. Indeed, our aim was the annihilation of the entire guard and to take their machine guns and mortar. We did not succeed in realizing the entire plan. It was fortunate that we got away without sustaining casualties." Tuvia Bielski in *Forest Jews*.

[18]Tuvia Bielski in *Forest Jews*. He also talked about these things during our meeting in his house, Personal Interview, Brooklyn, New York, 1987.

[19]Ibid.

[20]Eljezer Engelstern, Yad Vashem Testimony, No. 3249/233.

[21]Ibid.

[22]Ibid.

Bibliography

Arad, Yitzhak and Yisrael Gutman and Abraham Margaliot, eds., *Documents on the Holocaust Selected Sources on the Destruction of the Jews of Germany and Austria, Poland and the Soviet Union.* Jerusalem, Israel: Yad Vashem, 1981.

Calic, Edouard, *Reinhard Heydrich: The Chilling Story of the Man Who Masterminded the Nazi Death Camps.* Trans. by Lowell Bair. New York, NY: William Morrow & Company, Inc., 1982.

Carmichael, Joel, *The Satanizing of the Jews: Origin and Development of Mystical Anti-Semitism.* New York, NY: Fromm International Publishing Corporation, 1992.

Donat, Alexander, *The Holocaust Kingdom.* New York, NY: Holocaust Library, 1978.

Gutman, Yisrael, et. al., eds. *The Jews of Poland Between Two World Wars.* Hanover, NH: University Press of New England, 1989.

Halperin, William S., *Germany Tried Democracy: A Political History of the Reich from 1918 to 1933.* New York, NY: W.W. Norton & Company, Inc., 1946.

Hitler, Adolf, *Mein Kampf.* Trans. by Ralph Manheim. Boston, MA: Houghton Mifflin Company, 1971.

Hoess, Rudolf, *Commandant of Auschwitz: The Autobiography of Rudolf Hoess.* Trans. by Constantine FitzGibbon. Cleveland, OH: The World Publishing Company, 1951.

Kaes, Anton and Martin Jay and Edward Dimendberg, *The Weimar Republic Source Book.* Berkeley, CA: California Press, 1994.

Kleg, Milton, *Hate, Prejudice and Racism.* Albany, NY: State University of New York Press, 1993.

Lucas, James, *World War Two through German Eyes.* London, England: Arms & Armour Press, 1987.

Manstein, Field-Marshal Erich von, *Lost Victories.* Ed. and trans. by Anthony G. Powell. (Publisher not located.) Novato, CA.: 1982.

Meltzer, Milton, *A History of Jewish Life from Eastern Europe to America.* Northvale, NJ: Jason Aronson, Inc., 1996.

Orenstein, Henry, *I Shall Live*. New York, NY: Beaufort Books, 1987.

Rescue Attempts during the Holocaust: Proceedings of the Second Yad Vashem International Historical Conference. Israel, Jerusalem: 1977.

Rubinstein, Erna F., *The Survivor in Us All: Four Young Sisters in the Holocaust*. Hamden, CT: Archon Books, 1983.

Smelser, Ronald and Rainer Zitelmannn, eds., *The Nazi Elite*. Trans. by Mary Fischer. New York, NY: New York University Press, 1993.

Speer, Albert, *Inside The Third Reich Memoirs by Albert Speer*. Trans. by Richard and Clara Winston. New York, NY: Macmillan Co., Inc., 1970.

Tec, Nechama, *Defiance: The Bielski Partisans*. New York, NY: Oxford University Press, 1993.

Zelzer, Maria, *Weg Und Schicksal der Stuttgarter Juden*. Stuttgart, Germany: Ernst Klett Veriag, 1988.